SPIRITUAL CONFESSIONS
And my coming of age

My Sister,

Friends come and go, but a covenant friend is one sent by God that bears "His stamp of approval."

One who says... "I have made you two sisters and you will dwell together in my heart."

Sis. Mattai - you know the love I have for you. You have been a mother and a mentor; a friend and a Sister, but most importantly... you have become my heart.

Thank you for pushing me, praying with and for me, and keeping me in line. May God bless you and your family richly.

Love Always... Your Sister

Elaine M. White

ISBN 1-59113-284-3

Published by ELANA WHITE, 3908 Harlem Rd., #268,
Amherst, New York 14226

Printed in the United States of America.

Booklocker.com, Inc.
2004

SPIRITUAL CONFESSIONS
And my coming of age

ELANA WHITE

Dedication

I dedicate this book to all those hurt little children who are suffering within the souls of our adult beings. Life is precious and teaches us valuable lessons. We can choose to live and allow these lessons to make manifest mature beings and vessels of honor, or we can choose to give up and allow the problems in our lives to suffocate our very existence. You are important and your self-worth is priceless. You can survive. You can take it. By the power of the living God you can make it.

For out of much affliction and anguish of heart I wrote unto you with many tears. Not that ye should be grieved, but that ye might know the love which I have more abundantly unto you.
II Corinthian 2:4

M U S I K

My daddy was my musik, my orchestra and symphony.
As a child I danced to the S W E E T softness and the raptures of his
melody. Twirling and spinning in dreams made of gold,
Through heavy belts of laughter, timeless - aged - not old.
He was my violin - my flute – and my harp, wrapping me in love notes
of A and C sharp

Love that Jazz
Love that Jazz
My daddy was my musik
How I love that Jazz

I grew like a Lily - Like a note on a scale
When the tunes began to change…so sudden…
so R - A - P - I - D.   Confusion - D I L L U S I O N - and
intricate Intrusion…when I heard another sound
other than my father's musik. A song of love - A lustful melody,
stole my heart away from my Father's dream…Awkward sounds of the
Tuba, the Trumpet, and Trombone, belted from my Father's belly…
Rules in hateful tones.
Why?   Because I want to listen to my own musik, to pursue Life   -
Liberty - and what I know will make me happy.
So my husband became my orchestra and my S W E E T symphony

Love that Jazz
Love that Jazz
My daddy no longer my musik
How I love that Jazz

Days passed into years. Children came and family grew,
My daddy still playing his musik, but now he hears mine too.
I played my musik louder…the Viola, the Cello, and Saxophone

to drown out his relentless beats of the drum that flowed throughout my soul.
I didn't want to hear his musik, regaining his love was my goal.
I didn't understand the two were one, but now my husband had control.

We let by-gones go away…and I never stopped being his little girl,
But one day the musik stopped and so did everything in my world.
Now everywhere I go…I hear my Daddy playing every instrument with perfection, receiving his love without expressing my rejection.
Now I understand what his musik was all about. Now I wished I had listened and had no doubt.
As he sings in my heart and his musik sounds so sweet
I remember is laughter - his face - his memory - his beat

Love that Jazz
Love that Jazz
My Daddy is my musik
How I love His Jazz

Pain and agony…weeping over tragedies.
Hateful cries and an orchestra of classical lies
stole the beauty of my S W E E T symphony.
No longer my musik…No longer for me.
So where will my musik come from now…who will help me up when I don't know how?
Who will give me dreams made of gold?
Who will laugh with me while time and age unfold?

Love that jazz
Love that jazz
Swayed by Heaven's melody
How I love that jazz

The trials of life made me wise and gave me strength to realize
there's musik crying inside of me, heart felt words…
my S W E E T symphony.

SPIRITUAL CONFESSIONS
And my coming of age

Not the song of love that plagued my soul, that drowned out my musik with time and control, but a mellow sound that soothes my ears...warms my lips and dries my tears.
The sound I hear within my veins...of rushing water and runaway trains.
Tapping, proclaiming and drumming my own beat
with glorious music soft, but sweet. Playing the bass line of my heart...birthing new music to make a new start.

It's His musik that fills my ears, so soft and D E B O N A I R.
I weep with joy when in His presence, a love that can't compare in essence.
Ringing bells that were never rung and singing songs that were never sung...because when He called out my name
I answered without fear or shame. Embracing a love and life so pure...In Him I stand and can endure.

Love that Jazz
Love that Jazz
Jesus is forever my musik
How I love His Jazz

Foreword

This is an opportunity for me to tell you my story and witness to you how sinful and problematic we are and how wonderful God is. In spite of us, He still loves us. I want to tell you that no matter what you've been through and no matter what you're going through you are not defeated. As tragic as the problem may seem, you are more than a conqueror through Jesus Christ who strengthens you and these light afflictions are only for a moment. It is through our pains and our struggles that the Lord gives us our assignment. The assignment is not about you or what you feel you can do. It is about the ministry that's being birthed through you. Your assignment will lead you to your purpose and will also mold you into the image of our Lord and Savior. I testify to you right now that the only possible way I survived was because Jesus never left my side. Spiritual Confessions begins with my experiences as a child and takes the reader on a journey through a life saturated with sexual and emotional abuse. This is not a self-help book, and it is not just a book of empowerment. This book will show a childhood that although weighted with adversity and a longing to be loved, is still filled with excitement and laughter. As an adult I was also forced to deal with many tragic situations, which affected my marriage, my children and my life. After seeing how ugly the world and people can be, thoughts to give up tormented me. These thoughts walked with me during the day and chased me in my dreams at night. However, by the grace of God I was given the strength to face each passing day and all of its challenges. As I attempted to pick up the broken pieces of my life, I realized that my ability to love and to trust had been affected, and although at some point I accepted Jesus Christ as Lord and the Holy Spirit as my guide, I struggled with the trials I had to face. While developing a relationship with the Lord my life drastically changed, but then so did the people I loved most. Spiritual Confessions can help fill the void in the lives of all who find their troubled circumstances too difficult to handle. It also shares painful and funny experiences with the reader and demonstrates how psychological problems and concerns take root long before we know they're there. Walk with me as I triumph over the life events that have tried very hard to kill me and then celebrate my life with me as I finally learn who I am in Christ and what it really means to forgive and love unconditionally.

Acknowledgements

I would like to express supreme gratitude to my Lord and Savior, Jesus Christ. I thank you Lord for choosing me as one of your own and for molding me into a vessel of honor. Lord I thank you for showing me my purpose and giving me your strength. Most of all, I thank you for loving me.

To my Miracle and Inspiration, John jr. and Shantell, I will always love you and treasure your heart-warming smiles. Without you none of this would've been possible because you gave my life meaning when I felt like giving up.

To my Mama, I love you. Not only have you been the best mother one could ever ask for, you were right. Thank you for instilling positive values in me and teaching me how to be a woman of strength. Mama, you are everything to me; a treasure chest full of rubies, diamonds, and pearls that I didn't know I had until the Lord opened the eyes of my heart.

To my covenant friend, Evangelist, Dr. Barbara Huddelston-Mattai, you are truly a gift from God. Thank you for correcting me when I'm wrong. Thank you for your honesty, your friendship, and your love. God has truly put His Word in your mouth and anointed you to preach and spread His gospel. Thank you for giving me your heart and thank you for holding mine. When God made us friends, He gave me a special gift to be treasured always.

Thank you Lord, for blessing me with a wonderful father, dad, and friend who's gone on to be with you. I will always love you dad.

1
BUMPS AND BRUISES

My house, as horrid as it was, it was where I lived. I grew up in a small community on the east side of Detroit with my parents Sam and Theresa St. James, formerly known as Theresa Jones, along with my brother and two sisters. The prettiest houses on the block belonged to homeowners. Many of the homes were occupied by renters, which left some uncared for. I knew one day mama and daddy would buy us a big house with a big yard equipped with a huge swing set, but for now peeling paint, broken down steps, trash, and barren land was what I saw from our living room window. We lived in an upstairs apartment at 227 Stanton St. with three bedrooms. I shared a room with my younger sister, Lottie. There was a room for my brother Sam and the big bedroom was for mama and daddy. My baby sister Michelle slept in her crib in mama's room. Mama always kept our house clean and all of us kids too. All of our furniture was new and we never went ragged. Mama would always say, Just because you live in the ghetto don't mean you have to look like it or act like it. Mama would often times catch me staring at the pretty white house across the street all dressed in pretty flowers with a huge backyard full of the prettiest green grass I ever did see. Mama never said anything, but she knew what I was thinking. Why couldn't our home look like that? Why couldn't we grow grass? Why couldn't most of the homes over there grow grass? These questions rang in my mind like a thousand bells over and over again. Sometimes Sam would sit with me and gaze over at the pretty houses. I remember him saying, Diane, how come the sun only shines on the pretty houses across the street and down? I shrugged my shoulders and sucked my bucked teeth as loud as I could. I don't know Sam, maybe we ought to face it, aint' nothin' pretty over here. I looked up at that huge ball of fire and watched carefully as it stretched out its arms over the sky making those homes shine like brand new gold. They sparkled in my big brown eyes as tears rolled down my face because at that point and time it was evident to me that the sun don't shine on pity and some of the kids who lived in those houses really let us know that we were a pitiful sight.

I never saw a lot of white folk except for the old white couple next door to us. My daddy always said that all white people were mean and nasty, but I disagreed with his way of thinking. I called the old man next door Mr. George because I could never remember his name and I called his wife whatever nasty name came to my mind without verbalizing it. She was a very odd looking woman. She was short and stocky with no teeth. Her hair was short and thin with a blonde tint and she always wore those flowery house-dresses with white socks and slippers. Mr. George was a short man with hair as white as snow. He didn't wear anything other than his Blue Jean trousers, white socks and slippers day in and day out. He had a huge pigeon house in his backyard that was big enough for a clubhouse. It had openings where the pigeons could come and go as they pleased. I thought it was good of him not to keep them caged in because nobody likes being locked up, not even birds. I would watch him early in the morning carrying his pail of seeds to feed them. There had to be at least a hundred pigeons in that little house. I thought Mr. George was the nicest man I had ever met, even if he was white. He would always give all of us kids in the neighborhood candy and talk to us about his pigeons until his mean old wife would come out waving one hand at us while the other hand would be tightly gripped around that small glass of vodka. She always claimed to be drinking water, but water doesn't smell like sewage. She would yell and scream, Get away from my yard you little monkeys, and that's when I felt that my daddy was right about white folk, but Mr. George would always come to our rescue and make her go in the house. I especially liked it when he called her an old witch and told her to shut up, because although I couldn't stand the sight of her I could never bring myself to disrespect her. The only other white folk I'd seen were at school when I said good morning to all of the teachers. I didn't see any difference between us except their skin color was much lighter than mine and they talked funny. No one liked them, but I figured they couldn't be all that bad; after all, they came down here every morning just to teach us. I attended Public School #11. It was so boring I didn't really care if I went or not. It was the same everyday; good morning, good afternoon, and goodbye, but one day I walked in and all of the teachers were whispering and acting really strange. I just thought they were gossiping as usual, but when I entered my homeroom I had a new teacher. She was the reason for all the commotion. Her name was Mrs. Ruth, she was black and she was beautiful. All the kids sat in silence with their mouths propped wide open. I just sat there with this stupid smile on my face. I couldn't believe I had a black teacher. It made me feel good about myself and for the first time, I felt good about school. I tried to imagine that I was her standing in front of the class teaching and talking proper like white folk. I would be smart and successful, just like Mrs. Ruth and I had determined in my mind that school would no longer be boring. No one had asked about our old teacher, Mrs. Hanna. No one cared. She was a mean old miserable lady who was always serious about everything. It was a sin for Mrs. Hanna or anyone in the class to laugh or crack a smile, so we never did. When she talked she spit all over everywhere, including your desk, schoolwork, and all over you. My daddy said she did it on purpose, but mama said she had a spit mouth and couldn't help it. I squirmed in my seat all day long because I couldn't wait to tell my mama and my daddy the good news. When the bell rang I ran all the way home. I burst through the doors singing, I got a new teacher. I got a new teacher. Mama was inquisitive, but daddy kept eating his sandwich as if I wasn't even there. What's her name? Her name is Mrs. Ruth. She's nice, she's beautiful, she's proper, she's smart and she reminds me a lot of Grandma Jones. My grandma was a teacher and a fine one at that. That's where my mama got her smarts. I went on and on about what she taught us kids and how she taught.

Mama. Yes Diane. Mrs. Ruth is tall and skinny like a model and her hair is short and black. Oh, did I forget to mention; she's black. Daddy lifted his head up out of his plate for the first time since I had entered the room and said, black, beautiful, smart, and proper. Em...em...em you sho' can tell when colored folk get a little money cause' they talk like white folk. White folk is rich! Yo' teacher rich? Well dad, mama talk like she's white and we ain't got a cent. The only thing I remember after that was hitting the floor and peeling my face off daddy's hand. As I slowly picked myself up off the floor I could still hear my daddy rantin' and raven' about my smart mouth. I guess it wouldn't have been all that bad had I not placed my hands on my hips and twisted my head from side to side while saying what I said. Daddy never could compare his statements to my logical reasoning because words just sort of fell out of his mouth regardless of the order. No one wanted to risk getting a few lumps upside the head, so no one corrected him. Everyone agreed in unison, even mama. Uh huh, that's right dad. I'd say you sho' is a walking genius, ain't he Sam. My brother would tuck his head and say yep while we both giggled under our breath.

We really didn't play with the kids across the street unless they came over to our house because we were never allowed to travel over there. Most of the time I watched from the stairs of my house as they played in that yard laughing, tussling and running free. There was a little girl who lived in that pretty white house. Her name was Simone. Simone was 10 shades lighter than me. She had long pretty hair and her eyes were black as coal. All the boys fought over her while I idly stood by hoping someone would pay me a little attention, but no one ever did. When Simone had no one else to play with she'd come over to my house, and although I was being used I played anyway because to have a friend, real or not, meant a lot to me. My brother Sam was about the only faithful friend I had, but I used him as a playmate just as Simone had used me. When Simone was with her friends they would stand across the street and tease me until no end. My feelings would be hurt badly, but I couldn't tell mama because she would always tell me that Simone was not a true friend and to stop playing with her. Of course, I didn't always take heed to mama's warnings because loneliness always seemed to overpower me. One day I was sitting on the steps combing my dolls hair when I heard taunting chants echoing in my ear from Simone and her friends. Baldy, baldy; Diane don't have no hair. Buddies, buddies; they make her feet smell funny. Ugly, ugly; yes she is. I sat there frozen with my lip poked out as my eyes began to swell with tears. I must have batted my lashes a thousand times or more to hold them back, but soon my eyelids collapsed and the tears raced down the sides of my face. Then I saw a familiar face among the evil children, taunting, laughing, and pointing. I'd known that face all of my nine years of life. It was Sam. My own brother! How could he betray me for a few moments of pleasure? Simone didn't care for him, she was just stringing him along

4

to watch him pant over her like a helpless puppy. He wasn't supposed to be across the street anyway, so out of anger, rage, and frustration I brought mama into the picture. He told his side and I told mine. He yelled and I screamed. He pushed and I shoved. It didn't make a difference anyway because her soap opera was on and mama didn't want to be bothered. When it was all over she sentenced us both to a day in the house, no talking and no joking. He had to sit on the couch in the front room and I had to sit on the couch in the living room. Mama went back into the kitchen to prepare our dinner. She had one hand on her hip, the other hand was stirring our dinner, and her eyes were locked onto the 13 inch black and white television on the kitchen counter. My mama was a pretty lady. She wore the same kind of clothes that people wore on Soul Train with the nice psychedelic colors and she never left home without her afro-puff and platform shoes. Mama had smooth brown skin with a reddish glow and her eyes were warm, golden and brown. Mama's lips curved like the Euphrates River and her smile was everlasting. Mama was a beautiful African Queen in my eyes. Yeah, I may be ugly now, but I am destined to be beautiful just like my mama.

Mama had her back turned when Sam ran over to me, dug up his nose and wiped a boogie on my shirt then ran back to his seat. Sam was stupid. He knew he couldn't beat me in anything. Not sports, not anything. How many times does a person have to get beat up for common sense to kick in? I knew if I hit him mama would get me, so I politely told him to leave me alone. Sam continued to bother me, but I realized he was just trying to make up. We started talking and when mama didn't say anything we began to play. I soon forgot about Simone and her two faces as Sam and I played hide-go-seek. We played with his cars and then we began playing blindfold. In this game one of us would be blindfolded while trying to feel the way back to base on the others command of, you're getting hot or you're getting cold. After being blindfolded several times and making it back to base successfully I told Sam I didn't want to play anymore. Sam insisted, but I resisted. He poked me, pulled my hair, and then wiped another boogie on me. This time it was actually touching my skin. Anger riled up in me like fire. I began to remember what he, Simone, and the rest of the kids did to me. Pain and agony shone on my face. I was heart broken, humiliated, and aggravated. Then the opportunity for revenge arose.

Okay Sam I'll play one more time. Sam happily gave me the blindfold. It was his turn and he didn't have a clue. I almost felt sorry for him, so I gave it a second thought and after about two seconds I decided to go ahead with the plan. I blindfolded him as tight as I could and turned him around at least five times. While Sam tumbled around the room, bumping into walls and tables I quietly opened the door to the hallway and then tiptoed back to the couch. Sam you are freezing; turn around and come back this way some. Sam crashed into the orange hanging beads that separated mama and daddy's bedroom from the front room. The clinging sound of the beads caught mama's attention. What are you kids doing? Nothing mama! I jumped up and quickly shut the door. Well you better be sitting down before I whip your behinds. I took a peek at mama and then tiptoed to the hallway door and opened it again. Without Sam noticing I sat back down on the couch. Sam you are getting hot. You are so hot I could fry an egg on your forehead. I covered my mouth to muffle my giggles as he approached the hallway. I peeped into the kitchen to see if mama was looking. She wasn't. She was still in a trance, captured by the make believe lives that No One Lives. Sam you are burning up. He was in the hallway at the top of the stairs trying to feel something familiar. I contemplated whether or not I could do this to Sam. I couldn't help it. It's not my fault he's an idiot. Sam you are hotter than hot. Now turn left. Sam took one step to the left and all I heard were screams and thumps ringing in harmony with all 25 stairs, ringing with the satanic laughter within my soul. Before I knew it our dinner was in the air and mama was leaping over the kitchen table. She screamed my name pronouncing every syllable. I didn't do it mama. I swear it. I didn't do anything. Mama ran to Sam's rescue as I sort of just gazed at him from the top of the stairway. Somehow I just didn't think it was funny anymore. His frail body lay splattered at the bottom of the stairs like a broken egg. How could I have done this to Sam? Why did I do this? I began to choke on the mucus in the back of my throat while crying elephant tears. Oh God! Please let him be alright. I promise I'll never do it again. I hadn't thought of the consequences. I never thought about him getting hurt from a stupid, childish prank.

Revenge left a bitter taste in my mouth. Sam got up and slowly climbed the stairs. I tried apologizing, but he said nothing. As mama wiped the blood from his mouth and forehead she kept screaming at me. You could have killed him, what's the matter with you? Mama gave me such a cold look I felt chills running up my spine that let me know I was in line for the whipping of my life. I sat down thanking God for allowing my brother to be okay and thanking Him for not having mama knock me out, but just when everything seemed to settle down I heard daddy pulling in the driveway. I trembled to the mere sound of his voice. Mama ran to the door to greet him as usual, but this time it wasn't with a kiss. She gave him the whole run down of the entire incident in 30 seconds. My so-called African Queen turned out to be Benedict Arnold in disguise. My daddy was only 5 feet 6 inches tall and 250lbs., but back then he seemed like a giant. He had a big head with red hair and burnt orange skin. I used to think his head was swollen from his boxing years. Aside from that, he was a very handsome man whom I loved dearly. He talked in parables that only he understood, but when he opened his mouth we just did whatever we thought he told us to do. He reminded me of the cartoon Charlie Brown where every adult talked in muffling sounds with no real words.

While mama was talking daddy was taking off his belt. I would have run out the back door, but my feet were stuck to the rug like glue. Diane! You and uh huh girl you done gone crazy! I interpreted that as, Diane come over here because I'm going to whip your behind. I took position like a little soldier while daddy went wailing away. Whenever it came down to getting whipped I would try to act as if it didn't hurt, but this time was different. My rear end was on fire. I realized daddy wasn't stopping until I shed a tear. So I played the role. I jumped, I squealed, and I cried. Once my face got wet daddy stopped the madness. Now and uh huh you go and sit down somewhere and er ah stop acting like a nut. I walked past Sam giving him the evil eye and sat down next to him on the couch. As soon as mama and daddy went into the kitchen Sam made faces pretending to be me getting whipped. Out of anger I leaned toward him so he could hear me good. Sam you ain't nothin' but a mama's boy! This will teach you to never be nobody's sucker like you were mine today. Lottie got up and went into the kitchen. I didn't know the little

7

tattletale was turning me in. Sam stopped teasing and I had no idea why. I just didn't care. The only thing that mattered was sweet revenge, so I continued to give him a piece of my mind. Sam sat there with this silly look on his face and when I turned around to see where daddy was he was standing right behind me. Before I could bat an eye he slapped me upside my head. I went to bed with a sore rear end and a broken heart. I heard mama and daddy whispering amongst each other. Whispering about me and wondering if something was wrong with me. I heard my daddy bring up the time when Sam and I made Lottie and our cousin give the little girl downstairs some poison candy that I found in the garage. They brought up the time I acted as the ring- leader in getting Lottie, Sam and others to pull up Ms. Watson's Rose Garden. I thought they were the most beautiful flowers I had ever seen. We pulled them up and hid them behind the garage. When we were done her yard looked like someone had blown it up with five sticks of dynamite. As they compared these incidents they seriously questioned my sanity. I don't know why I did those things. I just did. I remember looking up at the stars from my bedroom window thinking about all that was said and done and for a moment I really cried because I knew I was wrong. I knew I had hurt the very people who loved and cared for me. I spoke to God that night. I asked Him If I was a bad seed and if there was something wrong with me. Although I didn't hear God speak to me audibly, He placed peace on my heart and in a sense I felt that everything was going to be all right.

2
LORD I'M SORRY

Summer had come and gone. Winter was now here. The snow was coming down hard, painting the city streets white. Snowflakes danced in the air like a thousand ballerinas and icicles hung from every rooftop (they were like precious diamonds). I glanced over at Simone's house and thought, now you can't tell the difference between the fortunate and the unfortunate because God blessed us all. Look, there's diamonds on every house, hanging from every rooftop, even mine. I often thought about my future; what would I be when I grew up. I gave up the desire to be a teacher like Mrs. Ruth. I'd see myself as a big time lawyer with fancy clothes and a nice car or an architect designing hi-tech offices and homes. Most of the time I would see myself as a track star. I'd be coming down the stretch towards the finish line, running neck and neck with my opponent. I'm pulling away. I'm going for first place and just before I cross the finish line I'd hear mama calling my name. Diane, stop all of that daydreaming and get your good intentions out of my window. You're messing up my drapery girl! It's time for you and Sam to get to school. That made me mad because every time I'd get to that point where I'm crossing the finish line someone would interrupt me and I never got to see If I won.

The school was only three big blocks away. We made snowballs and threw each other around in the snow along the way although mama said not to. Once we got to school there were hundreds of kids rolling around in the snow and having snowball fights. Sam and I decided to join in on the fun. I found my friend Sandy and we played and slid on the ice as if we were two polar bears. I heard mama's voice in the back of my head saying, Diane get up off the ground in your good coat; money don't grow on trees. I had on a brand new dress and as long as I didn't soil it or get the pretty ruffles wet nothing mama said mattered. Sandy and I lay side by side on the ground making angels in the snow when Mack and his thuggish friends walked up and kicked the snow in our faces. I was mad, but I was afraid of them so I said nothing. Mack attempted to get us to go behind the school with them saying he had something to show us. However, the air he carried made me feel uneasy. When I refused Mack said that they would beat us up after school, so Sandy went with them. The bell was ringing and everyone ran into the school. I tried to wait for Sandy and when she didn't show I proceeded around back to see where she was. When I got half way back there Mack and two of his friends grabbed me and pulled me to the rear of the school. I saw Sandy fighting with a strange boy whom I hadn't seen before. Everything in me told me I should've gone into the school instead of worrying about Sandy. I sensed fear and my eyes roamed, searching for a way out, but there was none. Mack was trying to kiss me while the other two pulled on my coat. I knew that I had to do something fast so I began to kick, punch and bite everyone who laid hands on me. My cries for help were of no avail. No one came to my rescue and my attempts to break free were soon overpowered. I was placed in a headlock, someone else grabbed my feet, and I was thrown to the ground. When I looked up there were at least 20 boys pulling on my coat and clothing. They pulled and tugged at my panties in their feeble attempts to get them off, but my hands were clinched to them like steel clamps. I thought to myself, why is this happening to me? How could they be so cruel? Through the wailing arms I saw Sam standing a far off. We made eye contact for about 30 seconds and in silence I said, Sam, go and get help. His eyes let me know he heard me and then he ran off. Tears poured out of my eyes, burning my face like red-hot flames of fire. My soul screamed out for help. Mama, please help me! Daddy you said you'd always be there for me; where are you? This is not supposed to happen. Oh God, please get them to stop. They are touching me where I don't want to be touched, but nevertheless God I won't let go. I won't let them get my panties off. Slowly I felt my dignity, worth, and self-esteem slip away. I couldn't hold onto all those things and my panties too, and since I refused to let go of my panties I decided to let go of me. As I continued to struggle with those demonic boys I felt the warmth in my heart subside and after a few minutes it was all gone. My heart was cold.

I glanced through the arms of my attackers once again hoping that help was coming. When Sam came back he had someone with him. It was Mr. Graves, the principal, but it was too late. Everything about me, defining who I was had been taken away from me. Each one of my attackers had a piece of me in their hands and there wasn't any left over for me to keep. Mr. Graves yelled out one time and those demons scattered like roaches running from raid. I lay there with my dress soiled, my panties twisted in knots and body frozen from the cold snow. I looked up to the heavens thinking, why? I got up feeling broken and indifferent. All of a sudden I had this anger that sort of hovered over me like a cloud and I could not rid myself of it. I couldn't hold my head up and something was wrong with my eyes. They refused to focus right and every thing seemed gray and ugly. I was taken to the principal's office with some of my attackers. The principal asked questions, but I couldn't utter a word without crying. Mr. Graves was a white man with gray hair and he had about a thousand wrinkles in his face. He grew angry because of my silence; however, I refused to answer him with my attackers standing next to me. So he said if you aren't going to say anything dear, then I can't do anything and since I can't do anything then you all can go to your class. He didn't call my parents or the police. His lack of concern only added salt to my open wounds. He wouldn't have treated me like this if I were a little white girl or his little girl. To him I was just another face. A black face with no distinction!

As I walked through the halls kids snickered and pointed at me. It amazed me as to how fast news traveled in that dungeon everyone called school. They called me names. I was called a prostitute and although none of us knew the true meaning of the word I knew it was something dirty and ugly. Mack and I were in the same class and he told them about the entire incident. They laughed and I cried. I felt dirty and I didn't want to be seen or heard. I just wanted to disappear. The day was long and when the bell rang to go home I was relieved. Sam tried to talk, but I refused to answer, so he walked home with his friends. I wanted to thank him. I wanted to tell him that I loved him and how much I appreciated him getting help, but whenever I opened my mouth I felt those hands around my neck, squeezing the life out of me. I felt the need to be by myself to think about how I was going to tell my mama that I let a bunch of ruthless young men abuse me. How could I have been so stupid? When I got home she took one look at me and said, Diane what's wrong with you and what happened to your dress? It's funny how parents can always tell when something is wrong with their child. I couldn't tell her. I tried, but every time I opened my mouth those hands rose up to my neck choking me into silence again. I stayed in my room for most of the afternoon and after several hours I decided to tell what happened. Daddy sat in a chair in the corner and mama stood next to him waiting for me to spill my guts. I stood front and center and told them every thing. I tripped over my words so badly I was beginning to sound like daddy. However, it felt good to get it all out. Mama and daddy asked questions and I could see what they were leading up to, but I calmed their fears when I told them that my panties were moved, pulled, and torn, but they didn't come down, and the only thing that touched me were hands. Mama grew angry. Why didn't Mr. Graves call us? I stood there shrugging my shoulders. Well I'm going down to that school tomorrow morning to straighten this mess out. Are you okay? Yes mama, I'm fine. Daddy just sat in silence. I felt his rage and pain bursting through the air and bouncing off our ugly gold and black velvet wallpaper. It was good to know that this time it wasn't directed towards me. Mama put her hands on her hip, sighed and went into the kitchen. Daddy followed. I stood there staring out into space wondering where the hug was. I really wasn't fine. Can't they see that I don't understand what happened to me or why it happened! I needed someone to talk to me and not at me. I needed someone to explain this in detail, but no one ever did. Where were the encouraging words that said I love you! I thought that maybe I could retrieve what I lost in the schoolyard in mama's arms. Maybe she was so distraught that she forgot. What about me, doesn't anybody care? Tears pounded at my eyelashes, but before anyone caught me I hid in my room. After everyone had gone to sleep I laid across my bed asking God to help me. How was I going to face that school tomorrow? How was I going to find the strength to get up? What reason would I have to get up? I couldn't figure out why this happened and then it dawned on me, maybe I was being punished for all of the wrong I've done. Shame ate a hole through my little heart and I began talking to this God that I really didn't know because no one else understood. They acted as if they couldn't hear me screaming. They wouldn't even listen to the pain in my voice. God I'm sorry for all of the bad things I did to my brother and my sister. I'm sorry for always getting into trouble. I'm sorry for making my mama and daddy mad. I'm sorry for what happened to me today. I'm sorry God, I'm really sorry. I closed my swollen eyes knowing that when I awoke my life would never be the same again.

Journal Insert

I am but a seed
Destined to be a flower
Growing stronger and stronger
Every minute and every hour
Rain coming down hard
Falling on my head
How much longer can I stand
When they all wish me dead
This is what I ask when I'm knocked down
But I can still smile with my face
On the ground
In the spring I dream
In the summer I sprout
In the fall I scream
In the winter I shout
I never thought
I'd hope to see tomorrow
When all I've had to look for
Is pain, suffering, and sorrow.

Diane.

3
<u>WHY DID YOU SAVE ME?</u>

It was Labor Day and my mama and daddy took the entire family; aunts, uncles, cousins, and grandparents to the beach for our end of the summer picnic. It was nice to spend time with family, especially Grandma and Grandpa Jones, but I found myself missing my daddy's parents, Grandma and Grandpa St. James. During times like these I wished they didn't live so far away. I wanted with me always. We made sand castles and covered each other with sand leaving only our heads showing. We ate, laughed, swam, and played games. My family sure knew how to have a good time. As a matter of fact, it was times like these that gave me an inner peace and allowed me to forget all of my problems. Just when I felt that nothing could spoil my day my two cousins, James and Tony threw Sam in the deep part of the water from the median. They knew Sam couldn't swim, but did it anyway. Sam's arms began to flap up and down like the flippers on a baby seal. As Sam gasped for air and struggled to stay a float I tried desperately to swim out to him, but I was too far away. Daddy plunged in just in time and pulled Sam from the water, saving him from the grips of death. I was glad Sam didn't go under. When daddy got out of the water James and Tony ran for cover because they knew if daddy ever caught them they were as good as dead. My cousin Sierra and I stayed in the water just about the entire time we were there. No one had to keep a close eye on us because we were both excellent swimmers. Sierra and I decided that we would see how far out we could go, however, mama expressed her concern loudly. Diane don't you go too far. I acknowledged her request, only I kept going anyway. After we had gone out a good distance I began to feel a little fatigued, so I slowed up to let Sierra know it was time to head back. I expressed to Sierra that my arms were tired and I needed to turn around. She agreed, but when we turned to go back we were so far out I could hardly see my family on the beach. Sierra put it in high gear and began swimming fast. Come on Diane, hurry up. I couldn't keep up with her and I began to panic. I couldn't muster up any energy to continue swimming. I tried, however I just couldn't get it together. My arms went numb and my mouth began to fill with the salty water around me. I flapped my arms and kicked my feet to stay a float, but I didn't have anything solid to hold onto. The water kept escaping through the cracks between my little fingers and refused to hold me up. I was determined to win this fight. Unfortunately my feeble attempts to save my own life failed. My body went limp and unlike Sam I went under. Slowly I tumbled under the surface of the waters. I watched carefully as the raging waters above me calmed as if nothing happened. I was then guided slowly into a world unknown to me. I remembered my mama's smile, my daddy's handsome face, Sam running to my rescue and Lottie's pooh bear laugh. I remembered all of the bad things that happened to me and I imagined all of the good things that would not come to be. It seemed as if I was falling forever, tumbling through memories and the mysteries of life. It's funny because I always thought dying would be painful, but I didn't feel anything. My heart began to beat louder and louder, ringing in my ears and throughout my soul. I knew I wasn't going to see any of my family again, but I felt a peace I'd never known before. A few seconds seemed like eternity. Then a bright light illuminated over me. It lit up the entire area around me. I couldn't figure out where it came from because there wasn't that much light on the surface of the water. As a matter of fact it was a cloudy day, but it was so bright down there I was able to see the beauty of the ocean floor. There were colorful plants on my left and in front of me were at least three women like figures. I thought I was seeing things until one of the figures swam over to me, wrapped me in her arms and took me to the surface of the water. When I got to the top I looked for her, but she was gone. I had my strength back and that panicky feeling I had before going under was completely gone. I swam until I reached the brown sandy beach where mama was waiting on shore yelling for me to come out of the water. Diane where have you been? Don't you ever go out that far again! Now go and sit down and do not go back in that water! It was evident that Sierra told them a different side of the story to take the blame off of her. I'm quite certain she didn't tell them that she panicked and left me to drown. I thought about that woman and the other figures I saw beneath the water. I assumed that it was my Aunt Cindy and her sister's because her touch was so familiar and I knew they were the only people crazy enough to be way out there. They all were excellent swimmers, besides, who else could it have been? I chalked the whole thing up as a coincidence that my aunts happened to come along at the right time. Nevertheless, I couldn't figure out how they made it back to the beach before me, so I walked over to my Aunt Cindy to ask her a few questions. How did you get back so fast and what were you all doing down there anyway? She looked at me strangely. What are you talking about girl? Oh, you didn't tell mama you saved me from drowning? Aunt Cindy and mama looked at me and started laughing then mama told me to quit acting silly and go play. I tried to convince them that I was drowning and someone saved me, but they didn't want to hear it. They refused to accept what I was telling them. Mama grew impatient with me and made me leave her sight. I walked away feeling confused. I sat in the dry sand with a towel wrapped around my green bathing suit, shivering until no end and staring out at the water. I wondered who it was that picked me up when I was falling. Who saved me from drowning? Who was it that breathed life into my childlike body? If it wasn't my aunt, then who was it? Dear God was it you? Did you send your angels to save me? Why didn't you let me drown? Look at me! I am nothing and nobody. For the first time in my life I finally felt a real peace. Why didn't you let me go? Why would you waste your time with someone like me? I sat still and pondered over the questions that ran through my mind. I thought about that light, how good it made me feel and how I would never forget what happened as long as I lived.

4
<u>ICE WILL BITE</u>

Mama waited patiently in the car for Sam to arrive from his Boy Scout's meeting because it was time to pick up daddy from work. Lottie and I sat in the back seat slapping each other's hands while singing "Rockin' Robin" as if it was going out of style. Michelle sat in her car seat sucking her thumb as mama's frustration became evident. For crying out loud, would y'all please stop it with the slappin' and clappin', you are driving me crazy. Okay mama we'll be quiet. Mama look! Here comes Sam and he's running like superman. In response she started the engine and began backing out of the driveway. Sam was yelling and pointing toward the crooked house we called home. Mama quickly rolled down her window. Boy what is the matter with you? I gotta go mama, real bad. Well you are just gonna have to wait. It is time for your daddy to get off work and I don't wanna hear his mouth, so come on. Mama, can I please just have a minute? Boy if you don't get in this car you won't see the next second of your life. Sam whined and hopped into the back seat. Mama drove off with Sam squirming in his seat passing gas as Lottie and I continued our rendition of Rockin' Robin in a soft whisper.
Daddy was standing on the curb in front of his job. His lips curved into a smile as he primped over to the driver's side. Mama jumped into the passenger seat and poked her lips out for daddy to kiss. In the midst of their smooching Sam whimpered. Oh my goodness I nearly forgot all about Sam. Can you take your son inside to use the bathroom? Nope! That boy can hold it. I'm not goin' back in there to look in that white man's face just because Sam has to go to the bathroom. He's gonna have to go somewhere because I wasn't planning on going home right away. Where do you have to go? I have to run out to the shopping center for a minute. Well sweetie, he can wait until we get there. Sam slid back in his seat and dared not frown. Before driving off daddy reached in his sack and pulled out a pair of ice skates. I leaped forward with enough ooohhhs and aaahhhs to cool a fire. This is for you Diane. You're the oldest and you're the only one whose feet are big enough to wear em'. I

love you daddy. Thank you, thank you, and thank you again. I kissed daddy on the cheek and he smiled, then he began to laugh. Spit leaped through the huge gap between his teeth, but I didn't care because my daddy gave me my first pair of ballerina skates. Something I've always wanted. Sam let out sarcastic remarks to make me feel bad. So what Diane! Don't nobody care about those stupid skates. Those things are old and they stink. I don't care what you say Sam, I can clean them. Lottie, of course, added in her two cents. You gonna get the feet disease cause' daddy found them nasty things in the garbage. Lottie be quiet. I don't care if flies were flying over them; this is my gift from daddy because I'm special. You kids be quiet. Ain't none of y'all no better than the other. But mama! But mama nothin', sit back and be quiet. Sam where did those skates come from? Mr. Owenoski had us cleanin' the attic and he said if there was anything worth findin', then it was worth takin'. So I took those skates for my daughter. They were gonna throw them out anyway. Well what about the rest of the children? What about them! I give them stuff all the time and she don't say a word, so now it's her turn. Man, that girl does not know how to ice skate, she's gonna end up breakin' her neck. Quit whinin' so much baby, she's gonna be okay. While mama and daddy conversed between each other I spit on my hands and began to wipe off my skates. I couldn't wait until we got home so that I could try them out. Sam and Lottie mocked me as I dreamed I was a princess dressed in pink and lace, skating my way out of the ghetto.

Daddy fought for a parking space and then cursed an old white woman because she took his spot. He mumbled and grumbled; I should wait until she climb outta her car and run her old behind over. We all laughed as daddy found another parking space. The shopping center was packed with all kinds of folk. Yellow folk, green folk, nice folk, and mean folk. White folk, brown folk, skinny folk, and round folk, each involved in their own conversation. Sam stood erect next to daddy as if he was going to explode. Daddy, can I go now? Yeah! Go on and find a bathroom, we'll be in one of these stores when you're done. Sam walked away with sweat pouring from his forehead. He would have run, but the possibility of having an accident was great. Mama desperately looked around the store trying to find a new Afro puff. She must have looked at

20 different styles and found 20 excuses as to why they didn't look right on her. Daddy sprayed assorted colognes all over him not realizing he smelled like Peppi Lapew. We were walking down the hall when we saw Sam approaching. His face hung low and his gait was slow. Hey boy! I know you feel 100% better. Where did you find a bathroom? I didn't. What do you mean you didn't? I couldn't find a bathroom. By the time I got there it was too late. Sam began to cry. Boy what's the matter with you? Be a man and stop snifflin'. Mama was fixing my ponytail when I smelled a foul odor in the air. I looked around and saw a brown streak going down Sam's pant leg. It resembled a brown river. Ughhh, Lottie look. Sam has dookie on his pants. Lottie laughed and daddy snatched Sam around to have a look for himself. Boy! Why didn't you wait until you found a toilet? Daddy, I've been waiting for two hours. I just couldn't hold it anymore. It came out all by itself. Mama shushed daddy when folk began to look and summoned us to quietly leave and head towards the car. Sam attempted to walk without bending his legs to keep his soiled pants from sticking to his skin. Quickly, I made up a song to humiliate Sam and coerced Lottie to join in. Walking through the mall when dookie starts to crawl...diarrhea – uh huh – diarrhea – uh –huh. Going down the gutter on a piece of bread and butter...diarrhea – uh huh – diarrhea - uh huh. Coming down slow when Sam screams OH NO, diarrhea – uh huh – diarrhea – uh huh. We taunted him like a stranger in a foreign land. When tears rolled down his face I realized I had hurt his feelings so I sang the song even louder. Mama and daddy stood at the car puzzled because they couldn't figure out where Sam was going to sit. Daddy went in the trunk and found an old filthy blanket. He placed it over the spot where Sam was going to sit. I asked mama if they could take us home and then come back later to get Sam, but daddy gave me that one more word and I'm going to knock you down look, so I closed my mouth and climbed into the back seat with Sam. I forced Lottie to sit in the middle seat next to him. She pressed against me as if her coat was going to disintegrate if she touched him. In the dead of winter daddy rolled down all the windows to air out the car. With our hands tightly gripped around our nose and mouth we drove all the way home with snow blowing in our faces.

Our street was covered in ice. It looked like a make-believe ice world; I could skate forever. When daddy pulled into the driveway the car died. Daddy cursed the car, but mama was happy that we made it home and didn't get stranded out in the cold. I was just happy to be home because now I could try out my new skates. My attention withdrew from tormenting Sam to the gift my daddy had given me. I ran up the squeaky stairs to our apartment, kicked off my boots, and rushed my new skates to the bathroom for a quick cleaning. I splashed water everywhere, soaking the fury sleeves of my coat. Diane if you don't get your tail outta that water I'm gonna beat you like you stole something. Woman, leave that girl alone. She ain't doin' nothin' wrong. She's just cleanin' the skates off some that's all. Well she's making a mess. Mama I promise to clean up when I'm done. After I'm finished can I please go outside to skate? Absolutely not! You are going to eat dinner and then you're going to bed. Besides, you've gotten your coat all wet and it's going to take all night to dry. Mama may I please go out? Can I please? Girl hush up and get your pajama's on. You have all winter to skate. When it was time to go to bed I took the skates and laid them beside the bed I shared with Lottie so they would be the first things I saw when I opened my eyes in the morning. Hours passed and still no sleep. The lights from cars passing by were gliding through my window and forming circles within circles upon my ceiling. Immediately I saw myself twirling, spinning, and even jumping in those circles with the blades of my skates sparkling upon the ice. Slowly my eyes closed as my mind drifted off into a world where I was free and happy to be whoever I wanted to be.

The smell of bacon slapped my face until I woke up. I looked up and the circles had disappeared from my ceiling. I looked to the left where Lottie lay still as a rock and then to the right where my skates were. They remained in the same position as I had left them. They stared at me, beckoning me to put them on. I smiled, jumped out of bed and headed for the bathroom. Mama was standing over the stove with one hand on her hip and the other hand equipped with a fork, turning that bacon as it sizzled in the pan. Good mornin' mama. Mornin'. Where's daddy? He's outside fixing on that old raggedy car of his. He's supposed to be shoveling that snow, but naw he's out there trying to fix what should be thrown away. Why are you up so bright and early Diane? No reason mama, but since I'm up I might as well get washed up and go outside to help daddy shovel. Em hem, so I guess those skates that you just sat by the door has absolutely nothing to do with you wanting to go outside. Oh those, well I figured since I would already be outside I might as well take the skates with me to make sure they work. Well before you see if they work grab the shovel and shovel that snow off my walkway. Ahhhh mama! Can I please do that after breakfast? No! See what deception does for you. You get yourself tangled up in a bunch of mess when you don't tell the truth. You were just on your heals a minute ago trying to get outside knowing good and well you didn't have any intention on helping your daddy. All you wanted to do was hop on those skates. You can skate your tail right on up that walkway with that shovel and I don't want to see a half done job either. With my lip poked out I dragged myself into the bathroom to get washed up. I could still hear mama talking a mile a minute. I wasted a whole hour listening to mama talk when I could've been skating. I put on three pairs of socks, sweatpants, a pair of jeans, a t-shirt, a turtleneck, a sweater, my coat and hat, two pairs of gloves, and the skates my daddy gave me. I felt like an Eskimo in Alaska. You be careful out there Diane. It's been storming all night long and most of the roads are shut down. I should keep you in because the newsman said no one should be out unless you have to. Mama I'll be fine, I promise. It was difficult for me to get down the stairs, but I held on tight to the railing until I made it to the lower level. I grabbed the shovel from the corner in the hallway and opened the door forgetting about the ice on the steps and the ice skates on my feet. One step is all it took for me to lose my balance. My left leg went to the right and my right leg flew up sending me in a spiral motion downward into a snow pile beside the stair well. I felt like an Olympic reject. I looked over at daddy and his head was buried under the hood of the car. I was glad to know he hadn't seen me fall because it would've been the last time I touched my skates. Hurriedly, I picked myself up and attempted to balance myself when daddy looked up. Hey baby, I see you are gettin' the hang of it. I knew you would. Look at you glide. It's just like roller-skatin' isn't it? Yes daddy. Why don't you go on and skate in the street. I looked up at our window for mama because I knew she would disapprove of the whole idea. I can't daddy. Why not? You and mama told me to stay away from the street cause' you said that crazy folk drive too. Oh don't worry about your mama; I got her in my back pocket. We laughed in unison as I drifted toward the curb. Go on girl or we'll never get a chance to see what those skates can do, especially if you limit them to the sidewalk. Just be careful. Okay daddy, how far can I go? You can go from Mr. Johnson's cleaners at the corner and back to our house. Thank you daddy, but mama told me to shovel first. Don't worry about nothin' I'll shovel this here snow. I darted out into the street as if I had been skating for years. Just when I had finally become familiar with it mama was calling us in to eat our breakfast.

The table was lined with food galore; scrambled eggs, home fries, ham, bacon, grits, and toast. As usual greedy Sam was sitting at the table first, pinching off pieces of bacon from the plates, and leaving the evidence of grease all around his mouth. Daddy was always served first, so we sat and watched him rip his teeth into his food while mama finished serving us. Daddy didn't wait on anyone. I never understood that rationality. He could at least wait until we were all served because by the time we were served he was done. And by the time mama sat down we were getting up, leaving her there to eat alone most of the time. I would sometimes eat in slow motion to keep her company, but not this morning. I had to get back outside. After loading my grits with sugar and butter and making a sandwich out of my toast, eggs, and bacon, I was able to finish my breakfast in a record time of two minutes. Girl if you don't stop stuffing your mouth and gruntin' like a pig I'm gonna make you stay in the house for the rest of the day. I don't know why you're rushing anyway because you have to clean this kitchen, so you better not darken that doorway until it is spic and span clean. I wondered, why is it that whenever you have your heart set on doing something your parents always find 50 million things for you do as if a little free time for play time is going to kill you. After the kitchen, I cleaned my room, and helped my mama with the dusting and other chores. At one o'clock mama finally cut me loose and allowed me to go outside. Daddy was sitting on the couch reading the newspaper. I slid next to him and whispered in his ear. Daddy can I please be allowed to go back out in the street. I promise to be extra careful, and besides, you can watch me from the window. Daddy nodded in agreement. I jumped up, threw on my coat, picked up my ice skates and ran down the stairs into the cold hallway. My warm, bare feet melted the clumps of snow on the hallway floor. I sat on the wet wooden stairs to put on my three pairs of socks. If mama knew I came down here half dressed I would get my behind tore up. After stuffing my feet into the skates I opened the big wooden door that led to the wonderful world of ice. I felt the brisk-cold air take hold of my face and as I inhaled my lungs chilled. Remembering the fall that I had taken earlier I sat on the frozen steps and slid all the way to the bottom. I looked to the left and then to the right before darting out into the street. I pushed off with my right foot and gained speed by swinging my arms in the air. I was gliding upon the ice with smooth strokes and pretty soon I was skating like a professional. Every so often I would look up and there in the shadow of the curtains was mama's silhouette watching over me like a hawk. Finally, after a few hours she called out to me. Diane. Yes mama. Aren't you cold? No mama. Girl, come on in and warm up some. Mama I'm not cold yet, please let me stay out a little while longer. Okay, but come in this house soon before you freeze to death. I knew then that my toes were tingling from the cold, but I didn't want to go in because mama wouldn't have allowed me back out. I rolled my hands up in my gloves, tightly tucked my toes in my skates and continued to be a professional skater. Soon Simone's older sister Tramaine emerged from her house with her ice skates on. Diane I didn't know you had ice skates. Had I known I would've asked you to skate with me a long time ago? This was a surprise because Tramaine never said a word to me. I was always beneath her. She was three years older and thought she was too mature to be seen with a child like me. However, I gladly accepted the company. The streetlights glistened upon the ice giving us the impression that we were standing on pure glass. Back and forth we went from the corner to my house giggling and talking as if we were the best of friends. My feet were no longer tingling. However, my ears rang as the cold air pounded upon the drums within them. I didn't care. I continued to skate anyway. Skish, skish, skish was the only sound in the air as the blades of my skates cut the ice into tiny pieces, scattering them all over the street like broken dreams.

Diane! Yes mama. You see those streetlights on girl? Yes mama. Well get your tail in here. Comin' mama! Tramaine I gotta go in now. I'll be out tomorrow. Okay I'll see you then. I strolled up the walkway and then I carefully climbed the stairs. The hallway was dark and wet. I shook off the excess snow that had become a part of my being before entering the second stairwell, which led to our upstairs apartment. I sat down on the steps and began to untie my laces. As the heat warmed my body the ice began to melt and trickle down my face. I tugged at my ice skates, but they wouldn't budge and my hands stung as I gripped the blade. On the third attempt the skates flew off and tumbled down the stairs. When I stood up to retrieve them pain shot through my feet and on up through my legs. Tears fell like rain and my feet felt like cinder blocks. I couldn't wiggle my toes or feel the softness of my skin. I pulled off my socks to find that my feet had lost their color. They had turned blue-gray with no signs of life, and they didn't look like mine. They looked like elephant feet. I crawled up the stairs moaning and calling for mama. I wanted to scream, but my lungs were frozen. The more the heat penetrated through my frozen skin the more painful it got. Mama heard my cries and helped me in. Daddy was sitting on the couch twisting the end of his mustache and shaking his leg as if he had some sort of nervous tick. Daddy took one look at my feet and his lip dropped to the floor. What in the world is the matter with your feet? They look like two blocks of purple ice. I know good and well you aint' that crazy to have stayed out in the cold where you would let yourself freeze to death. Didn't you feel your foolish-self getting cold? Didn't a bulb go off in that thick head of yours when your feet began to hurt? Yes daddy, but after a while, I just didn't feel anything. I tried talking over the tears, however, every last one of my words drowned. They were separated by sniffles, which sounded as if I was hyperventilating. Well I wonder why Diane!!! Could it be that your foolish behind had already frozen. Or maybe your brain froze keeping you from thinkin' right. Which one came first? Mama and daddy both began examining my feet, poking and prodding at them as if they were dissecting something dead. Sam I think we're gonna have to call a doctor. You are probably right cause' I think she has frost bite. Em hem, oh silly girl done did it this time and now they gonna have to cut off her feet. I began to scream and yelp-like a dog in trouble. Daddy, please don't let them cut off my feet. I need these feet. Please daddy, all I wanted to do was skate. I didn't mean for this to happen. Daddy gently laid his strong hands on my head, looked me in the eyes with concern in his and said that everything was going to be alright. Mama was standing in the doorway between the kitchen and the living room talking to a doctor on the telephone. She kept asking me questions and as I responded she relayed it back to the doctor. When mama hung up the telephone she had a worried look on her face. What's wrong baby? The doctor said he's 100% sure she has frostbite and needs medical attention as soon as possible. How are we going to get her to the hospital, all of the roads are closed and I ain't got that car fixed yet. I know all of that Sam and I've explained that to the doctor. Well if we can't get her to the hospital, then what are we going to do? The doctor also mentioned a home remedy, which entails soaking her feet in a pan of water to reduce the pain and swelling. If it doesn't get better within the next hour, then his advice is to bring her in immediately. Daddy jumped up and filled Michelle's old baby tub with water. Mama quickly grabbed some towels. When daddy placed my feet in the water I screamed uncontrollably. Mama wiped the tears from my face and after a while my screams broke the man-like shield that covered my daddy's heart and he got up, leaving my mother to take over so no one would see his pain. Mama rubbed my feet with her soft hands, caressing them as if they were her own. When she grew tired, once again daddy took over. Fear was chased away by mama and daddy's determination to save my feet. Sam, Lottie, and Michelle sat on the couch watching like three magpies. They quivered at the sound of my screams and batted their eyes several times to keep their tears from taking over. Mama and daddy changed places again and I could barely feel her touch for the pain, but the love mama and daddy put into my feet compensated for all the hurt in the world. Soon, the feeling came back into my feet and everyone blew a sigh of relief. They even rubbed and soaked my hands until the feeling came back in them also. Daddy grabbed the biggest spoon he could find, filled it with Castor Oil, and stuffed it in my mouth. I would've rather swallowed a lump of coal mixed with cement. I gagged and attempted to clear my airways while daddy repeated the same act with Lottie, Sam, and Michelle.

Mama wrapped my feet up in towels and daddy picked me up and placed me in the bed. Mama tucked me in after rubbing my chest with Vicks salve. The entire room smelled like a busy hospital. I watched carefully as Lottie helped mama pick up around the room. Mama wiped off my ice skates that my daddy gave me and threw them in the back of the closet to be remembered no more. She stood beside my bed and watched as I said my prayers. Now I lay me down to sleep, I pray the Lord my soul to keep and if I shall die before I wake, I pray the Lord my soul to take. God, please bless my mama, my daddy, Sam, Lottie, Michelle, my grandparent's, and even me. God thank you for saving my feet cause' I don't know what I would do without them. Thank you. I can feel my toes wiggling. They still feel funny, but I know it's gonna be alright, my daddy said so. Amen. Mama smiled, kissed us goodnight and then turned off the lights. As cars passed by in the street their lights formed circles across my ceiling. I watched as the shadows of the night danced within the circles, but this time they were dancing alone. This time they were without a partner as I lay still upon the ice. I couldn't dance and I couldn't skate because I had fallen victim to the cold. The ice I once skated on turned on me. Its feeble attempts to capture me and imprison me failed. I managed to escape, but before I did the fingertips of death touched my body, freezing my limbs and poisoning my system, but mama and daddy came to my rescue. I closed my eyes and exhaled softly, knowing I would wake up with healthy feet. Thank you for allowing me to survive this tragedy. Thank you again for not allowing me to lose my feet.

5
POISONOUS HANDS

I was pleased to be in a new school with a new setting to receive a new start. It took three years for the city to finally close School #11 for its health and safety violations. I could finally close that chapter of my life and start over. Most of the kids from school #11 were bused out, but Sam, Lottie, and I were sent to School #93. Mama got us into this newly built school by her working for the school board and all. This school was clean as a bill of health and there were much more black teachers than white. I was hesitant at first in making friends because these kids didn't seem any different from the kids at School #11. They just had different faces. They labeled me as weird and out of touch with reality because I kept to myself. I was teased because my mama dressed us real nice and although my sister was three years my younger, we were always dressed like twins. For Christmas my mama and daddy always bought us several gifts, one of mine included a brand new coat with a nice hat. I couldn't wait to wear my coat and hat to school. Everyone complemented me on how nice it looked and that made me feel good. When it was time to go home I went to my locker to put my hat on and this bully named Tammy snatched it off my head and put it on hers. Tammy was about my height and twice my weight. Her face was covered with scars from the many battles she'd been in, some of which were old knife wounds. I grabbed her and demanded she give back my hat. Within seconds I was surrounded by her five sisters and her other thuggish friends. She pushed me up against the locker and asked me if I was willing to do something about it. I took one look at them all and said nothing. In a twinkling of an eye old memories about School #11 flashed before my face and before I knew it hate was burning a hole in my heart again. It was clear to me that people were just evil beings and there was nothing I could do to change that. When the bell rang everyone burst through the big red doors and dove into the piles of snow in front of the yellow brick school. I didn't play, nor did I have the joy and laughter the other kids had. I stood in the snow and watched Tammy walk home with my new hat on her head as the cold air ripped through my pigtails. I cried all the way home and I told mama that I lost my hat and of course she was upset, but at least I didn't have to admit that I allowed someone to take what belonged to me from me. As usual, when I got home I sat down to release my pain within. With my pen and paper as my best friend I formed poetry out of hurt and tears. Poetry spoke to me when no one else would and it listened to me when no one else thought they should.

I loved my new teacher. Her name was Mrs. Williams. She was about 6'2" with black curly hair, shiny cocoa skin, and a smile so big and so beautiful that you couldn't help but to be good in her class. Mrs. Williams had our desks grouped in threes. I sat with Cindy and Angel and eventually Cindy and I became close. Angel was only nice because she and Cindy were friends first, but if the truth be told, she really hated my guts. They asked me if I wanted to be in their club. I of course, agreed. We called ourselves A.C.E, using the first letter of their names and the first letter of my middle name, which was Erma. They told me that they would be my guardian angels and if anyone bothered me they would be there to back me up. I was glad because I had someone on my side and because of it Tammy and her friends left me alone. Tammy was afraid of Angel and Cindy and after several months she joined the A.C.E with one stipulation; that I get the boot. I was at my locker retrieving some things when Angel and Cindy approached me. Diane we have something to tell you. Yeah O.K., but you are going to have to hurry up because I'm late for my art instruction. Mr. Price was giving me private lessons because he said my art was just as beautiful as my poetry. They got straight to the point. Well Diane it's like this, you don't ever have any money and we told you in the beginning you had to pay dues if you wanted to be in this club. How else are we going to get cigarettes and candy? Angel began to taunt me, poke and push me as Cindy continued to talk. And besides, we decided to put Tammy in your place. You are nothing but a goodie two-shoes and you are giving us a bad name. I directed my attention to Cindy because Angel was pushing all the wrong buttons and I couldn't stand the sight of her. Are you kicking me out? Angel said yes and poked me in my chest again. I am not talking to you Angel and you have one more time to touch me. Shut up Diane!

Everybody knows that you ain't gonna do a thing about it. Before Angel finished her sentence she poked me again. I thought about how they were just using me. They thought that since I dressed nice then I could probably get money from my parents whenever I wanted it. Pretty soon I didn't hear either one of them. Their words vanished through the hate that clouded my thinking and sense of judgment. I was tired of being picked on. I was tired of being misunderstood and I was tired of being raped of my integrity. Anger began to burn in me like never before and instead of allowing what I felt to escape through the tears in my eyes I allowed the anger in me to explode like a volcano. I hit Angel as hard as I could. I beat her down and stomped her face. Cindy just stood there screaming for Mrs. Williams because she knew she was next. Mrs. Williams, who was my favorite teacher in the whole world, broke up the fight and then paddled all three of us with a wooden paddle that looked like the oar to my grandpa's rowboat. I couldn't believe she was whooping me. She knew my plight. She heard all the bad things they said and the evil things they did to me, so why did she do this? Afterwards she made us all apologize to each other and clean the boards. I looked at Mrs. Williams with this huge question mark expression on my face. She acknowledged it and took me into the hallway. Diane I know you didn't expect me to hit you, but I expected much more from you. You know that your mother is a good friend of mine and I know she loves you and expects more out of you too, that's one of the reasons she brought you here. I will not accept this type of behavior from you or anyone else. Yes the kids bother you. Yes they say nasty things, but do you know why they do that? Softly I answered, no. They are jealous and I'm not saying that to say you are better than they are because you aren't. I'm saying that because I know they want to befriend you, but they don't know how. They bother you because they want what they perceive you to have and instead of complimenting you they make fun of you. I expect you to handle them the way you have been in your own meek and humble way. Do you understand? Yes Mrs. Williams, I understand. She hugged me and took me back into the classroom. The anger was gone, even toward her. She always said the right things at the right time. I didn't belong to A.C.E anymore and it didn't really matter because from that day forward no one bothered me not even Tammy and the rest of the bullies. I guess they thought I was crazy. No one expected me to lose it like I did and give Angel a beat down. I didn't feel like this weak, frail being anymore. I began to feel power in every step I took.

I made new friends and began missing many of my art lessons to hang out with them during free time. Mr. Price didn't like that. He always said that a real artist can't make it if they don't put forth the effort or time. Truthfully, I just didn't like the air he carried. I didn't like the way he touched me. I watched the way he touched the other female students that were being taught privately by him also and I didn't like it. All of the teachers were captivated by his smile and smooth talk; nonetheless, I saw something ugly underneath those pearly whites. Mr. Price was a beautiful black man whom I think was born with a paintbrush in his hand. He drew and painted with such wonderful expressions and he captivated the mind as well as the heart of the viewer. I wanted my pictures to come to life as his did, only I didn't think he had to touch me to teach me. As time went on I began to put more time and effort into my art. Mr. Price taught me everything he knew. He helped me to build my confidence in my abilities and in myself. He told me I could do anything I set my mind to. After each session he had some new compliment waiting for me. I didn't trust many people, but soon I let my guard down and I began to spend more time in the art room. Mr. Price was the only one who truly understood our artistic minds and our need to express our thoughts on paper. One Friday morning he asked that I come in after school with two other students instead of during free time because he had too many students coming in at the same time. However, when I arrived I found the classroom empty. Mr. Price was sitting behind this desk drawing as usual. I wondered where my usual sidekicks were, but didn't really pay it that much attention. Diane, if you don't mind before we start can you help me clean up this room a little bit. Sure Mr. Price. I cleaned the boards and straightened up the desks while some students in the hallway noisily worked on the school painting project. As always the pictures that were stretched across the walls captivated me, and I found myself drifting away inside of them. Blue, violet, yellow, and streaks of orange reflected the energy inside of me as it continued in each painting with no end. I realized that the freedom of expression and its ability to go on forever is what attracted me to it because in it I could be free to be whatever I wanted to be. Free of troubles and pain. Free to be me. I sat down at my desk and began to work on my art project. Mr. Price was looking over my shoulder. That's nice Diane. You are a wonderful artist. As long as you continue to let the visions in your mind flow onto this paper you won't have a problem. You really think I have what it takes? Yes, now come over to my desk. I want to show you something that I've been working on. I was very eager to see his work. As he sat down I looked at his pictures from the opposite side of his desk. Mr. Price these are beautiful. Diane you have the ability to do just as well. Mr. Price placed and empty drawing board on the desk. Now Diane I want you to draw what's in your mind. The instant I started drawing Mr. Price interrupted me. Diane I can't see what you're doing so come around to this side of my desk. I grabbed my pencils and hurriedly went to his side of the desk. I discontinued drawing when he slid his chair next to me and his furry arms came down on my left and then my right locking me in. To my surprise Mr. Price picked me up, sat me on his lap and then placed his hand over mine and started drawing. I froze as fear raced through my soul. I couldn't move. The red flashers were going off in my head screaming Danger! Danger! Danger! Why is he doing this? Somebody help me. Please God send someone in this classroom. His chin lay at rest on my shoulder while his hot breath moistened my neck. Diane you are doing excellent. You are a great artist and you are so beautiful. I was looking for a way out, but those hands kept getting in the way, only these hands were bigger. These hands were stronger. Every child like instinct told me to run, but I couldn't move. I just kept watching those hands touch my hands and then my neck, choking me into silence. I could hear the other kids in the hallway, only I couldn't scream because his hypnotic voice paralyzed my sense of judgment. I felt him pressing his body against mine while he continued to tell me what a wonderful artist I was. I hated him for attempting to take the little bit of me that I had left. With my mouth open wide I could hear myself screaming. However, the sound was imprisoned within. Beads of sweat rolled down my face while my eyes watched the door. My heart began to weep and lash out in silence. Mr. Price you are a liar! You are not interested in my art. You never were.

Get your hands off of me. Stop touching me. Leave me alone! He didn't hear me. Had he listened to my heart or had he seen what was in my eyes he would have heard me screaming. He would have felt my pain. What is with this species called male? Why are they always taking what does not belong to them? For ten minutes I struggled to fight back the tears and just when they began to surface one of the students entered the room to ask Mr. Price for some paint. This was my opportunity to escape. Those arms that had kept me prisoner were lifted and those ugly hands shifted. I jumped off his lap and headed for the door, never to return again. Several weeks later Mr. Price was fired for touching little girls. Although I never told a soul the girl who burst in his classroom sort of knew. She was the victim who turned him in. God in heaven, I thank you for helping me out. Thank you for coming to my rescue.

Journal Insert:
DRIVEN

Driven into a corner of darkness...Driven to the far edge of the sea...Traveled down that long road of hardship...Who understands me? Trying to keep all sanity...Trying to relieve myself of the silent pain...Misery and hopelessness, both tapping on my head like the beats of the pounding rain...I ask...What have I to gain? Given the opportunity to be what I am...Given the chance to be me...Triumph and the gracious life of living alone...Who shall I trust and who shall trust me? Poisoned by depression and distress ...Poisoned by life itself... Troubled nights and days go by... Nothing more and nothing less... What have I to confess? Sitting in this chair for years...After reaching inevitable success...The taste of salt from silent tears... Lord...I've tried my best...I ask again...What have I to confess? Dark corners peaking out at me... The loud sound of silence ringing in my ears...Four walls of captivity...I feel as though I've been institutionalized for years and years... What have I to confess? I am not sure...Insanity maybe...Perhaps a bit more.
Diane

6
<u>WHAT'S WRONG WITH THE CHITTLIN'S</u>

The smell of sugar and spices roamed about the house tickling the lining of my stomach.   Apples, cinnamon, pecan, and nutmeg danced throughout the air while dressing, turkey, black- eyed peas, and greens filled the crusted pots on the stove.   I sat on a stoop to watch mama create magic, turning all kinds of stuff into an excellent Thanksgiving dinner.   While mama was peeling, slicing, and mixing daddy practiced his Thanksgiving Day ritual that included football, beer, and pork rind skins.   During commercials daddy would mosey on into the kitchen, slip behind mama and wrap his arms around her waist.   Just before they began smooching I would turn my head in disgust or leave the room until they cleared the way.   This time I couldn't leave the room because I got caught up in the corner, so I placed my attention on the slimy chittlin's in the sink.   My eyes wrapped around every curve and went over every bump.   When I reached the end of the line I thought to myself, for you to taste so good, y'all stank.   That smell has to be from sitting in that nasty bucket too long.   Or maybe it's from the spices.   I wonder why mama don't clean these stankin' things with Ajax or something to get the smell out.   I snapped out of it when I heard daddy stumbling to get back to the television.   Touchdown! Touchdown! How did that happen so fast? I hate that team! You see what you made me miss by bein' in that kitchen foolin' around with you.   Mama threw her knife down and went to rantin' and ravin'.   Made you miss what?   Man, have you lost your cotton pickin' mind.   I was in here minding my own business when you came in here bothering me.   You are so ignorant!   Woman be quiet, can't you see I'm watching the game!   Michelle got up off the floor, went over to daddy and laid her head across his lap.   Daddy stopped yelling and mama ceased from fussing.   She picked up her knife and continued to clean and cut up those stankin' chittlin's.

Mama why does chittlin's stink so bad?   If I told you why, you wouldn't eat them.   Yes I would cause' they're good, especially with hot sauce.   Oh really!   Yes mama, so are you going to tell me?   They smell because they are the pig's intestines. Intestines! I know you don't mean the gut things. Isn't that the place where the #2 passes through? Yes it is. I can't believe I ate something like that. I will never eat chittlin's again. I'm getting sick and I think I'm gonna throw up. Diane be quiet and get out of my kitchen. You always have to go to the extreme with everything. Daddy grabbed his belly, fell back in his chair and began to laugh so hard I could see his tonsils. As he struggled to get a word out of his mouth spit flew out of the hole where a tooth used to be. I choked on the mere thought of eating something seasoned with pig mess. Daddy finally gained control of his laughter and offered his opinion. You should've never told that nut where chittlin's came from. You know how she is. Now you should make her stay right there with you so she can get some learnin'. When I heard what daddy said to mama I bent over like a sick dog and made myself gag all the more just so daddy wouldn't make me stay in the kitchen. When mucus slid from my mouth onto the carpet daddy stopped laughing and his face grew hard as a rock. Girl, get your crazy intentions outta my face and go back in there with your mama. When he stood up I ran around him like a frightened little rat and into the kitchen. Sam, Lottie, and Michelle were sitting on the floor in front of the television snickering. Every thing in me told me to slap those smiles off their faces, but since I had already been counted as sheep for slaughter, I ignored them. I began cutting onions and celery for the stuffing and when the oven was free I poured the cake batter into the cake pans. I was trying to leave a little extra batter in the bowl so that I could have it for myself, but mama caught me and practically scraped the bowl clean. I grabbed the spoon and began to lick it as fast as I could. Again, mama caught me and sounded the alarm for Sam, Lottie, and Michelle to come and get some of the treat. They stormed the kitchen like vultures, pushing and shoving as if they've never eaten before. Sam elbowed me, snatched the spoon out of my hand and began licking it. I pushed Lottie and Michelle out of the way and stuck my entire hand in the bowl, swiping the sides clean. Lottie grabbed my hand in a feeble attempt to get some of the batter off my fingers. I pushed her as hard as I could, but this time she went flying into the stoop that Michelle was sitting on, knocking her to the floor. Her screams silenced the house, which caused the rest of us to line up single file for the whipping mama said we had been asking for all day. Whenever it was time for a whipping I would always try to be last because I figured daddy would take out most of his anger on the first one in line and by the time he got to me he would be good and tired, but it didn't go as planned because daddy grabbed me first. After receiving our just due punishment we were all made to sit in silence until it was time for us to go to grandma's house for the big Thanksgiving dinner. Mama and daddy began talking about how foolish we were and since all of their frustration had been taken out on us they quickly forgot about their anger toward each other. Consequently, during half-time mama and daddy slipped away like criminals in the dark to spend some time alone. I felt this was my opportunity to make amends. I went to the bathroom, retrieved the Ajax and declared war on those stankin' chittlin's. I was going to get rid of that smell for good, besides; mama would appreciate the fact that I took the initiative to finish cleaning her chittlin's. Sam and Lottie began cleaning up the living room, Michelle turned the channel to cartoons, and I scrubbed away. I made those chittlin's super clean. Suddenly, the bedroom door crept open and then the bathroom door closed. Finally, when they emerged from the hallway they were amazed to see that we were actually doing something good. Daddy walked in with a proud look while mama kept her head down. Shame lit up her face and kept her from looking in mine. I wanted to say, so, where have you been? Were y'all cleaning up the room or did you think we were totally unaware as to what you two were doing, but instead I kept scrubbing away at those chittlin's.

Diane! Yes mama. What are you doing? I smiled greatly. So great, that every last one of my teeth was showing because I felt that I was doing a great service for her. A proud look hung over my face when I answered her. Well mother, you weren't done cleaning the chittlin's, so I figured I'd help you out. My lips sarcastically curved with every word. Well what is all this white stuff in the sink? Oh, that's my ancient Chinese secret called the "chittlin' stank cleanser." Diane quit playing with me and answer me girl. With my lip still wrapping around every syllable I answered with confidence. It's Ajax mama. She placed her hand on her hip and her eyebrow rose to her hairline. Her shamed face was replaced with an angry one and her voice rose 10 times above that of a bullhorn. Ajax! You mean to tell me you used cleanser to clean my chittlin's. You can't do that. You'll give us food poison and kill us all. I began shaking like a leaf. You would've thought the house was on fire or something the way daddy jumped out of his chair. I knew I was going to get it now. Daddy let out a loud roar that shook the house. Oh my goodness, not the chittlin's. Lord please say it aint so. He ran to the sink and began rinsing them in cold water. Mama laughed so hard she fell to the floor. She laughed until she cried. Daddy stood at the sink shirtless with his pants hanging past his waist showing his backside as plumbers usually do. As I eased away from them daddy angrily turned toward me. When they're done you gonna eat every last bit of it you crazy little girl. Something is wrong with that child. Who in their right mind would do something like this? Of course, Sam and Lottie were standing at the edge of the kitchen with their hands on their hips, shaking their heads from side to side as if they were disgusted with me. I drifted away into my room hoping I would just disappear. As I lay across my bed the smell of sugar and spices danced across my face. Apples, cinnamon, pecans, and nutmeg were playing the right tunes to my taste buds. Dressing, cranberry sauce, potato salad, and greens drifted under my nose. I couldn't wait to taste it. Just as I began to sink in my delicious thoughts an unfamiliar smell interrupted it. It wasn't as sweet and it wasn't as pleasant. As I lifted my hands to my nose the stench grew stronger. One sniff is all it took to remind me of what I did to my daddy's chittlin's. I could still hear his mouth going a mile per minute. As I looked back on the entire situation it was really kind of funny. I rolled around in my bed laughing and giggling to myself.

The house was quiet. There was a calm like no other. Hours of hard work lay still in assorted dishes; all packed up and ready to be devoured. We all piled into daddy's 1974 purple and white Grand Prix headed for Grandma Jones house. Daddy was fussin' at mama about being late and mama cut her eye at him so sharp I felt it. Daddy turned around and with a stern face he gave us our instructions. Now y'all better be on y'all best behavior cause' I ain't takin' no mess from y'all nappy headed kids tonight, and if any of you mention one word about them chittlin's I'm going to beat you like you stole somethin'...Do ya' hear me? We nodded in agreement and sat back as daddy pulled off. Mama turned the music on and we floated all the way to grandma's house aboard the rhythms of Earth, Wind, and Fire. When we pulled up I could see shadows upon the curtains of grandma's window, bobbing and weaving in laughter. The door flew open and Uncle George was standing there with a beer in his hand looking like J.J on Good Times screaming, what's happening. Uncle George is so skinny you could pick your teeth with him. Daddy put on his cool daddy act and began primping like a pigeon in shoes. Grandpa sat back in his brown lounge chair smoking his pipe, blowing rings of smoke into the air. The perfectly formed circles widened as they approached the ceiling, then stretched far apart until it was no more, disappearing into thin air like the laughter in the room. Grandma cackled like a hen. Ah eeh eeh eeh eeeee, rustled from her belly as she pulled me into her bosom, squeezing the life out of me. My eyes roamed the room as I wrapped my arms around my grandma. They rested on the blue, white, and gold print curtains, which hung stiff before the picture window in the front room against the wood paneled walls. I glanced over at the gold furniture that sat upon the gold rug and I smiled when I saw the little box for the television. It sat alone in the corner. The beaten trail on the carpet led to the dining room where the cherry table and chairs glistened under the light in front of the cherry china cabinet. Through the doorway was the kitchen that led to a hallway straight to the blue bathroom and the green bedrooms, which were cut into the walls on the opposite side of the room. The men threw curse words at each other and made up lies to make one seem better than the other. Mama called it trash talk. Grandma bounced around in the small kitchen where a small table sat between the stove and the refrigerator. The linoleum on the floor was chipped in several places and the yellow cabinets lined the wall on both sides of the window. Grandma delightfully hummed while banging her spoon against the pot as she checked her greens. In the dining room the women prepared the table and set the food out in nice arrangements. They whispered about how foolish the men were and exchanged secrets like silly little girls giggling in unison after every remark. As usual, the adults kicked all of us kids out of the living room and sent us to the back of the house where we couldn't hear their garbage being slung back and forth. We entertained ourselves by turning out all of the lights in the back room to play ghost.

We screamed as if someone was killing us and when we were bored with that we eavesdropped on the adult conversation being passed around.

The house was filled with words and laughter, childlike giggles, and plenty of sniggles. After everyone had gotten acquainted with each other, as if for the first time, we gathered around the huge dining room table to bless the food. When Uncle George, already drunk from the night before offered to lead the prayer everyone sighed, but quickly joined hands as he stepped up to the plate. Would everyone bow all eyes pleeze? Dear Lawd, most precious and h-e-a-v-e-n-l-y Father God. I know it was you; y-e-s you, who gave us dis' here food to eat. Everythang' is lovely. Lawd thank ya for da' yams, I thank ya for da' turkey, da' greens, and er ah even all da' drinks which is good to my soul, dat's why you wept and dat's why I thank ya. In Jesus name we pray, and let the people say Amen. By the time he was done half of the circle was in tears from trying to hold back laughter. Mama was on her knees and when she could no longer keep her laughter in it burst forth. The next thing I knew she was rolling across the floor chuckling like a broken down hyena. Sam joined in with the rest of the kids and began to laugh. I wanted to play it safe so I held onto a straight face. The adults looked around at all of the kids laughing and grabbed the child closest to them. For five minutes they yelled at them about being disrespectful because they laughed at an adult even if he was incorrect. I sat in a corner chair with a huge smirk across my face. I was glad I didn't laugh. I learned two important lessons in a matter of minutes. I learned to wait before opening my mouth and I found out what the meaning of hypocrisy was. I waltzed around Sam and Lottie with a proud look on my face that said, It was you who got into trouble this time, not good ole' me. Sam went to punch me, but realized one more peep out of him and daddy would sentence him to visit Mr. Belt, so he withdrew his fist. When all the confusion had ended everyone went around the table in single file overloading their plates as if they wouldn't be allowed to go back for seconds. Michelle was on the other side of the table eating her food as mama placed it on her plate. Mama dropped a scoop of chittlin's on Michelle's plate and she started crying. Mama leaned over so that Michelle could see the look in her eyes, but Michelle couldn't see her because she had shut hers, so mama questioned her as quiet as she could.

What is your problem child? I don't want those chittlin's mama. Sam and I slowly looked over at daddy. The hair in his mustache was sticking straight out over the chicken bone protruding from his mouth. His eyes had bulged out and he began to bat them as if he had a nervous tick or something. Sam and I looked at Michelle and really felt sorry for her. Grandma walked over to Michelle and began talking to her. Child you know good and well you like chittlin's. What's so different now? They're just nasty grandma. Nasty! They have never been nasty before. Uh huh, they are nasty because Diane put Ajax on it. Everyone yelled the word Ajax as if it was the number one answer on Family Feud. That chicken bone that was in daddy's mouth hit the wall. Daddy's face was so red you would've thought someone burned him with a torch. Mama hesitated before offering her reply. That girl lie, em em em, that don't make any sense for a child to make up stuff like that. I'm gonna whip your tail when you get home. Now I've told you about making up stories. You know good and well Diane didn't put Ajax on this food. Mama talked nice and loud so no one could hear Michelle refuting what she was saying and kindly escorted her to the bathroom. Lottie followed mama and Michelle and placed her ear to the door. Sam and I knew Michelle was going to get smacked. Uncle George picked at daddy's chittlin's with a fork looking for traces of Ajax and pretty soon those chittlin's grew cold and hard as they sat there all alone. I went into the kitchen to get some dressing, but Lottie and my cousin Chole were standing over it making faces. Chole what's wrong with you and Lottie? There's nothing wrong with us, but if you looked close at the dressing you will see that there is something wrong with it. I examined the dressing and couldn't find anything. Lottie kept pushing my face closer asking me if I saw it. What am I looking for? A Roach! Yeah right...where is it? It's in the dressing. Chole pointed to a particular spot in the pan. It's a Roach! Sam ran over and tried to pick it out with a fork and like doctor's performing surgery we all stood around dissecting the dressing. That is disgusting, who made this dressing? You know who. No I don't, why don't you tell me. The nasty house upstairs made it! Who, Cousin Sally? You got it. I decided to make a song about the whole incident. Sally Mae was cookin' some food early Thursday and brought it to the table because she was hungry...she didn't know that a roach jumped in and now it's lookin' at us with a stupid grin. We all laughed and sang the song in unison. Grandma stormed towards us wiping her hands on her apron. What are y'all doing? The smiles quickly slid off our faces. As I stepped forward to answer for the younger ones, I decided to take an intellectual approach with grandma. Again, my lips sarcastically curved around each word. Well grandma it's like this. We were trying to get some of this wonderful dressing when we noticed some legs sticking out of it and after further investigation we found that the legs belonged to the roach lying in the pan. Roach! That ain't no roach. Sam and I looked at each other and wondered if grandma was looking at the same thing. Grandma went on and on about how that wasn't a roach. I knew without a doubt she convinced her eyes they were lying to her. Grandma if that ain't no roach, then what is it? I said it ain't no roach and I mean it! Y'all only say that cause' you know Cousin Sally got roaches. Well so do half the world, so wake up and smell the coffee. Y'all are some simple kids. You know good and well there ain't no roach in that food. That's nothing but a burnt onion. I thought; the only thing that was burned to a crisp was her eyesight. Grandma, have you ever seen an onion with legs and antennas before? Grandma ignored me, scooped up the dressing and placed it on our plates. Chole started crying. What's the matter with you child? Chole screeched…there's a roach in that dressing. Oh hush up talking stupid before you get a whippin'. Y'all better eat everything on those plates. Sam looked at me and whispered to make sure he wasn't overheard. Now I see where mama gets it from. I agreed. We marched to the table under grandma's command with sagging faces and tears in our eyes. Our feeble attempts to get mama's attention went unnoticed, so we hurriedly ate the roach infested food and prayed we wouldn't crunch on that roach.

On the way home we told mama and daddy the whole story. Mama choked off the mere thought of it and daddy complained all the way home. I can't believe what I'm hearin'. That couldn't have been a roach. Yes it was daddy. Well, why in the world would y'all silly kids eat that mess and why didn't y'all say somethin' to me or your mama? I don't care what your grandma told you to do, use common sense next time. I think I'm gonna be sick. That's why I don't eat other folks cookin'! How nasty can you be? How in the world did a roach get in her food? What did she do, mistake it for a raisin? And who ever heard of dressing with raisins? Daddy was so outraged that he forgot all about Michelle telling everyone about the chittlin's. His mouth went a mile per minute. Michelle and Lottie were sound asleep and between mama's gags she laughed. Sam and I communicated by eye contact only. We didn't want to risk all that anger being turned on us. As daddy slowly drove through the city the cool breeze drifted through the window onto our faces. We inhaled the intoxicating, but peaceful scents of the night, closed our eyes and drifted off to sleep in the back seat of daddy's purple Grand Prix.

7
__ROAD TRIP__

School was just about over and summer was here. My class was going to Washington D.C for one week. I couldn't wait to venture out on my own. Everything seemed to be falling into place for me. I was going to high school soon and mama and daddy had just bought a new house in an all white neighborhood on Park Place Boulevard. My dreams were finally coming true. The house was white with green trim. It had four bedrooms, a large living room, dining room, and a family room to watch television. This house had a huge backyard equipped with a red, white, and blue swing set and a basketball hoop hanging over the garage, waiting for me to dunk in Sam's face. Finally, the sun was shining bright and I could feel its warmth all over me. Mama said that by the time I got back from Washington the move would be complete and we would be in our new home. So, before I left I said good-bye to all of my friends, Simmone included. As the bus pulled off from the school we drove through the neighborhood to get to the highway. I watched carefully as the broken down homes and buildings began to fade away, only to become part of my past. We drove down Stanton Street and then by my old school. I waved good-bye to the shattered memories of my childhood. I waved good-bye to the broken pieces of my life that had been scattered over this neighborhood like dirt and decided not to take any of it with me. Laughter echoed throughout the bus and music danced in our ears as we celebrated our freedom from parental guidance. I wanted to share a room with a new friend I had met. Her name was Joyce, but she chose to room with Tammy and the rest of the bullies because Tammy was her cousin. Being that I was one of the leftovers without a roommate I was placed with Arlene and Debora (two beauty queen rejects) and a girl named Alecia who acted, looked, and even dressed like a boy. The kids talked about Alecia all the time. They teased her continuously, but most of the time it was done behind her back because she also fought as a boy would. I felt sorry for her because I knew how it felt to be taunted and teased about things that weren't true, but I couldn't necessarily say whether or not all of the things that were said about Alecia weren't true. She grabbed her private parts like a boy; pimped like a boy, and told us her mother dressed her in her brother's clothing purposely. So one could only assume that she was what they said she was.

Each room was equipped with two king size beds, a television and a bathroom. Since there were four kids per room we had to pair up for sleeping arrangements. Arlene and Debora paired up immediately so neither one of them would have to sleep with Alecia; as if someone wanted to sleep with them anyway, but I most definitely didn't want to sleep with Alecia. Arlene and Debora teased me all night about how Alecia was going to rape me while I was sleeping. I ignored them and did my sit ups as usual before taking my shower and retiring for the evening. Eventually I joined in on their conversation and began to talk about Alecia in the worst way just to get them to leave me alone. The three of us laughed all night long leaving Alecia outside of our inner circle. I could almost hear Alecia saying, "You idiot, don't you know you aren't part of their inner circle either!" What was I doing? I knew these people weren't my friends and I knew the minute I turned my back they would stab me in it. How could I treat another human being like this? Although it felt good not to be the one being taunted I still couldn't help thinking, how could I have stooped so low? Debora began talking about Alecia's hair and how much of a mess it was. Laughter shook the walls of our room. I was laughing so hard tears began to fall from my eyes and when I glanced over at Alecia I saw tears swelling in hers. She was trying to act as if we weren't bothering her, but everything in me told me that she was hurting. Hate plastered her face like wallpaper. I knew that look well, except I wear mine on the inside now. My smile slid off my face and her pain I did embrace. I felt bad about what I had done to Alecia and I wanted to apologize to her, but I just couldn't talk myself into doing it. Alecia went to bed long before the rest of us with a broken heart. Arlene and Debora kept talking about her and when I refused to entertain any more of their conversation, they began to talk about me. Hey Diane I heard that the reason why you don't have no hair is because your mama is a pigmy. Arlene and Debora laughed and teased me for the duration of the night. Their sneers echoed in my mind and like Alecia I laid my head down on my pillow with a broken heart. The two of them finally went to bed about 2:00 in the a.m. I chose not to say my prayers on my knees that night because I didn't want any of them looking at me strangely. I didn't want to give them something else to talk about since none of them believed in saying their prayers. I slept on the edge of the bed to make sure my body parts, not even my feet, would touch Alecia's. I whispered a prayer to God, curled up into a fetus like ball, and rocked myself to sleep as I did every night like a little baby in my mama's arms. We all woke up around the same time. Arlene and Debora were snickering amongst themselves, however, Alecia decided to confront them. I'm not taking any of your garbage today, so y'all better leave me alone. Arlene and Debora started to laugh hysterically when Arlene walked over to Alecia and me with a silly grin on her face. Diane did you two have a good time last night? What are you talking about Arlene? Well, Debora and I saw those covers moving back and forth last night and couldn't believe what you two were doing. For your information I have to rock myself to sleep or else I can't go to sleep. You know how far apart we slept from one another, so what is it that you thought we were doing. Debora opened her mouth wide and screamed, SEX! Alecia bawled up her fists and began to shout obscenities at the two of them then stormed out of the room. I pushed Arlene as hard as I could. What are you trying to say? I know you don't think Alecia and I were "..." I know you aren't insinuating that the two of us "..." What's the matter Diane? Is your tongue twisted or is the shame of being raped by Alecia causing you to react this way? I really wanted to kill the both of them for being so ignorant and foolish. Their crazy insinuations held my words prisoner. I was tired of being misunderstood, but once again I swallowed everything that had been dished out to me and pretended not to care. They couldn't spell sex if they wanted to, let alone, give a definition to the word. Their huge vocabulary of obscene verbs and adverbs really let me know they were totally ignorant when it came down to explaining sex or anything about sexual relations. It took me a long time, but I figured out that kids only bother and tease others to cover up their own faults and lack of acceptance within themselves. However, their lies cut me. The pain was very real, but that's what I get for compromising with the devil. After everyone had gotten dressed for the day we all boarded the bus for our sight seeing trip. Before the bus driver could get the key in the ignition Debora and Arlene were telling everyone on the bus that Alecia and I were an item and that we had a very romantic evening. Although we both told everyone they made up the entire story no one believed us. We became the butt of everyone's joke while on the bus. After several attempts to persuade them otherwise I sat back in my seat in silence, dreaming about home. My plans for having a nice time faded away and for the remainder of the trip I kept to myself. I counted the days as if I was in prison serving time. I had no one to hang out with and no one to talk to. Even Joyce abandoned me. No one wanted to take the chance of being ridiculed, so they jumped on the bandwagon and rode my back like everyone else. Alecia was going through the exact same thing as I, but we couldn't and we wouldn't talk to each other because of the lie Arlene and Deborah made up for a laugh. When the day finally came to return home I was the happiest person on the planet. I couldn't wait to get home to see my new house and pull into my new driveway. There was nothing anyone could say to me to upset me today. My main focus was getting home and seeing my family. Alecia, on the other hand saw this day as a day of reckoning. As we all were preparing to take our showers Debora walked around Alecia and purposely bumped her shoulder telling her to move out of the way. Before Debora could get another word out of her mouth Alecia put her fist in it. The next thing I knew Debora had been laid out on the floor and Alecia was on top of her pounding her face inside out. Arlene ran out of the room to get a chaperone while I sat there filled with laughter. The chaperone burst through the door and attempted to separate the two, but Alecia continued to throw punches, striking both Debora and the chaperone. Debora's face was filled with blood and tears. It wasn't all that funny, but I continued to laugh anyway so that she could see how it felt to be hurt and then taunted by someone. By this time we had a crowd standing at our door trying to gain ringside seats. Eventually Alecia jumped on Arlene and began pulling her hair out. The Hotel security guards stormed the room and broke up the fight, making everyone go to their own rooms. After which, the chaperone's did gain control of the children.

While the bus driver threw our luggage into the lower compartments, we boarded the bus, pushing and shoving in line to get the seats in the back of the bus. The back of the bus was where members of the in-crowd got together to cut up. Since I wasn't in the in-crowd I sat closer to the front of the bus where I wouldn't be bothered by Arlene and Debora, although they were somewhat quieted by the constant reminder of their cuts and bruises given to them by Alecia. The scenery on the highway was all the same, mountains, trees, and more mountains. I gazed out the small window next to my seat thinking about mama, daddy, Sam, Lottie, and Michelle. I didn't think I would, but I missed them all. Sam had gone on a camping trip shortly after I had left, so I knew he wouldn't be there when I got back and as much as he got on my nerves I still missed him. I began to imagine myself sitting in my huge bedroom that I was going to share with Lottie. Michelle had a bedroom all to herself next to mama and daddy's room. I didn't think that was fair because I was the oldest. I should have had a room to myself, but mama and daddy didn't want any grown kids sleeping next to their bedroom. It seemed as though we were driving for hours and not getting anywhere, so I figured if I closed my eyes and went to sleep the time would pass by much faster. When I awoke everyone was standing outside of the bus in front of the school. I was excited to see mama and daddy searching the crowds for me. When I reached for my jacket hair began to fall from my shoulders. I placed my hands at the top of my head to feel for my hair, only to have it all fall to the floor. I began to scream as loud as I could. Arlene and Debora got back on the bus with the other kids following them. They began chanting vile things. Diane don't have no hair, she's baldheaded, baldy, baldheaded Diane. They picked the hair up off the floor and began stuffing it in my face and pounding it on my head. I wept, not because of what they had done to me, or what they had taken away from me, but because I felt as if my life was over. The only thing I had left was my body, an empty shell-a useless piece of art. I could hear mama and daddy calling my name off in a distance, but I had fallen to the floor at the hands of my enemies. When I looked up mama and daddy were standing over me, pulling me up off the floor. Daddy kept shaking me and calling my name over and over again. When I was finally able to open my eyes fully I saw Mrs. Smith, who was one of the chaperones.

She was shaking me and telling me to get up and to stop talking in my sleep. I glanced out the window and watched all of the parents waving at us as we pulled up. Mama and daddy had big kool-aid smiles on their faces. I was glad that I was just dreaming because I had more than enough problems to deal with.

8
WHAT'S WRONG WITH ME?

It seemed as though we were driving all night long, but we finally arrived in Ohio at 3:00 in the A.M. Daddy drove down the highway showing all of his teeth. He was proud of his new car and wanted everyone to see it. It wasn't brand spankin' new, but it was newer than the one we had before. Mama, Sam, Lottie, and Michelle were all opening their slumber filled eyes. They slept the entire way as I stayed up to keep my daddy company. I was his eyes and ears for the police while he deliberately went over the speed limit, besides, I couldn't wait to see my grandma and grandpa. I couldn't wait to be taken up in their arms. Daddy pulled into the alley beside their home and parked. As we sat patiently in the car daddy pounded on their door to get them to wake up, and when they didn't he grabbed a handful of rocks from the alley and began throwing them at their bedroom window. Mama what are we gonna do if they don't wake up? I guess we'll have to sleep in the car until day breaks. Sam whined, ah man! Don't nobody wanna sleep in no car; I wanna see grandma and grandpa right now! Boy you hush up your mouth right now! I put my head down to keep myself from bursting into laughter. Let me serve notice on all four of you. Just because you're at your grandparents does not mean I won't knock fire from you. Start showing off and you'll find out that I mean business. We sat as still as pigeons on a stoop because the cracks in mama's face said she was serious. When she turned her head we exhaled and began breathing again. I looked up at the house and a light came on, then I heard the screen door fly open. Hey dad, how are you doing? Well I was sleepin', but it's mighty good ta' see all of ya'. We jumped out of the car and wrapped ourselves around grandpa. Grandma soaked mama and daddy with kisses and left over pillow slob while grandpa pulled our bags from the trunk of the car. Dad leave those bags alone, these kids can get that stuff in the morning. Naw, you all go inside; I'll get the bags. These kids will be here for the entire summer and seeing how we only get ta' see them once a year, I'm gonna spoil them ta' death.

Mama and daddy stayed the weekend, but early Sunday morning they rose and prepared to go back home. Diane, Sam, Lottie, and Michelle come here please. Yes mama. Your daddy and I are leaving. I want you all to mind your grandparents and act like you got some sense; do you hear me? Yes mama. Diane you stay out of that alley because ain't nobody gonna fool with you and poison ivy too. Yes mama, I understand. Your daddy and I will be back in four weeks to pick you up. Just before mama and daddy got in the car Uncle Ted pulled up and hurriedly ran toward daddy. They embraced as if they weren't going to see each other again. Uncle Ted was my daddy's only brother and they loved each other very much. Although Uncle Ted was the oldest my daddy was the biggest and bravest and everyone knew it because Uncle Ted acted like a wimp at times. Daddy drove away very slowly. He and mama waved their arms in the wind as we chased the car down the road until it disappeared, then as if nothing ever happened we began playing like four maniacs who'd just escaped from a mental institution. As time passed I went into the house to spend time with grandma. I sat under her watching soap operas and snapping green beans. On Sundays grandma and grandpa took us to church where we stayed for most of the day. Grandpa said Sundays were to be respected. That meant no yelling, no playing, no running, and no jumping. On Sundays after church we were bored to death. With grandpa as the pastor of the church some people pretended to be nice to us just to get closer to him, but their phony expressions of love couldn't hide the evil in their hearts. We saw right through them and so did grandma and grandpa. There were, however, some that expressed genuine love, nerve wrecking, but genuine. People would pinch our cheeks and squeeze us until we would just about pass out. The old ladies liked to kiss Sam all over his face and pinch him on his rear end. Sam hated it and I deemed it to be very abnormal. When they were finished with him he had lipstick everywhere. He soon began running from all of them and hiding in the bathrooms until the coast was clear. Grandpa was a different person when he was in the pulpit. His bold and powerful demeanor scared us. He preached a lot on the Love of God, His judgment, and His standards for holiness. Grandma was the choir director. She always looked so beautiful in her white choir robe and her long gray spiral curls. Her right hand twirled around in the air as she pointed to each section of the choir to let them know when to sing. Her left hand rested upon her hip as her foot slapped the ground, pounding out the beats to that good ole' country gospel music. Grandma's voice was soft and sweet. Melodic tunes flowed from her belly and into our hearts. I loved watching her and wanted very much to be in her choir. Lottie and myself swayed with the music as Sam entertained a beat of his own, and Michelle fell asleep as soon as grandpa said, Amen. We were caught off guard when the church suddenly went into praise and worship. People were yelling and calling on God and out of the blue some woman leaped out of our pew and began dancing, shaking, jerking, and crying. Like daddy, my eyebrow raised two inches as if to say, what in the world is wrong with her? Hey Diane, are you thinking what I'm thinking? Yeah Sam, that woman has got some demons in her and they seem to be fighting to get out. Let's get outta here Diane before we get what she's got. Boy you better leave that lady and her demons alone because if we move grandpa is going to knock fire from us. Don't you see him watching us from the pulpit? Little did we know that woman was happy with the Holy Ghost; she didn't have a demon, she had Jesus!

The summer was passing by fast. The days were long and hot and the nights were as cool as a polar bears breath. The moon rested on our faces as we ran through the tall green grass with glass jars in our hands. We preyed on lightening bugs and imprisoned them within our jars. It amazed me how their small beings were filled with so bright a light. How did it get in there anyway? With my nose pressed against the jar I watched as its wings fluttered in desperate attempts to escape through the air holes at the top of the jar. Little lightening bug I only captured you so I could take you back home with me. I want to show my friends that you exist because we don't have lightening bugs back home. His light captivated me and I couldn't take my eyes off him. I then realized he was too beautiful to be kept locked up just so people could stare at him, so I set him free. While Lottie, Sam, and Michelle were trying to catch more lightening bugs I opened their jars and set all of the lightening bugs free. We had only a few weeks left before mama and daddy would be back to pick us up. Sam spent the days with grandpa and other male cousins paving concrete and driving the tractors. Grandma had us girls helping her around the house with the cooking, cleaning, and washing. Before noon each day we made grandpa and Sam lunch and took it to their work site as if that's all we were good for. Grandma this isn't fair. What's not fair Diane! This so called be a slave to the men thing. Girl hush up your mouth before your grandpa hears you and knocks you on your romp. For what, I didn't do anything wrong! Diane your mouth is going to get you into trouble someday. Well grandma you tell me if this makes sense to you. Sam gets paid to work with grandpa and all we get is…girl, hurry up with that sandwich, or give me a little more ice with my lemonade. It's not fair for Sam to be sitting up there with his chest poked out waiting for me to serve him. Humph, I am not his slave and he ain't nobody special. Grandpa got a whiff of my attitude clogging up the air and decided to question me about it. What's all the commotion about girl? His heavy words stifled me. You heard me girl, watcha' talkin' 'bout. Grandpa I don't think it's fair that Sam gets paid for his work and we don't get a cent for ours. Sam is doing a man's job and you're doing what you're supposed to be doing. Common sense held back the sarcasm I was accustomed to giving out without notice and wisdom showed me how to get what I wanted. I lowered my eyes and spoke in a lighter tone to plead my case. Grandpa can't you give us something else to do? I can do twice the job that Sam does and you know it. I've told you a hundred times Diane, this particular job is not for women, but I'll tell you what I'll do. I'll pay you and your sisters five dollars a day to help your grandma clean out the basement until it's done. I was all for it until I got a good look at the basement. It looked like a dim and damp dungeon of the oldest castle in the world. Cobwebs draped the doorways and all sorts of creepy crawly things ran across our path. Michelle cried so loud she received a get out of work pass to go straight to the cartoons. Lottie wanted to do the same thing, but I quickly reminded her of the cash promised to us.

Okay girls pick a spot and start cleanin'. Grandma how can we pick a spot, there's junk everywhere. Girl you better hush up and get busy. I need to have all this stuff put out at the curb before mornin'. Why? I don't wanna miss the garbage collector. Diane, guess what I found. What is it Lottie? I found a treasure. My eyes widened as Lottie pointed out the treasure. There were rows and rows of toys and games all covered in dust and cobwebs. Those were your daddy's and Uncle Ted's toys. Wow grandma you still have it after all this time; we can't throw this stuff away, it's too valuable. I'm not keepin' this junk any longer. We flooded grandma with nicely dressed pleas until she gave in. Okay, you all can keep a few things, but only if you promise to clean them up good. We promise grandma. We finished our cleaning and when we were done our pile of keeps was taller than the pile of trash, so grandma rummaged through it and left us with two things a piece then we dragged the last bag to the curb and piled it on top of the rest. There was so much trash it looked liked someone had cleaned out every basement on the street. Grandpa pulled up in his truck with Sam trailing behind in the tractor. He laughed as he turned into the alley. His laugh sounded like a cat scratching against a wall and when his mouth opened you could see his shiny gold tooth. It sparkled against his face, which looked like it was covered in grease when the sun sat upon it. Are you girls finished already? Yes sir, we sure are. Let me take a look–see. Grandpa climbed off his truck and went into the basement. Well I'll be a monkey's uncle; it's clean. I can see the floor, the ceiling, and the shelves. Grandpa, are you pleased? Very much so! Pleased enough to give us a raise? What do you need a raise for? I need a raise so that I can buy something from the store. What is it that you want to buy Diane? I want to buy a brand new, not someone else's pair of All-Star sneakers. Is that all? Yep. Then you got it. We were all too tired to prepare dinner so while we were all getting cleaned up grandpa ran out and got a big box of fried chicken and French fries. After feeding my hungry face I went to bed. My entire body was aching from the heavy lifting I had done earlier. My stomach was also cramping and it gradually worsened through the night. My back felt like someone was jabbing a knife into it and when I awoke the bed beneath me along with my pajamas were soiled. I knew my time was coming, I just didn't know when. I remembered the stories from other girls in school about their period and suddenly fear overshadowed me. Not only was I unlearned about the entire subject matter, but I felt shame. Instead of asking grandma for help I tried wishing it away on a daily basis. I used tissue to prevent my clothes from soiling, but that didn't always work. Grandma discovered my secret while we were separating the laundry, but she never said a word. In a way I hoped she

54

would say something because I needed sanitary items and I wanted someone to explain to me what was going on with my body. I guess she figured my mama would handle it when I got home. A few days passed and to my surprise it was over. I forgot about the whole thing and in a few days we were on our way home.

It felt good to be home again. I missed my basketball hoop and all of my friends. Mostly, I missed sleeping in my own bed and the dreams I left on my pillow. I wasn't home a month before my period showed up again. This time would be different though because now my mama was here to give me that long talk I'd been waiting for practically all of my life. I sat on the toilet crouched over in agony. Mama! Mama! What do you want Diane? I need you to come in here for a minute. Mama opened the door and stood there filled with all the answers to my questions. What's wrong Diane? I'm bleeding mama. When did that start? It happened when I was away at grandma and grandpa's house. Did you tell your grandmother? No. Diane how in the world did you get your sanitary napkins? I didn't. What do you mean you didn't; what did you use? I used toilet tissue. Mama stood there with a puzzled look on her face, and then she left and went to the store. When she came back she handed me the items I needed. She gave me instructions on the usage and disposal of them, how long my cycle should last, and how to keep track of it. She turned to walk away, but I looked at her with an expression of expectancy and she turned back toward me. Diane. Yes mama. Do you know what sex is? Yes, I think so. Well don't have it. Mama turned and walked out closing the door behind her. I sat there staring at the door for a few minutes hoping she would come back, but she never did. I felt like a lost ball in tall grass. I sat there with my head hung low trying to figure out what just happened. What happened to our talk? She was supposed to sit down with me and explain the birds and the bees. We would talk, then laugh, and then talk some more. I don't really know about sex, what it is and what it entails. I only know what my friends told me and I don't think they really know. Maybe I should go to her and tell her I don't know anything. Would she talk to me then? Will she embrace me and tell me about the facts of life? Disappointed, I showered and went to bed. Mama made an appointment for me to see a gynecologist. My friends told me about their horrible experiences at these places and how you are made to feel like some sort of scientific experiment, being probed and prodded like a dead piece of meat and I dreaded the whole thing. When they called my name mama and I were placed in a small white room with a black table in the middle of the white floor. A black chair sat in front of the black table. Mama sat in the chair and the white nurse with a white dress put a clean piece of white paper on the table and handed me a white paper gown. She told me to get undressed and to put it on. The white nurse left and I put the white paper gown on and sat on top of the white paper that was on the black table. Two white male doctors in white jackets walked in, one was older and the other was a young student doctor. The older doctor had gray and white hair mixed together and he was very polite to mama and me. The younger doctor had black hair, which he'd soaked in mouse before coming to work. He had an ugly smirk plastered on his face. After the older doctor examined me he began telling my mother I was a very healthy young lady. He looked at me and then turned to mama. Does Diane know about sex and does she understand it? Mama said, yes. I wanted to say no I don't, would someone please tell me! The older doctor stood by the door and explained that the younger doctor was a student. Diane if you don't mind please lye back down so Dr. Hutchins can examine you. I really didn't want to go through that experience again, but I complied anyway. As I laid my head back Dr. Hutchins made sure his eyes met mine; they were cold looking and his perversion smothered his smile. I wanted him to stop looking at me the way that he did especially since he had to touch me where he did. Instead of touching me, he rubbed me and instead of examining me he began to sexually abuse me. His smile transformed into a silent grin and as he chuckled to himself my eyes searched for mama's to let her know I was in trouble, but the other doctor was standing in the way and I couldn't find her face. She was so engrossed in conversation with him that neither one of them paid attention to what was going on. We left the hospital and I never uttered a word to mama about what happened to me. I felt dirty and cheap and I wondered if there was something drastically wrong with me. I seem to be like a magnet that only attracts abuse. My first gynecological exam turned out to be the most hideous experience one could ever go through. Who would believe me? I'm a twelve-year old black girl, he's white, he's a doctor, and there were other people in the room. He exemplified confidence when he raped me of my identity with my mama and his mentor in the room. His smirk dared me to say something and the act kept me silent. I looked around the room and took notice that everything was white except for the table, chair, and me and mama. All of the black things could be moved and pushed around, but the white was always there. It seemed to be the basis of everything. It was everywhere, on the walls, on the floors, and on their faces. My eyes even reflected the whiteness of my surroundings and I realized that it was in control. On the way home I could feel hate and anger eating away at my inner most being and at that point I just wanted to die. Several months later I began to develop cysts commonly known as boils. They formed at the top of my head, on my rear end, and in between my legs, which made it difficult to walk or sit when they came upon me. At first mama and daddy thought they were tumors, but the doctor said they were just pimples tripled in size. Not one doctor could tell me why I was being inflicted with these cysts. They said some people just get them and they don't exactly know why, but I hadn't heard of anyone except myself having these cysts. I had surgery after surgery and I was tired of being cut on. I was tired of being placed under a microscope as if I was someone's guinea pig. Embarrassment set in because of the location of the cysts and the fact that they oozed all of the time. It bothered me because I didn't know if I would ever have a normal cyst-free life. These ugly lumps made me feel different, as if I wasn't a normal young woman. I didn't think any one would understand what I was going through and I felt like I was the only one suffering from this condition, so I didn't talk about it to anyone. In my ignorance I came to the conclusion that these things were probably happening to me as a punishment from God. A punishment I knew I deserved.

9
<u>EYES WIDE SHUT</u>

We spent a lot of time at grandma and Grandpa Jones house and we enjoyed every minute of it. Every Sunday morning grandma would get everyone up for Sunday service by ringing the doorbell like a mad woman. Ringing and yelling, time to get up, time to praise the Lord this beautiful morning. Grandma was a round woman with dark skin and pearly white teeth. Her face was as round as a melon and her smile glowed like the moon at night. Her laugh was so original and warm it was unforgettable. Her kisses were like sweet treats and her touch was as soft as the hand of an angel. Mama and daddy were out in the street; each with their own friends doing who knows what, and grandpa was gone hunting with his shotgun and two shot glasses. We spent some weekends with grandma and grandpa, but Friday nights were considered our family night out. I really enjoyed these times because mama and daddy took us out to eat and to see a movie or something instead of venturing out on their own, but sometimes mama and daddy would have parties at our house. Our apartment would be packed with folk. The women wore either afro-puffs or a bushy wig. Short skirts and platform shoes were the style while the men wore bellbottoms, afros and attitudes. We would have to go to bed early, but Lottie and I would always leave our door cracked to watch the adults do their weird dances. We covered our mouths with our hands as giggles spilled out while watching Aunt Betsy twist her 500-pound hips from side to side as the sounds of Al Greene and Marvin Gaye shook our walls. Our laughter grew louder and louder as we imitated mama's guest. After being overheard mama would storm into our room, but her anger was overtaken by laughter after witnessing our awkward imitations of everyone. She would make us go to bed and shut the door completely not realizing that as soon as she left we opened it back up.

I always thought my grandparents were funny; they were either chuckling about something or arguing about nothing. If grandma said the sky was blue, grandpa said it was purple. All in all, their love was genuine. I felt that their neighborhood was just as crummy as ours. The entire neighborhood looked as if it was covered with a gray blanket. All of the houses were gray, the grassless front yards were gray, and the destitute faces were gray. Regardless of the surroundings, grandma and grandpa were full of springtime joy. They had this air about themselves that made me want to breathe it in all the time. Grandma would never have to wake me on Sunday mornings because I would already be up listening to her sing, but since me, Sam, Lottie, and Michelle were used to sleeping in on Sunday we acted as if we couldn't hear that wretched bell ringing. I just lay there listening to grandma hum and sing like a canary. I could never figure out what the song was and I don't think she knew either. She just hummed whatever good thing she was feeling. She hummed and pranced around the kitchen while the bacon sizzled in a pan full of grease. To the ear it may have sounded like a bunch of twisted jargon, but to the heart it was an orchestra of love. For a while I would be at peace, not concerning myself with the world outside no matter how trying it was. I always felt that the Lord and his angels were singing to grandma's spirit and in turn she sang to mine. Although the sun refused to shine outside it didn't matter to me because my grandma always found a way to bring it into her home and our hearts. After Sunday morning service we returned to their home searching for something to eat as if we were starving to death. The first stop was always the cookie jar. Sugar bear was always a good soldier, but he couldn't protect the cookies from those nasty roaches. I always wondered how on earth they got inside. There were no holes in the jar and the top was always fastened shut. Sugar bear didn't let his guard down, so how did they get in? Lottie thought grandma let them in to get something to eat seeming how she was so kind to everyone and everything. Sam disagreed, grabbed a handful of cookies, flicked off the roaches and said, God made dirt and roaches, so roaches and dirt won't hurt, then he stuffed his mouth and left the kitchen. Sam was so repulsive he made me sick. I closed the cookie jar and rushed to the cabinet to satisfy my hunger with crackers, but the roaches seemed to like crackers better since it was twice as many in the cracker box than in the cookie jar. My stomach was screaming for something so I marched back to the cookie jar, swallowed my pride and did the same repulsive thing that Sam did. After wiping my mouth of the evidence Sam jumped out from behind the refrigerator laughing at me. Ah ha ah ha you swallowed Mr. Roach and all his cousins. Sam, leave me alone! If I ate them, then so did you. I didn't really eat them. I only wanted to make you think I did. Sam you ate them and you know it. No I didn't. Sam pulled a bunch of cookies from his pocket and at that very moment I wanted to throw up, but instead I punched Sam in the mouth and put him in a chokehold. When Sam began to choke I smiled. Grandma was in her room changing her clothes. However, with the thumping and bumping going on in the kitchen she came running out half dressed. Before I could let Sam go she was wailing at my legs with the strap that grandpa used to sharpen his razor and it sure felt like it had razors in it. I grabbed the strap to keep her from hitting me until I could tell her what happened. Surely she would understand. Her smooth face turned from cocoa to black ice and when her brow rose, I let go of the strap and ceased from explaining. Sam and Lottie ran out of the kitchen to take cover from the bomb that was about to explode. What did I want to do that for? I might as well have just smacked her instead. Steam emitted from her nose and anger painted her eyes dead red. Then the volcano erupted. It was no use in me trying to explain, besides grandma hated the way we acted as if roaches were going to kill us. To her that demonstrated that we thought we were better than her, so to tell her what happened would only make things worse for me. Girl you must have lost your mind! How dare you try and snatch the strap from me and try to hit me. My eyebrow rose higher than hers, only mine came with an inquisitive look. Hit her? I would never do that. Grown ups always add to things to make the situation seem a little more dramatic than it really is. I knew I was in for it now. Grandma raised her hand and beat me as if her life depended on it. Her mouth ran a mile a minute and the strap didn't have a problem keeping up. My whole body was sore by the time grandma finished with me. My anger grew greater than the pain because I knew the misunderstanding about me attempting to hit her when I grabbed the strap would travel to my mama and daddy and back to my rear end. I went outside while grandma cooled off. I sat in the dirt flicking rocks, watching the cars turn the corner and as each one drove by I exhaled loudly with relief that it wasn't mama and daddy.

Grandpa was home by now. He stood in the kitchen taking the skin off of something wild. I assumed this something was our dinner. My grandpa's philosophy was, if it's moving and you catch it, then you kill it and eat it. You knew when grandpa was home because you could smell his pipe a mile away and he was always conjuring up something to eat. His favorite meal was midnight stew. It was a combination of whatever was leftover in the refrigerator and whatever else he found to mix with it. One night I was curious in trying it. He mixed some greens, cut up hot dogs, rice and cornbread and placed it in a pot with hot sauce. After heating it up for about 15 minutes it was ready to be served. I thought the ingredients were disgusting, but the taste was pretty good. Grandpa was a peculiar man and very handsome. He was 6'2" with reddish brown skin. Grandpa's hair was gray and white, he had a gray mustache, and dimples lined the sides of his face. He spent most of his time fishing and hunting and when he wasn't doing that he was drinking with the boys. I guess that's what got on my grandma's nerves the most. She never liked him getting drunk because when he was drunk he always talked silly, which made good for an argument. After a while she would just wave her hand at him and walk away saying, a drunk ain't worth two cents. It bothered me to hear grown folk argue about nonsense. My parents did the exact same thing, only with a more violent tone. That was one of the reasons I didn't like them hanging out on the weekends. If my father made it in before my mother, then he would fight with her about coming in so late. If my mother made it in before my father, then she would fight with him about where he had been. I grew tired of awakening in the middle of the night to hear them fuss and fight. Consequently, as we got older the need to stay at grandma and grandpa's house diminished. Daddy said we were old enough to watch our own selves. Diane! Yes mama. I want you to fix pork & beans and hot dogs for you all to eat later. I'll be back late. How late mama? Don't you worry about it just go to bed at a decent hour! Can we at least go outside? Absolutely not! Why not, it's not even dark out yet and all the kids are out playing kickball. Diane, you, Sam, Lottie and your cousin Chole have to keep an eye on Michelle and your cousin Charmaine; so no you can't go out. Keep the doors shut and locked. Do not answer the door for anyone. But mama, we can watch Michelle and Charmaine outside. I'll make sure everything is fine. Besides, Michelle is four years old now. It's not like she's a baby; and why do we have to watch Charmaine anyway, that's Chole's sister! This ain't 1-800-babysitter! You better watch your mouth Diane before I keep you in this house for the entire summer. You will watch who I tell you to watch do you understand me? Yes mama, I understand. When daddy came home from work on the weekend he was drunk. He got dressed and went back out to get drunk some more so we knew he wouldn't be coming home any time soon. Mama, her sister, and their friends always hung out in the next town so they wouldn't bump into daddy and his friends. Therefore, we knew that we would be playing kickball with our friends regardless of the instructions we received. Mama left not too long after daddy. We watched carefully and patiently as her car disappeared down the street. Sam dashed outside the instant the car turned the corner. I got some cookies and juice and sat Michelle and Charmaine upstairs in front of the television giving them strict orders not to move from their seats unless I told them to. We took turns checking on them because we knew if we took them outside or if they found out we were outside they would spill their guts, so we took 20-minute shifts watching Michelle and Charmaine. Our post was in the front room next to the front door and near the stairs leading to the upper where the brats were. Every time they would attempt to come down the stairs they were ordered back up. It was Chole's shift and Sam, Lottie and I were two doors down hanging out with our friends, laughing and talking silly. Every time a car would pass by our street we would sprint towards the house only to find that it was a false alarm. We were talking about going to the store when Sam jumped up and took off running. Lottie and I were wondering if something was the matter with him until daddy passed by us, pulling up in our driveway. The smiles slid off our faces and our so-called friends began to taunt and tease us. Sam has always been a turncoat. He could have warned us or said something, but he chose to save himself instead, forgetting that we were all in this together. Didn't he know that if we got caught then he was going to get into trouble also? Sam just didn't care. Lottie and I hid behind some bushes trying to figure out what to do. What was daddy doing home? He never comes back home for anything. Fear stabbed me in my side like a knife with a thousand ridges. Lottie began to cry uncontrollably. We are going to get it; I knew I should have stayed in the house. I made a split decision, grabbed her arm and ran toward the house. Daddy had pulled up to the side door and went into the house. Lottie and I weren't too far behind him, but we went in through the front door. I wasn't sure whether he had seen us or not, he would've had to have been blind not to have seen us. When daddy approached me I was standing in the front room panting like a jackrabbit. Diane why are you breathing so hard? Oh we were just playing around. Well don't play so hard. You know how your mother feels about you playing in her front room. A sigh of relief came over me. He hadn't seen us. You need me to get you something dad (like some glasses)? No, I forgot my wallet that's all. The brats began chanting the words…they were outside…over and over again. I pinched Michelle and told her to be quiet. When she started to cry my dad ran to her rescue to see what was wrong. I thought for sure she would tell, but the little stinker didn't utter another word. After daddy left we went right back outside to play hide go seek and other games. We allowed Michelle and Charmaine to sit on the porch to get some air as a treat for not telling on us. At about ten o'clock we all went in, ate our pork & beans and hot dogs, and popped popcorn while watching videos. I woke up about two o'clock in the morning only to find that the television was watching all of us instead of us watching it and mama and daddy still weren't home. I made everyone get in the bed including myself. At 5:30 A.M I heard someone pacing the floor. The sound of those shoes on that wooden floor echoed in my ears. I prayed to God that those shoes belonged to my mama, but as loud and as heavy as they were I knew they were my daddy's. Please God don't let them fight tonight. Mama where are you? Please just come home. I tried to close my eyes to go back to sleep, but I couldn't, I kept hearing those angry shoes walk back and forth from the kitchen to the hallway. Each step grew louder and louder, echoing in my mind and ringing in my ears. After a while my weary eyes closed only to be awakened by yelling and screaming. I don't remember exactly what the words were saying. All I know is that it hurt me to hear them and if it hurt me then I knew it was hurting them. Mama ran in the bathroom, but daddy caught her. Before she could close the door I heard him hit her. The sound of flesh striking flesh echoed throughout the entire house and silenced the night. Mama's weeps and moans broke that silence and broke my heart. God why does it have to be like this? Why...why... why...why do people hurt each other the way they do? As I listened to my mama cry tears fell out of the holes in my face. I looked around the room over at Lottie and she was sound asleep or at least pretending to be. I couldn't understand how two people who loved each other could bring themselves to hurt each other like this. Before I closed my weeping eyes I vowed that when I got married my husband and I would never hurt each other as my parents did. My marriage would not be based on lies, deceitfulness, lack of trust, or infidelity. I will not fall victim on their battlegrounds. My marriage will not be a faux pas. Where is the love they once had? Where has it gone? My silent tears soaked my pillow and I slept on a river of sorrow, floating away, drifting further and further away from reality.

I was slow getting up the next morning. I didn't want to face either one of them, so I wrote a sign and placed it on my back. It said, don't speak to me because I won't speak back. My mama was sitting in the chair combing Michelle's hair in silence. A stream of tears continuously rolled down her face, seeping out of a blackened eye. I sat next to mama with anger in my heart. I watched my dad as he cooked breakfast in silence. He couldn't even look me in the face. No one said a word. The only thing talking was the television. My thoughts pounded in my mind like drums. Why did you do this dad? What! Do you think hitting on a woman makes you feel like a big man? Why dad? Why did you do this to my mama? I felt the tears bubbling up in my eyes so I got up and went into the bathroom. When breakfast was ready I sat down at the table. I had completely forgotten about the sign I taped to my back until my mama tried to knock my head off. That did it. I hate this house and everyone in it.

Journal Insert:
GRANDMA'S KITCHEN

Cold floor chills my feet as my brother, my sisters
And I stumble into the kitchen like four little Mag
Pies. All dressed in our p.j's from an overnight stay
watching grandma cook the dinner for the day.
The aroma was nice and tickled my nose, then my
belly and even my toes. Ox tail stew grandma said with a
smile. We begged for a taste, and then stood single file. We
smiled and ran off except my sister of two
She said - that tastes pretty good for Fcx tail stew.

(Remembering the good times helps me to forget the bad)
Diane

10
<u>HEY GIRLIE!</u>

High school was a different experience for me. A chance to become someone other than the person people thought I was in grade school. I went into Lavella High School determined to portray myself as a mature young adult. Lavella High was an old building and it looked like a Roman Palace. The doorways were at least 10 ft. high and the woodwork was carefully carved out by hand. I was excited about this new school, but apprehensive in allowing anyone to know I was a freshman because I heard how upper classmen tormented new freshmen. On the very first day I walked in with Joyce, who was my very best friend. Neither one of us was over 5ft. tall, but together we felt really big. There was chaos all around us. Freshmen were being chased, beat up, and splattered with eggs and milk. We walked by everyone with our noses stuck up in the air. Although I wasn't allowed to wear makeup, Joyce said if I wore it, then we would look older and no one would bother us. We pretended to know where we were going with our faces painted like clowns in a circus when three white boys approached us with a handful of eggs. They all were at least six feet tall and wore football jerseys. They lifted their hands to pound us with eggs when Joyce placed her hands on her hips, stepped forward and gave them a piece of her mind. You better put those eggs down. I don't know who you think we are, but we're not freshmen. The strange boys looked confused. We have never seen you girls here before and we are all seniors who've been here since freshmen year you little liar! I took a step back and looked for a way out. If my daddy didn't teach me anything else he taught me how to use the sense God gave me, and my senses were saying, RUN. Joyce cursed the boys and told them we were transfers from another school. The boys looked puzzled and began putting their eggs back into their bags. A smile formed on my face. With tenacity I politely asked them to move out of our way and within seconds they stepped aside. We were only three feet away when one of them yelled, wait a minute! What school did you come from? Joyce and I looked at each other and began tripping over our words because we couldn't think of a school. The boys cursed and laughed at us in a wicked and demeaning way after realizing that we were indeed freshmen. Joyce and I were incoming track stars, so we turned and ran through the halls as if fire was at our backs. They didn't give up for anything, not even after we ran out of the front door. Once we were outside we hit the mile long sidewalk as if our lives depended on it and I opened up my wings and turned on the after burners. In seconds I was so far ahead of them they had no choice but to give up. We decided not to get on the bus right away and walked around the neighborhood pretending to belong there. I gazed at the mansion size homes and wondered who lived in them. There were expensive cars in the long and circular driveways. I imagined myself pulling my Mercedes Benz around the circular driveway. My lovely husband would greet me at the door with a hug and a kiss and as I gather my briefcase and coat my children run out and thrash me with hugs as we walk into the house. I realized I was daydreaming and although it seemed like a fairy tale, it was all I wanted. As we walked on Joyce pulled some funny looking cigarette out of her purse. In response I questioned her. Joyce what are you doing? Girl, I'm getting high. Since when do you get high? Since the summer! I tried it at my Uncle Fred's house and girl it makes you feel goozood! Whatever Joyce! Diane you are such a square. I bet you are afraid to take a hit aren't you. No I'm not! I just don't want to. Why not? I have a cousin who cracked up because of her drug use and I'm not trying to be like that. Girl, ain't no little joint gonna do that to you. How do you know? Cause' I've been smokin' it and I'm still the same. Well how do you smoke it? All you do is inhale; sucking it in until your air is gone. Then hold your breath and blow it out. Joyce stuck the joint in her mouth, went through the motions she described to me and then handed it to me. I took one look at the tip where I was supposed to place my mouth and turned up my lip because Joyce's saliva covered the entire thing. I took the end of my shirt and attempted to wipe it off. Joyce rolled her eyes and blew the smoke out of her nostrils. I put the funny cigarette up to my mouth and hesitated when the smoke made my eyes water. Go on you woos. I opened my mouth, sucked in the smoke, held my breath, and after repeating this act two or three times I began to see double and laugh uncontrollably. I knew something was wrong with me

67

and if I knew it, then mama and daddy would definitely know it. I panicked because I didn't want to end up in a body bag, but Joyce insisted that by the time I got home the high would be gone. Stupidity told us to knock on those rich folks door and run. Cruelty told us to curse them, and defiance told us to forget about our home raising. We stopped at a corner store several blocks away, eyes glassy and half closed. We piled chips, cookies, and a soda a piece on the counter. We ate as if we hadn't been fed in a month. Randy, Joyce's boyfriend met us outside the store. Joyce tried to get me to go to some apartment building with them down the street, but I didn't want to. They just wanted to have sex in the elevator and Joyce wanted to use me as her alibi.

Joyce my mama is gonna whip my butt if I'm too late. We'll mine will too, so come on Diane quit being a square; we can both tell our parents we were together. It wouldn't be a lie, plus you need time for your high to clear up. I agreed. When we arrived at the apartment building I stood outside to wait for them. There were three old white women congregating on a park bench outside the building. One of them got my attention by yelling out to me. Hey girlie! I looked around as if I knew she couldn't be referring to me. Hey girlie in the red slacks! I looked down at my clothing and knew for certain the old woman was talking to me, so I walked over to see what she wanted. Excuse me, but are you talking to me. Yes I'm talking to you. You're the only colored girl standin' over here with red slacks on aren't you? The high was beginning to wear off, but I could still hear a voice telling me to knock her off that bench. My eyes cringed at her and my smile ran away. So girlie, how old are you? I'm 14 years old and my name is Diane. The women looked at each other and giggled as if something was funny. Well girlie how would you like a job? You mean a real job! Yes, of course. What kind of job? Oh, helping with things around my apartment like cleaning, doing dishes, and small errands. I would have to get permission from my parents first, but I would love to have the job. How much would you pay me? Well I would need you every Saturday, so let's say $25.00 per week. That sounds fine. Here girlie take my telephone number. My name is Ms. Willa, when you come back go in through those doors and take the elevator all the way up to the eighth floor. When you get off come to apartment #822 and don't forget now;

come bright and early Saturday morning. What is bright and early, eight or nine o'clock in the A.M? Nine is fine girlie. The old women got up and went into the building. I sat on the bench watching the minutes tick by on my watch, contemplating leaving Joyce before I ended up in hot water. The high that hung over my head began to drift away with the wind. I wasn't as giddy, just a little dizzy. I determined within myself not to ever do that again. Finally, Joyce and Randy surfaced. I thought they were so disgusting and pitiful, but Joyce didn't seem to care. Randy walked with us to the bus stop and when the bus came he kissed Joyce and went home. Joyce I think you're playing with fire. Girl shut up. Don't tell me to shut up Joyce; I'm only trying to help you. What if you get pregnant? I'm not going to get pregnant! What if you do? If I do then I'll just take care of the problem, why don't you mind your own business and leave me alone anyway. Joyce began to brag about what she and Randy did. Humph, I know I am a woman. Can you say the same Diane? Oh, my bad. I forgot you are still a little virgin girl. Joyce I really don't care what you say about me because I'm not having sex until I get married. Oh shut up, you just don't want to do it because you're afraid and you ain't got nobody! Out of anger I refused to talk to her anymore. Joyce's stop came up; she waved good-bye and got off. I was thinking about my new job and all the outfits I would buy with my money. I couldn't wait to tell daddy and mama that I was now a workingwoman. I got off the bus and stood in front of the candy store window peering at my reflection trying to see if there was a difference in my appearance. As I stood there gazing at my silly face a fine brother waltzed by me. His staring made me so nervous I was afraid to turn around, besides I didn't want him to catch me drooling at the mouth. As he passed I turned to see where he had gone, but he hadn't gone anywhere. He was just standing a few feet away staring at me and me at him. Finally he said hello and I smiled and walked away. My heart was beating a mile per minute. He was so fine, so full of muscles that his smile warmed my soul. I fell in love instantly. I was upset with myself that I didn't at least stay to find out his name. I thought about him all the way home. I wondered if I would ever see him again because I felt that he was just right for me.

I walked up the driveway in slow motion, stretching my eyes wide open so mama wouldn't be able to tell that I was a little high. Before I put the key in the door she snatched it open. She stood there with her hand on her hip while her lip tossed my name around in her mouth. Diane where in carnations have you been? It is 5:30 and you should've been home two hours ago! Answer me child, where have you been? I stood there bucking my big eyes as my heart began to pound against my chest. I thought she would've at least moved out of the doorway and let me in. I missed my bus mama. Missed your bus, why? This was the perfect opportunity to place the blame on those white boys. Mama I didn't mean to be late, some white boys chased Joyce and me from the school. They were throwing eggs at us and trying to beat us up. Daddy began screaming in the background. Some white boys did what! I knew there would be a problem sending you over there to that school. They are lucky I wasn't there. I think we ought to go to that racist school before I kill me somebody. Oh Sam be quiet. That's typical behavior in high school for the first few weeks. Well they better not lay a hand on her. Mama moved away from the door and proceeded up the stairs. Good comeback Diane, I thought she would never move. When I entered the kitchen I told mama and daddy about being chased through the mansion lined streets and how we out ran them. I had to assure daddy that the boys didn't intend on harming us so he wouldn't take it any further than it ought to go. Mama looked at me kind of weird. Diane! Yes mama. What's wrong with you? Nothin' mama! You are acting rather funny. No I'm not; I've got something to tell you. What is that? I got a job. Daddy chuckled. A job! You're only 14 years old, who on earth is going to hire you? I pulled the little piece of paper from my pocket that the old white woman gave me and handed it to mama. Carefully, she looked it over. Where did you meet her Diane? I was stumped. I forgot to prepare a lie for that one. Uhhhhhh, I, uhhhhh. After we were chased we ended up on Chelsea Road and these old ladies were sitting on the bench talking. When we walked by one of the women called out to me saying, hey girlie. Daddy yelped, girlie! She must be white. Yes daddy, she is, but... But my foot, I bet you she's a bigot. No daddy she's just an old woman who doesn't know any better. Mama can you call her and check it out? What does she want you to do Diane? She said some

cleaning and small errands for which she'll give me $25.00 per week.
How many days a week? Only one mama, and that's on Saturday
mornings. I don't know. This woman might be a quack or something.
Mama can I please have the job? You won't have to buy so much of my
things because I'll have the money to buy it. Mama called the woman to
interrogate her, but found her to be a sweet old woman who needed help.
Mama allowed me to take the job without any more hesitation. I
couldn't wait until Saturday. I was so excited I called Joyce to tell her
that my mama said I could have the job, nevertheless, Joyce was still
acting funny and her response to my news was cold. So what Diane!
Did you tell your mama how high you got or how you ended up meeting
the woman? If I did you better believe she would be talking to yo' mama
right now. Oh shut up Diane! You think you're all that; you make me
sick! You make me sicker, you nasty hoochie! DIANE!!! If you can't
talk on the telephone like you have sense then GET OFF!!! Okay mama.
Right now Diane! Joyce I gotta go. After hanging up the telephone
mama badgered me about the conversation I had with Joyce as if she
wasn't aware that the conversation was personal and private. What were
you and Joyce arguing about? Nothin' mama! Don't tell me nothin'. It
had to be something. Now tell me what it was? Mama! It was really
nothin', she's just jealous because I have a job and she doesn't. I tucked
my head and walked away. Well I don't care what she said; you just
better not let me hear you talking like that ever again! Do you hear me
Diane? Yes mama, loud and clear. Now you all get ready so we can go
and eat. Lottie fix your clothes, Michelle you come here, Sam go wash
under your arms, and Diane comb your nappy hair because you look like
you stuck your fingers in an electric socket twice. Daddy laughed and
began making him a sandwich. Sam what on earth are you doing? I'm
makin' me a dog-on sandwich woman; y'all take too long. I'll be done
starved to death waitin' on y'all. You are so ignorant! You act as if you
can't wait 10 minutes. Woman, don't worry about me; you and your
kids just hurry up.

I went into the bathroom to comb my hair. Sam was in front of the
sink swishing soap everywhere. Sam cut it out; you are getting soap on
everyone's toothbrush. I slid the canister full of toothbrushes to the side
when I noticed that one of them looked like it had been burned twice

71

over. Ugghhh! Sam whose toothbrush is this? Diane hush up, you know that's daddy's toothbrush. We laughed. Well what does he use it for...cleanin' his car tires? I could tell you one thing he doesn't use it for and that's brushin' his teeth. Hey Diane, that's why his teeth are so yellow. I'm sure you're right. The brother has 18 karat gold teeth and breath that spells halitosis backwards. I think that's what killed his toothbrush. Man, this toothbrush is so brown and dry it looks like he scrubbed the toilet with it. He couldn't have because it would at least have gotten wet. We laughed so hard we were crying. When I looked up daddy was standing in the doorway of the bathroom. What are you two knuckleheads doing in here? Nothin' daddy! Well hurry up outta' here so I can get washed up. Okay daddy. I attempted to put his toothbrush back in the holder when he caught me. Diane what are you doing with my toothbrush. Oh, I thought it was mine, but then I realized that it wasn't because the bristles on my toothbrush aren't that particular color. A smirk like expression slid across my face and Sam ran out of the bathroom because he thought I was going to get smacked, but daddy didn't catch onto my sarcasm. He just said okay and shut the door behind him. After everyone was ready we all piled up in the car. Daddy took us to his favorite place, "The Ponderosa." We walked in and the menu was on the wall with pictures of the food. Instantly, Sam pointed to the steak and fries. Daddy looked at mama and then back to Sam. Boy you got a job that I'm not aware of? No daddy, but those kiddy meals don't fill me up anymore. I agreed. Daddy and mama talked it over and allowed Sam and myself to have adult meals, leaving Lottie and Michelle restricted to the kiddy menu. We ate, laughed, and had a wonderful time. As usual, after dinner we went for a family drive through the city and ended up at the waterfront. Leaning on the rails before the endless waters, I gazed up into the dark sky and attempted to count all the stars above me. I couldn't do it. Only God knows how many of them are up there because He placed them there and He knows them all by name, just like all of us. Michelle played with her doll in the grass and Lottie hid behind a tree dodging the rocks Sam was throwing at her. Mama and daddy sat in the car talking and kissing. Sam why don't you stop throwing those rocks before you get into trouble! Shut up Diane, you think you are everybody's mama, but you ain't. Whatever

Sam, regardless of what you think I'm the oldest and I'm telling you to put those rocks down. I'm the man and I'm telling you to shut up and mind your own business. If you tell me to shut up one more time I'm gonna shove those rocks down your throat. Sam lifted up his hand and threw every rock he had at me. Although I tried to block them one hit me in the face, another in the leg, and one to the head. I charged at Sam as if I were a raging bull, under bushes, around trees, in circles, and between cars. Anger motivated me, but fear wouldn't allow Sam to be caught, so I picked up some rocks and stoned him until he screamed. When daddy called out to us I got rid of the evidence. Sam waited until I got in the car before he came back because our anger toward one another was evident. Daddy turned to me and gave me a piece of his mind. Diane you and Sam are getting too old to be acting so silly, NOW CUT IT OUT! Daddy got us all settled then drove down to the ice cream stand and got us all a double deck cone. Our angry faces quickly disappeared and there wasn't a sound in the car except the sweet sound of our tongues slapping up against the melting ice cream. We acted like crying babies who were just given a warm bottle to settle us down and as our stomach slowly filled up with ice cream our eyes gently closed. I looked up into the rearview mirror one last time and saw daddy grinning from ear to ear. Those are still my babies. I don't care how old they get; they are still my babies.

Saturday morning came rather quickly. Excitement about my new job got me dressed in a half hour. Daddy I'm ready. Ready for what! I need you to take me to my job. Oh, I forgot all about it. I can't be late daddy. Give me a minute Diane. Daddy got dressed and took me to Ms. Willa's apartment. You want me to wait for you? No daddy, I am getting older and I need to learn how to take care of myself. I just wanna' make sure you're okay. I'll be fine daddy. I'll call you when I'm ready. Daddy drove off and I stood there waving good-bye. I went inside and took the elevator up to the eighth floor. The hallway was dim and the carpet was dark. A mildew smell remained stagnant throughout the hallway along with a hint of old food. I walked up to a door with the numbers 822 spread across the face of it. I pulled the wrinkled piece of paper out of my pocket and began to examine it carefully to make sure I was in the right place. Lightly, I knocked on the door and waited for her to answer.

When she didn't come to the door I knocked a little harder. Finally, the little old lady surfaced. Yes, can I help you? Ms. Willa It's me, Diane. She stood there staring at me as if she had gone crazy. I'm the girl you hired to clean. Oh, hello girlie. My skin cringed to that word. Come on in. She walked away from the door and led me into the kitchen where she kept her back to me. The galley-like kitchen was so small there was only enough room for her so I stood behind her. She was cleaning chicken and cutting them up in small pieces. So, Miss. Willa where do you want me to start or shall I say what is it that you need help with? I filled the room with a million and one questions when I noticed she wasn't paying me any attention. I tried to squeeze by her to look her in the face because I didn't think she could hear well. Excuse me Ms. Willa, but what is it that I'm supposed to do? There's nothing for you to do right now girlie. I have a lot of guests coming over and I need to get this food cooked. Who's coming over Miss. Willa? I don't know, whatcha' talkin' about girlie! Uhhhh, you just said you were having guests over and... I couldn't finish my sentence because my eyes carefully watched her as she picked up a butcher knife and began chopping the chicken like a mad woman. Who are you anyway girlie? I, I, I, ummm, I'm the nice girlie that you hired to help you. I said it proudly as if it were my name. She waved the butcher knife in the air while talking to me. Well what do you want with me? My eyebrow rose to my hairline and my eyes began searching for the way out. Uhhhh, I don't want anything, but I think I better leave. I turned and headed for the door when she grabbed my arm. No! Please help me clean the chicken for my guest. I was beginning to wish my daddy had stayed, but I knew he was long gone. I patted the woman on the hand and agreed to help her. We went back into the kitchen where I washed my hands and began to help her. STOP! What are you doing girlie? I'm helping you. I don't need no help and your hands are dirty and nasty. I heard my mind say, okay we're outta' here and before I knew it my feet were moving my body toward the door. I don't think I closed the door behind me. I ran down the stairs instead of waiting for the elevator, out the door, and down the street to the pay phone.

Hello mama. What's wrong Diane? Can you tell Daddy to come and get me? Diane you can't be ready you just got there. Mama this lady is crazy. I think she came straight out of a sci-fi movie. I'll tell you all about it when I get home. Okay, where are you? Tell daddy I'll wait for him on the corner of Main and Jefferson St. My thoughts began to trouble me as I stood there waiting for daddy to pick me up. Ms. Willa wasn't crazy. She was just a lonely and confused old woman who needed help. Where was her family? It bothered me that there was no one, not even a grandchild. Why do some people end up alone with no one to talk to and no one to laugh with? There was no one to hold, no one to help clean the chicken or get you to a doctor when your mind has left for good. I considered Lottie to be a pest, Michelle a nuisance, and Sam was a pain in my brain. However, I always had someone to talk to. I had someone to listen to me and laugh with me. I had someone to hold and love. Loneliness is like a disease that eats you up on the inside until there's no more you. It was loneliness that was killing Ms. Willa.

<u>Journal Insert</u>
(To my grandparents with a heartfelt love)

I close my eyes to be with you
For the times I miss your face
I hold you in my heart and dream
And wait for your embrace
I do not want you to feel alone
Or as if no one really cares
I just want you to know you're loved
And I will always be here
Thank you for always teaching me
About the things I just don't know
And thank you for loving me
And giving me seeds to sow
Your wisdom surpasses my knowledge
Your beauty shines like the sun
I'll hold you forever in my heart
Even when this world is done
Diane

11
<u>COMING OF AGE</u>

I was bubbling with joy when my coach told me I was a candidate for a track scholarship. I went over to Joyce's house to share my good news, but she acted as if it wasn't important. The only time she gets excited about something is when it involves her. She gave me a bunch of so what's and quickly reminded me that we were still juniors and that I might change my mind before senior year. I stayed for a little while longer and decided to walk home by myself because she was getting on my nerves. It was cold and dark, so I picked up the pace especially when I came across a group of hormones standing on the corner. While crossing the street one of the guys with a green snorkel coat approached me. He was trying to kick it to me, however my focus was on my scholarship and I felt I didn't have any room in my life for a boyfriend. He introduced himself as Eddie Camden and as he talked I attempted to get a glimpse of his face, but the hood of his snorkel kept it hidden from me. When He asked for my telephone number I attempted to give him a fake one and ended up tripping over the number because I couldn't think of one. He caught me off guard and didn't afford me any room to lie. If you are going to lie, then I would prefer that you just not give me your number. There was something about his voice that made me give him my real telephone number; it was warm and sincere. A few weeks later I decided to allow him to come to my house so that we could sit and talk. It was all so strange because I didn't even know what he looked like, but our conversations over the telephone let me know that he was really interested in what I had to say and he communicated well. He wasn't shallow like some of the other guys I knew. He had a pure and genuine heart.

The doorbell rang and my heart stopped. I was a little nervous in meeting him because I didn't know what to expect. When I opened the door I thought I was dreaming. Could it really be him? I couldn't believe it! It was the handsome guy I'd met in front of the candy store a few years ago. I tried not to blush, but it was too late; my smile turned into a grin and before I knew it all of my teeth were showing. When he sat down and shed his coat I thought I was going to pass out. Not only was he intelligent and handsome, he was built like a miniature Hercules. His hands were strong, yet soft as a baby's bottom. We talked for hours and at the close of the evening I came to the conclusion that I was very attracted to Eddie Camden. He had everything I needed and wanted in a man and I knew I was falling in love with him. As time went on mama and daddy fussed a lot about me spending too much time with Eddie. They said I was putting all of my eggs in one basket and that I had a whole life ahead of me to meet other people. However, they failed to realize one important factor, Eddie and I truly loved each other. Our relationship began with a friendship and our friendship blossomed by keeping an open line of communication. Eddie wasn't just my significant other he was my best friend. When we went to church mama and daddy assumed we were using that as an excuse to go and do other things. Physically, we only knew each other by a kiss, but mama and daddy thought we were having sex. Besides, I made a promise to myself when I was 12 years old. I swore I would not have sex until I was married. Our dates consisted of long walks to the show, the closest burger place around the corner, and long talks in mama and daddy's living room. A day didn't go by that we didn't see each other. Daddy would position his chair in the corner of the dining room adjacent from Eddie and me to make sure we weren't up to anything. He would sit there with a big frown on his face bouncing his right leg up and down as he did whenever he was nervous or putting a baby to sleep. One eye would be on the television and the other eye would be on us.

Diane! Yes daddy. Visiting hours is over and yo' company gotta go. Eddie and I were both heartbroken because we wanted to be together always and forever. Let me walk you to the door Eddie. Are you sure your daddy aint' gonna get mad? Man please! Once we got in the hallway we talked for 10 more minutes then Eddie gently kissed me goodnight for almost 10 more minutes. I hesitated when it was time to go back into the house because I knew daddy had a mouth full of complaints. Diane I am sick and tired of seein' that boy's face. Every time I come home from work he's sittin' up in here like he lives here. Don't he have a home? I would like to be able to sit around my house in peace and not have to look into your silly faces; he just can't come over here everyday! Y'all ain't married and you're only 17 years old. The only time daddy took a breath was when mama interjected with her em hems and Amen's. Eddie and I had been together for just about a year and we began to discuss the issue about sex quite often. I would rationalize why we shouldn't and Eddie would give me theories on why we should. I wanted to wait until I got married and Eddie felt that since he wanted to be my husband, then sex with him was okay. Birth control was Eddie's suggestion. However, the mere thought of asking mama gave me indigestion. I might as well have packed my bags in preparation for her answer. Mama's solution to birth control was abstinence, but at the age of 17 I needed something much stronger than that. I placed all of my burdens within the balances. I weighed what little I knew about God, the difference between a good choice and a bad choice, my future, and any possible disappointments I may cause mama and daddy against my love for Eddie and the lust that was now overpowering my entire being. I never thought I would lose my virginity on the back stairs in mama and daddy's hallway. I always pictured myself being carried over the threshold after the wedding, where a soft bed of roses would welcome Eddie and I. Instead I made my bed upon a cold and hard stairwell where cold hard reality set in and let me know the choice I made was not a good one. I realized I gave up my most valued possession, my hope and my dream, for five minutes of pleasure. Foolishly I played with fire as if I was invincible, playing house and doctor in secret places. Before I knew it the fire had consumed me and I got burned. We sat on Eddie's front porch in silence. Eddie stared at the ground with his arm wrapped around me, and I gazed up at the sun as if the solution to my predicament was going to fall out of heaven and right into my hands. What am I going to do Eddie? What do you mean? We're in this together Diane. I know, I guess what I'm trying to say is, how in the world am I going to explain this to my parents? I did the very thing I said I wouldn't do. What am I going to do about school? I have a track scholarship waiting for me. My future is waiting for me, and now I have a baby waiting for me. You can still do all of those things Diane. I'm going to take care of you and my child, but first you have to talk to your parents because sooner or later they are going to find out. The mere thought of talking to mama and daddy paralyzed my thoughts and caused my mind to go blank. Eddie if I tell mama now it will really hurt her. She's already dealing with grandpa's illness. I just can't do it. Eddie and I cuddled in silence when his brother Jason walked up with his fat man laugh. Ah ah ah ah. What's so funny Jason? You and Eddie are funny; y'all crack me up. You act like it's the end of the world. Ain't no sense in cryin' over spilt milk now cause' what's done is done. Eddie grew angry at Jason's insensitive words and yelled at him. Jason shut up and leave us alone! You can't make me daddy, I mean Eddie. Of course, I had to add my two cents. Eddie, don't let his ignant' self get to you. Well I'd rather be ignant' than pregnant, ah ah ah ah. I just came out here to tell you that my mama wants to talk to you. Who are you referring to, Eddie or me? I'm referring to you Diane; she wants to talk to you. I was puzzled as to why Mrs. C. sent Jason out to get me. Jason walked away laughing as if he was pleased to have tormented us. Eddie I'm not going in there. What does your mother want with me? Just go and see Diane. Why should I? Diane just do this for me. Slowly, I arose and went into the house. Mrs. Camden was standing in the kitchen cooking. Hello Mrs. C. How are you? I'm fine and what about you? I'm good. Diane why don't you step into the other room with me? Excuse me! I said...why don't you step into the other room with me; I would like to have a word with you. Oh, no problem Mrs. C. I cut my eyes at Eddie for setting me up. Now I knew without a doubt he told her. I walked into her living room and stood in the middle of the floor with my head hanging from my shoulders. She placed her right hand on her hip and stood before me with a look of authority. Diane, I'm gonna ask you something and I want you to tell me the truth. Yes Ma'am. Eddie tells me you're pregnant and I want to know if it's true. I tried to answer her, but my lip wouldn't stop quivering. Is that true Diane? Her loud voice startled me so I quickly answered her. Yes Ma'am it's true. How far long are you? I don't know, maybe two months. What were you thinking? How could you let this happen? Don't think I'm picking on you because I'm not. I gave Eddie the same lecture I'm giving you. I thought you were smarter than this. Tell me somethin', how are you and Eddie going to raise a child and you're only children yourselves? I don't know Mrs. C.; I guess I didn't give it that much thought. Eddie walked in and began pleading with his mama to stop badgering me. Mama please! Eddie get out, I don't want to hear a word from you! I'm talking to Diane, but if you want to stick around I'm sure I'll have a little something left over for you! Eddie looked at me as if to say that he was sorry for asking me to come inside before turning to walk out of the room. Mrs. C. you have to believe me, I didn't mean for this to happen. But it did, so now what! What did your parents say? Panic flushed my face white and fear lowered my eyes to the floor. I began dropping so many tears I could see my reflection on the plush red carpet beneath me. Oh my Lord! You didn't tell your parents did you. Instead of answering her I wept. Well, by your reaction I can tell you haven't said a word to them. What are you waiting for child? I just need a little time. Time! You don't have that much time left. Are you afraid of how your daddy might take it? I'm afraid of what I'll see in my daddy's eyes. They expected so much more out of me. Well, do you want me to tell them? No! I'll do it. I promise I'll do it. It would be better if it came from me. Okay, but if you don't tell them soon I'm gonna call your mama and tell her myself do you understand? Yes Ma'am, I understand. Eddie wanted to walk me home, but I chose to walk alone. How am I going to fix my mouth to tell mama and daddy that a baby was growing inside of me? How am I going to explain how it got there? I kept to myself for most of the day. I was trying to figure out the right moment to tell them, but after carefully weighing the situation I decided not to. Days turned into weeks and before I knew it school was over. I went to a local college two weeks after graduation. Mama and daddy thought I turned my track scholarship down to stay in Eddie's face, but I turned it down because of my pregnancy and I also didn't want to run for the rest of my life. I didn't want my college education to be dependent on my ability to perform for them. Of course, taking a maternity leave in the middle of the first year would also hinder my scholarship. All of the pressure I was feeling took the excitement out of running. I also went through what I call the "What if syndrome." What if I got hurt? What if I grew tired and decided not to run, would I be allowed to stay at the school or would I get the boot. I thought about taking the baby with me and trying to wing it, but after thinking it all through I decided to stay home. Foolishly, I tried to ignore my condition as if it was going to go away or something. For months I kept my secret locked behind my belly button unwilling to let it out and unwilling to acknowledge it as something real until I got morning sickness. I don't understand why it's called morning sickness because I wasn't only sick in the morning, I was sick all day and all night. Sickness seemed to govern my days. I flooded my system with Ginger-Ale and crackers. Nevertheless that only gave me temporary relief. When at home I retreated to my bedroom, hung my head out of the window and let my guts out, only to hose it up later. During dinner I made several trips to the bathroom and vomited as quiet as I could. To lie and be deceitful was surely hard work and I prayed for all of this to be over soon. Finally, after what seemed to be eternity the sickness stopped. Mama and daddy began staring at me as if my skin was turning colors. At first I thought someone told them, maybe Mrs. C., but I quickly wiped that thought clear from my mind. I assumed it impossible for them to know my secret because I thought I hid it well.

It was hot and I had been in class for most of the day. I boarded the bus with two friends Joyce and Carmen. As usual we sat in the rear of the bus and cut up. Laughter shook the windows as the three of us reminisced about our high school days. Hey Diane, isn't college jive okay? Yeah. Do you regret turning down your scholarship? Not really, you know the story behind it. Carmen rolled her head around as she spoke. Girl please, I would've taken it in a heartbeat. Joyce turned and added her ten cents. What is she gonna do, run around the track bumping into people with her big belly? We laughed insanely, me more than them to cover my hurt. So Diane, are you beginning to feel the baby kick? Yes, it's strange because it takes me by surprise. Joyce sat back throwing her sarcastic comments at me as usual and burst into laughter after Carmen's next question. We want to know the juicy stuff, tell us how your parents took it when you told them you were pregnant. I, uhhh, haven't gotten around to doing that yet. What do you mean Diane? I mean I haven't told them yet. Carmen joined Joyce in their hideous laughter toward me. Wait a minute! Wait a minute! Let me get this straight. You haven't told them and you're walking around them looking like you swallowed two watermelons. Her last statement literally shocked me. Oh my goodness, am I showing? Carmen fell on the floor of the bus laughing and gagging on her own saliva. Joyce fell across the seats in the back of the bus, while I sat there examining my stomach. That must be why mama and daddy have been looking at me as if I just fell from the moon. Oooh, do you think they know! I became sickened with Carmen's sarcasm. Well if they don't, then they are just as crazy as you are. Joyce, what am I going to do? I can't go home. You two ain't a bit of help. This is not a laughing matter; I really need help. Joyce sat up and looked over at me. Well Diane if you'd gone to my doctor like I told you to he would've taken care of your problem. I told you I don't believe in that Joyce now get out of my face talkin' stupid! My child is a part of me and I love my baby, so I don't care what y'all think. Diane don't yell at her you're the one whose five months pregnant. Did you expect to go through the entire pregnancy without showing? Their laughter had begun to irk me and out of anger I cursed them and got off the bus. When I reached the corner of my street I stopped and peered at my body in the big shiny glass of the beauty shop. I turned from side to side and then looked up at the expression on my broken face. I could've bought myself for a penny and got change. Who is that pregnant woman? I recognized the face, but the body was unfamiliar to me. It wasn't a stranger's body. It wasn't the woman in the beauty shop. It was me, myself, and I. How could I have been so blind? I walked slowly, eating pretzel rods and drinking apple juice. There's no use in trying to hide something as visible as this, but I don't think mama and daddy know. I will tell mama today. I got home and made myself comfortable. I pulled a chair to the table and munched on my pretzels while watching television. I sat there thinking about my life and my future. Now that I had a child on the way I desperately wanted a right now career. I didn't want to wait eight years to finish college and law school. I needed to provide for my child's needs as well as desires. I wanted to prove to mama and daddy that Eddie and I could make it. Then a commercial caught my eye. There were men and women dressed like soldiers marching in synch and singing a military song. They were police recruits and the police department was seeking men and women to join the force. It seemed as if they had marched right into my living room. This was it. This was the answer to my prayers. I would be a policewoman. This would be my career until I could finish school. Then I heard mama coming in the door.

Hello mama. There was no answer. In silence mama walked around my chair and then back into the kitchen. I sat in a wooden chair watching television, content that my secret was safe from her for now, I thought. She just kept pacing back and forth, glancing over me with those scornful eyes. Every child-like instinct told me she knew because she just kept killing me over and over again with those scornful eyes. After wearing a hole in the rug she pulled a chair in front of me and sat down in silence. She knows...She knows...She knows; rang in my mind like a thousand bells over and over again. I didn't look at her because I couldn't. I fixed my eyes on a spot on the television and began to stuff my mouth with the salty pretzel sticks. Bite down, chew, chew; no swallow. She asked if I had anything to tell her as she watched me with those scornful eyes. I couldn't speak and I couldn't swallow because the pretzels dried up my mouth and my hand kept stuffing my mouth with pretzels. Lips burning from the salt...heart burning inside, while her question rang in my mind like a thousand bells over and over again. For five months I made myself invisible. I actually believed my round belly went unseen. Who did I think I was foolin'? Nobody! Not her and not my self-righteous, self-satisfied, selfish, self. My eyes swelled and filled with tears as my secret began to unravel, rolling off her tongue as the steamy tears rolled down my face. The words, Are you Pregnant...Pregnant...Pregnant stabbed through my heart like a bolt of lightening. I began to choke on those salty pretzels over and over again. She leaned toward me with those scornful eyes, burning a hole through my mind, reading my secret thoughts I thought were hidden. I couldn't take it anymore so I reached down deep inside my soul and grabbed as much courage as I could and I screamed out, Yes I Am Pregnant... Pregnant...Pregnant! The words rang in her mind like a thousand bells over and over again. I was accused of being a liar. I was accused of being deceitful. She shouted, how could you, why would you, why did you let someone talk you into Sex...Sex...Sex?" First year of college and already a Statistic...Statistic...Statistic. The words rang in my mind like a thousand bells over and over again. I dragged myself into my four-cornered room trying to figure out how I was going to make things better for her, my mother. I drowned in my own relentless tears and slept on a bed of sorrow as I was awakened by my own screams of:

GRANDPA. I must have been having a bad dream. The night had fallen on the earth like a black blanket. It only made me aware that he was home, but why wasn't he screaming? Why wasn't he yelling for me to come down those stairs? Not as his little girl, but as a woman with child. Why was there silence when there shouldn't have been? My curiosity got the best of me. I eased off my bed, down the stairs to the place where he sat in a wooden chair beside the television. He looked at me out of the corner of those scornful eyes. In them I saw disappointment, then a tear surfacing in those scornful eyes. They all sat in silence with looks of insanity, my brother and sisters too. Something was wrong. I couldn't look him or her (that man and that woman) in the eye, so I looked to my sister. She said, GRANDPA is Dead...Dead...Dead. It rang in my mind like a thousand bells over and over again. I sat still, frozen by the shocking pain of death. I glanced over at my mother. Pain and agony shone on her weeping face. Now I felt shame. Now I felt responsible for all of her pain. I never wanted to hurt her or him, my father, although I went unnoticed and invisible to everyone. Especially them! The funeral had come and gone. Several days passed and still no mention about my condition. Not a word was spoken until he finally lifted up his head. I only remember the word Abortion...Abortion...Abortion as it rang in my mind like a thousand bells over and over again. He asked if I heard him. How could I not hear him? I was standing right in front of him, and that woman, she just kept wiping the kitchen table. Wipe...Wipe...Wipe as if she had no part in the decision. What makes them think they can decide for MY LIFE, MY FUTURE, and MY BABY? IT IS MY DECISION! How could they do this and why would they do this? They are not thinking about me. They are just thinking about their self-righteous, self-satisfied, selfish, selves. What about what I want? What about what the love of my life wants? I guess that doesn't matter because we're young and I guess that makes us incapable of making decisions. Nobody said nothin' about marriage, but if you want to make it your CHOICE, then go right ahead. I'll have your abortion, but don't expect me to agree with it, condone it, or accept it.

Silently, I sat on the windowsill in that place, glancing over the world with my face pressed against the cold window. The rain slapped the glass and then my face. I wondered whether the world was crying for me since my tears were being held captive within me. I cannot cry. I refuse to cry and I refuse to ever utter another word for as long as I live since they are Taking...Taking...Taking a part of me and throwing it away. The nurse asked questions that I refused to answer. I just kept watching the world's tears slap the glass and then slap my face. And that woman, she sat in the chair behind me tripping over the answers to the nurse's questions, watching me as I sat in Silence...Silence...Silence. It rang in my mind like a thousand bells over and over again. Hours went by and darkness fell as I sat still in that place, watching the lights of the city dazzle in my eyes. I thought if I got up and left in the middle of the night no one would notice. I've always been invisible to him, to her, and to the world. They only think they see me, but they don't. They don't even know me; who I am, what I believe, what I want, what I like, what I hate. They only know of me. Well, I won't be here in the morning when the butcher comes. I will be long gone. As I slowly clothed my swollen body thoughts swarmed around my head like bees in a beehive; my mother's face and her scornful eyes, my father's words of disappointment, television watching me and pretzels poisoning me. Scornful eyes and Lies...Lies...Lies! Grandpa is in a coffin, and now...my baby? Tears began drowning me and my thoughts began killing me over and over again while the rain came down hard slapping the glass and ringing as it hit the metal awning. It rang in my mind like a thousand bells over and over again. Waiting, watching, waiting for the rain to stop, then I would go. Then I could breathe in life, whatever life was. My eyes closed from watching and sleep arose from waiting. The sun peeped through the worn cracks in my eyelids. I knew then that it was too late. As I opened my inquisitive eyes a man-like figure stood at the foot of that bed, but he wore no white coat. It was he, my father. Had he returned to make sure his deed was done? No, he spoke the words "Let's Go Home" and it echoed in my mind like a thousand bells over and over again. We left and for the first time I was visible to them, to me, and to the world. I AM A LIVING-HUMAN BEING. I HAVE AN OPINION. I HAVE A CHOICE. I HAVE A VOICE. MY LOVE WILL BE MY HUSBAND. MY BABY IS MY MIRACLE SON. I AM NOT A STATISTIC...STATISTIC... STATISTIC!

<u>Journal Insert</u>

Growing up sure isn't easy, but I used to think it was fun
Until I became a young woman, my childhood was over and done.
Mama put away my dolls and all my Barbie rings
Gave me my old cradle and lots of baby things.
Pretty yellow, green, and pink; blankets, socks, and shoes
Too late to turn back now, too late to get the blues.
Now I sit and watch the days all pass me by
I question many times…why me, why this, why now, why?
There's no one here to answer, no one here but I
Feeling so alone, my heart begins to cry.
I never meant to hurt her or lie to her so long
I guess I made that choice that God considers wrong.
I gotta go to work now to provide for me and mine
Stay in school and study, mama said I'd be fine.
I didn't think they understood all the things I'd gone through
That's why I didn't say a word while the baby inside me grew.
Get that education she said…leave them boys alone
All of that foolish behavior I will definitely not condone!
Life is about choices, life is full of tests
I don't always admit it, but mama always knows what's best.

Diane

12
<u>LEARNING TO HATE</u>

Daddy was very protective when it came down to his children. In spite of our differences he loved me and only wanted what was best for me. He said the police force was too dangerous for me and mama wasn't happy about the decision I'd made concerning my future. I guess they felt that I hadn't considered the consequences of that type of job and they were right. My concentration was on the money I'd make and the benefits I'd receive. Also, I felt my life wasn't moving fast enough for me. I was working two jobs and balancing the job of a mother and full time student. Daddy wanted me to be the lawyer I said I would be and I assured him I would finish after I graduated from the Academy.

How much longer before you graduate Diane? I'll be done with it in a few months. I want you to be careful Diane. The world isn't like you and you still have a lot to learn about people. Daddy I'm gonna be fine. Well at least they're paying you well so I guess I can't complain. It was a nice day so I decided to walk to Eddie's house to pick up our son Xavier instead of waiting for him to pick me up. I enjoyed walking; it relaxed me and gave me a chance to commune with myself. I was nearly four blocks away when I saw a large crowd gathering around a police car. My stroll turned into a fast paced walk. As I drew closer I saw Eddie standing in the front yard of a yellow house. I followed his eyes and they led my own upon a yellow porch. A black man was beating on two police officers, one white and the other black. I couldn't believe my eyes. He was tall and obviously very strong. There were five small children in the doorway of that yellow house and his wife was on the yellow porch yelling for her husband to stop. Their accent told me they were of African decent. Eddie, did someone call 911 to get help for those officers? Yes, the little white officer broke loose, ran to his car, and called for help. I guess you're right, listen at all those sirens riding on the wings of the wind. When the man threw the black officer into the wall his wife jumped on him to keep him from hurting the officers. Eddie laughed. Diane you should assist your fellow officers. I can't, they told me not to get involved in anything while in the academy. Oh hush Diane, I was only kidding anyway. In the blink of an eye several police cars pulled up. They didn't care that they almost ran every last one of us over. They gave us a look as if to say, "Get out of the way." None of them got out of the car empty handed, some had flashlights and some had clubs. There were so many police officers charging the porch area I couldn't count them. We all thought it was mighty brave of the woman to help the police in subduing her husband. Wait! What's happening? Their weapons were raised in unison and came down hard upon the woman's head. Then they beat her husband. She resisted and tried to give an explanation, but they continued to strike her. The crowd, including myself roared at the men and women in blue because of the injustice they were inflicting upon her. We were on their side until they did the unthinkable. The woman's hands were no longer wailing against her husband to help the police. Now she clinched his arms of steel to seek protection from the law. The children ran around the porch screaming and attempting to get to their mother. The woman reached out for her children, but before she could grab hold of them one of the black officer's took her flashlight and knocked the woman in the head. A split ran from her left eyebrow to the middle part of her head. Her beautiful brown skin was now covered in blood. Enraged, the man gained more strength. He looked like a combination of Mohamed Ali and Bruce Lee, however, he was outnumbered and his fury was over. The angry crowd was threatened by the police to either leave or be locked up and as the angry crowd grew louder I realized that I had the loudest mouth of them all. We're not going anywhere! That woman didn't do anything wrong. You all just got out of your cars swinging at whoever was in your sight. Diane you better be quiet before you lose your job; you see how they are! I don't care! It's a matter of principal. I looked to the white officer who actually benefited from the woman's help to see if he would step up and tell the others that they made a terrible mistake, but instead he lowered his cowardly face and looked away. I yelled out to him, and was quickly silenced when he threatened to arrest me. We stood there staring each other in the eye until Eddie snatched me away. Come on Diane, it ain't worth it. I turned and walked away with Eddie. You sure better hope they don't remember your face when you get out of the academy. Eddie

I could care less because right is right and wrong is wrong, and those police officers were dead wrong. Diane, are you absolutely sure this is the type of job you want? I am very sure, now more than ever before. Why? It gives me a purpose and a chance to change the negative perceptions people have about the police into something positive and I want to make a difference, besides, all of this brutality has to stop. I'll make sure of it! Eddie and I took a slow walk to his house. Anger embraced us both and silence captured our words. How could people be so insensitive, uncaring, and brutal? Two of those officers knew fully well that woman was not fighting against them. Regardless, they stood by and watched as she got her head beaten in. As a matter of fact they joined in on the beating. Would it have been so difficult to say, no, don't strike her because she was only helping. I don't understand people and why they do what they do. I'm joining the force, but I pray to God I don't become one of them.

I learned early on to keep my chin up and my mouth shut. There was favoritism, separatism, and there was racism, but I watched with a scrupulous eye looking over the ills of the department and saw room for improvement. I stood by while some of the women in the academy flaunted their bodies in front of the instructors, selling themselves for a passing grade. What was going on in those back rooms during lunchtime? Why were their clothes disorganized when they came out? Could it be that they were involved in an extra credit assignment that didn't include anyone else? All I knew was that I didn't want to do any extra credit. After several weeks of training and tests it was time to graduate. Our superiors made it mandatory to go through what I call a brainwashing session where we were told to bring our spouses or significant other. We were told that policing was very stressful and the majority of us would end up in divorce court or a bad relationship. They told us that most of us would end up as alcoholics or drug addicts. It was stressed to us that we were now police officers and our only friends were other police officers. We were told that we were now blue. Not white, not black, not brown, and not pink, but blue. It was impressed upon us that the police department was our family now and it was important for family to stick together because no one likes a rat. They stressed that no one will understand us and no one would want to be around us because we were now of a different species. As the round, bald man continued to speak I remember saying to myself, you're wrong man, and I'm not falling for it.

The transition from the academy to the precinct house proved to be an awful experience. I walked in through the front doors of the most violent precinct in the city. There seemed to be a lot of confusion brewing in the air. There were a large number of officers, mostly male; hanging around like silly boys on a playground. Some reading the newspaper, some drinking either coffee or vodka with a tinge of coffee, and some were just horsing around. My first impression of the place was that of low morale. There were pictures of nude women spread eagle all over the walls. There were pictures and cartoons of male organs on the walls with the names of other police officers plastered all over them. I was disgusted by it and I wanted to turn around and go home. There were only a few female officers assigned to this particular precinct along with myself, and while we idly stood by trying to fit into a male dominated profession, the men made bets on whom they were going to get in bed first. As a rookie I expected a little teasing, however, some of it got real ugly. In the beginning I did very little patrol, so my assignments included walking the beat and working as the desk officer. While managing the desk several white officers would always make it a point to gather around my desk and make up the most hideous jokes depicting black people as "Jigs" and "Nigs." They would laugh and point at me, whether I would acknowledge their presence or not. I would continue typing as if they weren't there, showing no emotion on the outside, but crying elephant tears on the inside. Several black officers from the other platoon thought it necessary to tell me on several occasions they were going to rape me. When I didn't pay them any attention they would grab my arm or do something stupid to gain my full attention. I began to wonder if this job was worth all the aggravation. I was told on several occasions the reason they bothered me was because I didn't go along with the program and they felt I treated them as if they were beneath me. That was too much like standing up to them and they didn't like that, but because I rarely had to see them I didn't take their idle threats seriously. Day in and day out I was humiliated and harassed and I was tired of it. I was ready to take my complaints to the captain and lieutenant of the precinct; however

I found them to be condoning this behavior. They had that "boys will be boys" mentality. Most of the time these things were being done right in front of my superiors and I knew then they thought it was normal to behave like barbarians. All of the female officers were picked on. Some enjoyed the attention and others despised it, only they were too afraid to say anything. Night after night I went home to Eddie in tears with the desire to never return to that hole again. Nevertheless, after receiving rest and talking it over with him I somehow gained the strength I needed to return.

It was a busy day and I had a lot of work to do. As I was typing at my desk I looked up and that same group of white officers quickly approached me. I placed my face in my work pretending not to hear them as they started with the "Jig" and "Nig" jokes again. One of the voices was a familiar one. It was one that I had come to know as friend. I looked up and questioned him as to why he was acting like them. He told me to shut up and started walking toward the back room cracking those hideous jokes. When peer pressure sets in people begin to change and they end up hurting others just to receive the golden seal of approval from their peers. I walked to the doorway and placed my hand on my hip. None of you would like it if I called you a bunch of honkies or white trash now would you? The room silenced and faces began dropping to the floor. The officer I thought was a friend ran toward me, grabbed me, and dragged me to the back briefing table. When he picked me up I put him in one of my headlocks. Sam couldn't get out of my headlocks, so I knew this little wimp of an officer wouldn't be able to either. He slammed me on the back table and began to punch me in my sides several times, but his head was locked in the clutches of my arms. I remember looking to all the officers who stood around the table watching and I wondered if someone, anyone was going to pull this man off me. Red faces, white faces, brown faces, and black faces of both male and female stood by and watched as my ribs began to cave in. Fearing for my life I let go of his head, but I grabbed my knife out of my utility belt and began ramming it into his stomach area. One of the officers, seeing this, pulled him off me. Another officer grabbed me and snatched the knife from me. My ex-friend began yelling obscenities at me and thought I was crazy. It was only by the hand of God that he had on his bulletproof vest. I didn't really want to hurt him. I couldn't hurt anyone. I just wanted to scare him so that he would stop hurting me, but I thank God it didn't penetrate his skin because I didn't consider the consequences of my actions until after it was over. I ran to the telephone to call an attorney, the inspector, and the local news station. Out of fear a black officer who was my senior walked up to me calm and collective. You know if you report this you will be the one to get into trouble. Why do you think that? Regardless of how it was started, you're a female and he's a male, you're black and he's white, and you pulled out a knife. You're on probation and I can almost guarantee you that all of the blame will be placed on you, and they will fire you for just being involved. I hung up the phone and sat at my desk in a confused and furious state. This was all just a game to them, a game that had no winners. I knew if I told what happened they would make it worse for me, so once again I held my chin up and kept my mouth shut. A few hours later that officer walked up to me to apologize for his actions and thanked me for not reporting the incident. He stretched out his hand and we shook on it. The rest of the group was a little leery in saying anything to me. They all thought I was crazy. My mental state was deteriorating and I felt as though I needed a change, so I transferred to the other platoon, which was made up mostly of black officers. As usual, I sat at my desk preparing the paperwork for the day when a group of black officers surrounded my desk. They were just as bad as their white counterparts. The tiny hairs on the back of my neck stood straight up. I sensed danger, but couldn't see a way out. My heart knocked on my chest as if it wanted to get out and I felt like a rat cornered by five hungry cats. Well, well, well if it ain't little Diane. We told you that you couldn't make it on that other platoon, but you didn't want to listen to us. You belong to us now, but you have to pass our initiation before we can accept you on this platoon. I don't have to pass anything and I would appreciate it if you would get off my desk because I have work to do. The senior female officer who was working the desk with me snickered and sneered at me as the crowd of officers grew angry regarding my last remark. What did you say and who do you think you're talking to? I am talking to every last one of you. I'm not afraid of you, so leave me alone. Girl you have lost your mind. We told you we would catch up with you one day, but you didn't think we'd ever get you, did you? You are gonna learn to listen to us and respect your elders. Two of them grabbed my arms and two of them grabbed my feet, however, they didn't take me without a fight. I kicked at them and even caught one of them in the face. I pulled and pushed and I almost got away. In spite of my feeble attempts to gain victory they overpowered me. As they carried me away I called for help from the senior desk officer, but she only responded in a negative way. Don't look to me to help you. We all had to go through it and I told you once before to roll with the punches, but you gotta play hardball like you're better than everybody. I couldn't believe this was happening. What had I done to deserve all of this torture? They told me they were going to rape me. I didn't believe them and now it was happening. They carried me into the exercise room, closed the door, threw me on the weight bench, and held me down. They taunted me and told me what they were going to do to me. I looked into their faces and my mind glanced back to my childhood years. I saw the schoolyard and all those hands touching me, and then Mr. Price imprisoning me. Had they seen what was in my eyes or listened to my heart they would've heard me screaming. They would've felt my pain. What is with this species called male? Why are they always taking what does not belong to them? I began to scream for them to let me go, louder and louder. One of them posted at the door as the look out while the others were trying to decide who was going to rape me first. The tears I kept prisoner for so long broke loose and began to surface in the white of my eyes. They loosened their pants and then turned off the lights. My heart stopped and the ghosts of my past entered the room also. Their hands wrapped around my neck and choked me into silence. Frantically, my eyes roamed the room when suddenly the door flew open and they all ran out laughing, including the ghosts of my past. I got up asking God to help me as I hurriedly wiped the tears from my face. I was sure no one had seen the tears and I wasn't about to let them know there was a crack in my face. As I walked back to the front of the precinct they were all standing around my desk laughing. My desk partner had a crooked smirk stretched across her face. I wanted to rip it off, but then I came to the conclusion that it would be better if I'd killed every last one of them, however, I regained my senses, held my chin up and kept my mouth shut.

I went home and cried myself to sleep as usual, but this time it was different. I was learning how to hate and I was beginning not to care for anything or anyone, not even for my own safety. I was doing exactly what I didn't want to do. I was becoming one of them or at least I was starting to feel like one of them. My life had become a living nightmare and I didn't think I'd ever wake up.

13
<u>THE POWER OF GOD</u>

Eddie asked me to marry him and of course I said yes. My love for him was great and I wanted to spend the rest of my life with him. Everything was going just right until I received a telephone call the night before the wedding. Hello Diane this is Monique. I know who you are; I thought I told you not to call my house anymore. I know what you said, but I feel you ought to know something about your future husband. I don't care to hear it Monique. Please just listen to what I have to say Diane! Eddie and I have been friends for a long time and I just want you to know it's more than just a friendship. What do you mean, more than just a friendship? You know exactly what I mean. Are you trying to tell me you and Eddie slept together? Diane that's none of your business! Excuse me but you made it my business when you decided to call me with your garbage. Well I'm not telling you my personal business, but I will tell you I love him. Monique I've listened to you and now you're going to listen to me. You probably do love Eddie, but if Eddie truly wanted you or loved you he wouldn't be marrying me tomorrow. I don't believe Eddie slept with you. However, I do believe you thought that if you called me with this trash I'd dump him so you'd be there to pick up the pieces. Now why would you call me with this lie? Monique began to cry and apologized before hanging up. I sat there in the dark for hours waiting for Eddie to show up so I could give him a piece of my mind. I felt if he hadn't tried to play on both sides of the fence then none of us would be in this situation right now. I was livid and by the time he showed up I was ready to take his head off. My words were brutal, cold, and sharp and when I finished yelling I grabbed my coat to leave.

Diane, please don't leave me. I will tell you the truth. I know I should've nipped this in the bud a long time ago, but I liked the attention Monique gave me. Did you sleep with her? Well, almost. What do you mean, almost! Either you did or you didn't. I swear to you I didn't sleep with her, but I started to. Diane I love you with all my heart and I can't stand the thought of losing you. You're the only woman for me; you've got to believe me. Why can't you just be right Eddie? Why do you always have to be doing something stupid? Diane, I'm telling you I didn't sleep with her. Oh, I believe you, but I'm not crazy enough to believe that you're innocent either. As much as I love you I cannot and I will not enter into a marriage under false pretenses. Diane, please say you'll show up at the wedding tomorrow. I can't say that Eddie because I don't think I'll be there. Please say that you'll show up; I'll be waiting for you. I grabbed my coat and left. I drove through the streets for hours drinking foolishly and talking to myself. Anger rifled throughout my entire being and the tears fell without notice. I couldn't figure out what I should do. I hadn't stopped loving Eddie, but I hated him for what he did. While weighing my decision mama and daddy's faces popped up before me. Then Xavier's laughter and thoughts of the house we purchased together. They all played important roles in making my decision and after gazing into my heart I saw Eddie standing there in the midst of it all. I realized the love I had for him outweighed everything else, even Monique. The Bridesmaids were dressed in satin-royal blue gowns and the men were all dressed in white with satin-royal blue cummerbunds. Eddie and I were dressed in all white. I arrived at the church one hour late. My nerves were a wreck and I wanted to make sure that the second thoughts I thought I was having were really my nerves. Girl where have you been? Daddy you are making me very nervous with all of your yelling. I was just getting myself together. Well if you haven't gotten yourself together by now then something is wrong. I started down the stairs to the parlor. Where are you going girl? I'm going to the parlor for a minute daddy! I swear, you are gonna be late for your own funeral, that boy has been waitin' for you since three o'clock. Well, tell him I'm here and they can get started. I paced the floor for 15 minutes and watched as my Bridesmaids all lined up. Aunt Betsy freshened up my lipstick for me. Sweetie don't chew on your lips, your lipstick keeps coming off. Oh, I know. I can't help it. I'll just be glad when all of this is over. She smiled as she sensed my nervousness. Well honey, In order for this all to be over you've got to get up, so come on because it's time. Daddy met me in the hallway and we watched with my arm in his, as the wedding party began walking down the isle. Xavier stood idly by like a miniature-sized man all dressed up and as handsome as can be. When it was time for him to go he smiled at everyone as he carried the ring down the isle. Daddy tugged at my arm and gave me an inquisitive look. Are you ready Diane? Yes daddy, I'm ready. You know there's no turning back once you say I do, so if you're having second thoughts now is the time to speak up. Daddy I'm fine. Mama opened the big glass doors for daddy and me. As I approached the doors my foot froze and I pulled on daddy's arm to make him stop. Girl what is your problem? Uhhh, they're not playing here comes the bride. How can they play it if they don't see you? Well I'm gonna wait until they start playing it. Mama held the door wide open and gave me the eye as people began to wonder what was wrong. Mama thought she was whispering, but the entire church heard her. Diane you get up here right now! I'm coming mama. Daddy tried yanking me, but I didn't budge. Diane, what's the matter? I don't know mama, there's a lot of people up there and I don't want them staring at me. Girl, have you lost your mind? Why would you wait until now to start having second thoughts? I'm not having second thoughts mama, I was just thinking some things through that's all. Daddy put his hand over my hand and somehow that calmed my fears. I remembered Eddie's beautiful smile and how much I loved him; this erased the contempt I had for him and I knew I wanted to spend the rest of my life with him. Then suddenly, my feet were moving and the next thing I knew Daddy was handing me over to Eddie. Eddie and I both looked worried and very nervous, but all of that subsided when he locked his arm in my arm. We exchanged our vows and were pronounced man and wife. When the minister said you may now kiss the bride Eddie and I both looked to see if our parents were looking before we kissed, but when we looked into each other's eyes we forgot all about them, especially Monique. Passionately we kissed then hand in hand we led the bridal party out of the church. The musician was supposed to play a special selection Eddie and I picked out. However, he played the wrong song and we ended up walking out on, "What a mistake I've made." I thought, what a profound moment.

The reception was packed with people, food, pictures, and loud conversations. At the tender age of two Xavier took charge of the dance floor, as usual. All eyes were on the little dancing machine. I was amazed at the lack of fear he exhibited and the overwhelming sense of confidence he demonstrated. In my heart I knew Xavier was going somewhere in his life, he had to, he was my miracle. Suddenly, a woman whom we hadn't met, but we soon got to know well, pulled Eddie and me aside. I want you two to listen to me good. Yes Ma'am. I know you don't know me; however I do know both of your parents. I'm going to give you some good advice someone gave me 30 years ago. I took it and believe me it works. Don't go to sleep angry. Make sure you apologize and get that thing straight before you close your eyes at night. Keep mama and daddy out of your business, both of you. If you have an argument don't y'all go running home to your parents! They'll still be holding onto that thing when you've already forgiven each other and gotten over it. Always keep an open line of communication. Eddie, Diane is your best friend and Diane, Eddie is your best friend. And don't be afraid to love and let go. I wrapped my arms around this stranger and kissed her on the cheek. You have given us a wonderful gift and we will cherish it for the rest of our lives, thank you. We had a wonderful time at the reception; however, the time came for us to depart. We left Xavier with mama and daddy and went on our way. Our room was filled with cards and boxed gifts. We started the evening out with reading the cards to each other and talking about the funny things that happened at the reception, but when the time came to consummate the marriage we had a difference of opinion. Eddie wanted to consummate the marriage by having me sit with him and watch pornographic movies so that we could copy what they were doing. I wanted to consummate the marriage the traditional way with no additives. I wanted us to make our own music and not duplicate someone else's. After realizing our indifference I exhaled, and wondered, what in the world have I gotten myself into? I also knew Eddie was thinking the same thing. This odd situation made a strong connection to the song we ended up walking out of the church on, "What a mistake I've made." How could we have been so far off track regarding our expectations of each other in this marriage? We were together for six years and married for 9 hours, and within these last 9 hours I've found that Eddie had another closet full of trash, which he failed to reveal in the six years we were together. Maybe I refused to see it because my love for him blinded me to his little idiosyncrasies.

One year after the wedding Eddie and I had a baby girl and we named her Kayla Divine Camden. We gave her the middle name Divine because there was something special about her. She looked like a little angel and her skin was the color of ebony and amber mixed together, which was as soft as the clouds. She was so beautiful and precious her smile made my heart melt. She gave me peace and inspired me to laugh in the midst of some rough times. Xavier was a handsome and intelligent little boy. His eyes reflected innocence and love. He carried a special light that drew people to him. He was my miracle, my hope, and my dream, and the gray patch in his head showed me that he had been given great wisdom from birth. I thank you Lord for my two beautiful children.

The beginning of our marriage was very difficult. I thought I knew Eddie and he thought he knew me, unfortunately we really only knew of each other. Eddie wanted to hang out until the break of dawn with his friends and whomever else, and I wanted quiet time with my husband, long walks through the park, and dinner as a family. Eddie hardly spent any time at home, so I began hanging out all night because at least then I had people around me who wanted to spend time with me. At least then I had someone to talk to and someone to talk back to me. At times I would sit at home and discuss my problems with Xavier or myself. I knew he didn't understand anything I said. On the other hand, my loneliness drove me to those extremes. I realized the marriage I'd always dreamt about was only a figment of my imagination. We both had expectations that weren't met, not because we didn't want to meet them, but because we didn't know how. With the pressure from my job along with the disappointments in my life and marriage my imagination got the best of me. I began to imagine life without me. Suicide laughed at me and told me that it was entertaining thoughts concerning me. I had hit an all time low in my life. Although I tried talking to Eddie he didn't hear me. He was too concerned about himself. I couldn't run home to talk to mama and daddy because they would only use it against me to prove that they were right and I was wrong, and Sam, Lottie, and Michelle would say that I was just trippin' and because I didn't feel they would ever understand I ended up suffering in silence. Depression was rocking me to sleep and loneliness whispered demented lies to my soul.

Eddie was staying out just about every night and I no longer felt like a wife. I felt like a live-in maid. It was as if I had married a ghost. His spirit was there, I knew he lived there, but physically he wasn't there. He wouldn't call home and there were many times where he would make himself totally unavailable to us, so on the nights I got off work at 11:30, I would head straight for the bars and by midnight I was drinking and dancing. Usually I would dance with Sam because strange men would sometimes interpret a dance for a date. Hanging out and imitating the behavior of a lunatic wasn't as fun as everyone tried to make it seem. It was becoming a little monotonous. However, because it was the only way I knew to wind down and that's where everyone else was I continued to do it. One evening I decided to do something special for Eddie. I prepared a nice candle light diner for two; T-bone steak, baked potatoes, garden salad, and a side dish of shrimp scampi. Jazz filled the air while Xavier and Kayla slept soundly in their beds. At 6:00 P.M Eddie called to let me know he was on his way home. I told him I had a special diner waiting for him and at 2:00 A.M I sat alone. The food had gotten cold and the candles were no more. I was so angry I thought my head was going to explode. Why does he do this to me? Why do I continually allow him to do this to me? Time after time after time Eddie stands me up and leaves me foolishly waiting for him like someone desperate for a date. Life had become too painful to cherish and I felt as though I couldn't do it anymore. My marriage, my family, and my job had gotten too heavy to carry and the bad began to outweigh the good. Sobbing, I dragged myself into my bedroom carrying a bottle of the most potent liquor I could find. I grabbed one of my bottles of prescription pills and poured it out over my nightstand. I sat on my bed, took my wedding band off my finger and held it before my face. My mind went back to the wedding and I remembered the minister telling me to hold the ring close to my face and to really look at it. He said; see how the ring forms a complete circle without any breaks or separations! I remember Eddie and me nodding in agreement. The minister continued. So shall your marriage be. Marriage is holy. It is symbolic of the marriage between Jesus Christ and the church. You two are now one. I remembered everything the minister said to us on that day and I realize now that Eddie and I weren't one anymore. The question that came to mind was, had we ever been? Our oneness had been shattered by our ignorance and selfishness, which fragmented the marriage relationship. Disappointed I sat the ring amongst the pills. Could I really do this? Maybe! Do I really want to do this? No, I just want to show Eddie what he has done to me and to let him know I'm tired. Do I really care? No, not really. I picked up one of the pills and gazed at it for a long time as I held a cup of that stankin' alcohol in my other hand. As I searched my memory to find something good in my life, something worth living for I heard a voice speaking and the hands that held my life in its grips lowered. You know you don't really want to do this. You only need someone to love you, take care of you, and spend time with you. It sounded good, but it wasn't enough. I needed to deal with the here and now, so I began gulping down the alcohol like water as I scooped more pills into the palms of my hands. As I raised the pills to my mouth I heard a scream and then a cry. Xavier was having a bad dream. I placed the pills and alcohol on my nightstand and went to attend to him. I didn't turn on the light and I hid my face from him because I didn't want him to know I'd been crying. After comforting him and assuring him that everything was going to be fine I turned to walk out of his room. Xavier calmly asked me not to leave. I assured him that I would be close by and I wasn't going anywhere. Mama, do you promise? Yes Xavier, now go back to sleep. Kayla lifted her head and said, mama do you promise me too? I said yes and blew her a kiss. I went back to my room and sat on the edge of that bed. When I looked at the pills I saw Xavier's face and I remembered the promise. When I attempted to pick up the glass of alcohol, Kayla's smile made me put it down. Although my meaningless life was saved I decided to leave the evidence on the nightstand to scare Eddie to death and when he finally came home it did just that. Eddie screamed and shook me violently to wake me. My eyes opened wide and peered into his. I saw fear in his and he saw confusion and contempt in mine. When he realized I hadn't done the inevitable he dropped me from his arms onto the bed. Enraged, he began screaming very loudly and questioning as to how I could do this to him? He thought I was crazy and needed help. He wanted me to talk to someone concerning my mental state, but when I tried talking to him; once again, he didn't want to listen. We slept on a bed of anger and our bodies didn't touch. I thought, now Eddie sees how I feel. It hurts to love someone deeply and then not be loved in return; and it hurts to face the possibility of losing that person forever. Xavier's scream stuck in my mind. I pondered over the entire ordeal and realized when I wouldn't listen to the still voice speaking to me God used my miracle and my divine inspiration to save my life. It couldn't have been anyone else. God why do you keep saving my life? Why do you even bother with me? I'm useless. From as far back as I can remember I've been nothing but trouble. Nobody understands me. I've always been different and invisible to everyone, to my husband, my parents, and to the world. I'm just a woman without a face. Nobody sees me, nor does anyone hear me screaming. Help me God. Do you hear me screaming?

Journal Insert
Faceless

Silently I sit under the moonlight
Just to get away…I find peace in the night.
Tears filling the wells of my sunken eyes
Darkness is watching and I cannot cry.
It is pain that I feel echoing in my heart
The true meaning of emptiness and the shadow of a broken heart.

Took away my name, my soul embraced
For I am a woman without a face.
Took away my heart, my love disgraced
For I am a woman without a face.

The cool brisk air chills my soul
Wind whispering in my ear about the love he stole.
Laughter brushing through the trees
Evil faces pass by in the breeze.
Silence ringing in my ears, darkness is lifting
My face filled with tears.

Took away my name, my soul embraced
For I am a woman without a face.
Took away my heart, my love disgraced
For I am a woman without a face

Diane

14
A BULLET HAS NO NAMES

I loaded the trunk with a picnic basket full of food and sodas. Xavier and Kayla filled the back seat with balls, balloons, toys, and of course, water pistols. We had everything we needed for our games and to keep cool under the hot sun. Eddie and his brother were sanding my floors and were glad to see us go. The park was so crowded you could hardly see the grass. Xavier you look out to the right and Kayla you look on my side to see if you guys can spot grandpa's car. Frantically, Kayla pointed out of her window. Mama there they are. Where Kayla? There they are mama. That's not them. Are you sure mama? Yes Kayla I'm sure. Well are you really sure it's not them? Kayla! Yes mama. What color is your skin? Brown! And what color are those people that you're assuming is our family? I think pink and white mama. Exactly! Well that man still looks like grandpa to me, the only difference is he's pink and grandpa is orange and brown. Xavier twisted his lips and threw words at Kayla. Be quiet Kayla, you are so confused. Xavier don't you talk to your sister like that. She's only voicing her opinion. Okay mama, but while you were talking you passed grandpa and the rest of them. I turned the car around and saw daddy waving his arms in the air to get my attention. I parked my car in the grass near the shelter. Xavier and Kayla dashed from the car straight towards daddy. They wrapped themselves around his waist and his leg as if he was a movie star or something. Daddy really loved his grandchildren and wasn't ashamed to show it. My entire family had packed themselves under the shelter like sardines. Some of the kids were playing football and the rest of them were on the swings. My attention had fallen on most of the adults who were playing cards and making bets as if they were at a Las Vegas Casino. Losing caused them to yell and alcohol brought about violence. The rest of us laughed and talked about each other while eating everything in our site. When no one was looking I eased out to my car and grabbed my super soaker with a backpack full of water. They never saw me coming. I wet everyone under the shelter including the food. Sam ran to my car and passed out the rest of my ammunition, but I was still as fast as I was in high school. No one could catch me except for Eddie and he wasn't there. I saw mama sitting in a lawn chair and casually walked up to her. Diane, get away from me. But mama, I just wanna be close to you. Girl if you don't take that water somewhere else the only thing you're going to be close to is that ground. Oh such violence mother; maybe you need some cool down time. You know, the time out period after a good butt whoopin' that you used to give us when we were kids. Mama cut her eyes at me real slow then she sat her soda on the ground. My Aunts began to laugh. I pulled back on the pump slightly and wet the tip of mama's nose. She laughed and sarcastically turned her head as if she was daring me to do it. Oh, you don't believe I'll do it. I pulled back on the pump again with giggles bubbling in my throat. This time a bigger spurt of water came forth wetting mama's shirt. She jumped up and moved towards me like lightening. I pulled back on the pump, wetting mama in the face. I turned to run, but everyone else was running toward me and I couldn't stop because the Bride of Frankenstein was on my heels. I pulled back on the pump to fire upon all those attacking me; only this time a burst of air came forth instead of water. I was all out. I dipped and dodged. I was almost free until I ran into daddy. I forgot I couldn't out run him either. He held me while the others emptied their buckets of water on top of me. After drenching me from head to toe they all walked away laughing. I smiled and began poking my hair with my fingers to try and get the curl back into my jerri. I sat down next to my grandma. She always had the prettiest smile and the happiest laugh. Eeeh eeeh eeeeh, I see you got some of your own medicine Diane. Yep, I sure did grandma, but they would've never caught me if daddy hadn't grabbed me. Eeeh eeeh eeeeh, I thought Sam was going to have a heart attack out there running with y'all young folks. Not my daddy, he's in excellent shape. Besides, he taught me everything I know. Grandma, are you going with us to the waterfront to see the fireworks? Naw baby. Your grandma is tired and I'm going home. Are you sure? Yes I'm sure. You need to be going home too as wet as you are. Do you have a change of clothes? Yes grandma. I'm going to change right now. Make sure you change Xavier and Kayla before they catch the death of pneumonia. Yes grandma. As I walked over to my car I began to feel nauseous and my head was hurting. A migraine was coming on and I knew it was time for me to sit down. I changed and sat in silence. Mama was watching me and casually approached. Diane your face looks flushed, what's wrong? Mama my head hurts. Girl you know you can't be running around like a nut in this heat. It'll go away mama. All I have to do is be still. As the minutes ticked away it only grew worse. I couldn't blink or swallow. No matter what I did my head ached. Concerned, mama interjected once more. Diane maybe you should go home and rest and I'll take the kids to see the fireworks. It's alright mama, I think I can make it. Girl you know you have to go to work tonight. I know mama, but I can manage. I'll go home and lie down for about an hour and I should be okay after that. I demanded silence all the way home. I climbed in my bed hoping to sleep the headache away although Eddie was still sanding the floors. The noise kept me awake and the lack of sleep caused me to get sicker. Every thump, every bump, every laugh, and every word amplified in my head 20 times the norm. 40 minutes later the thumping in my head was reduced to throbs, however, the nausea was still there. I laid there in agony when at the bottom of my leg I felt a pat and then a tug. What is it Xavier. Are you taking us to see the fireworks? I don't know; I'm sick. Please mama, grandma and grandpa are waiting for us and I don't want them to leave us. Okay Xavier, give me a minute. He ran down the stairs shouting to Kayla to get ready. How am I going to make it to work tonight when I feel like a sick scraggly dog with one leg and no teeth? I can't tell Xavier and Kayla no, they've been waiting to see the fireworks all day and I want to take them. I peeled myself off the bed, showered and got dressed. I was the last one to make it to mama and daddy's house. Sam and all of his friends went ahead of us. Lottie, Michelle and the rest of the family piled in cars and we headed out. Parking was scarce. Nevertheless, we all found something one mile away from the park. I was so sick I wanted to puke. My heart began to pound within my head. Daddy always gets nervous whenever one of us is sick and he watches over us like a hawk. Hey sweetheart, are you okay? No daddy these migraines hurt and I feel dizzy. Well maybe you should stay in the car and rest. No dad I can make it. I'll stay for a little while, then I'm gonna have to go because I need some sleep before I go to work. Girl by the time we get outta here you won't have time to sleep. I'll be okay daddy. He backed off, but kept me within arms distance. We walked down the hill and over a bridge before we made it to the park entrance. There had to be at least 10,000 people entering the park and it seemed as if they were all talking and bumping into me. I could hear every conversation at the same time in my head, which made the pain escalate. I thought I was losing my mind. I plugged my ears with my fingers and asked mama to hold onto my arm so that I could walk with my eyes closed. That helped ease the pain some. Finally we made it to the center of the park and found a spot in the grass that we claimed as our own.

The park floated on a blanket of noise and some people threw obscene words at one another. Daddy beckoned for me to lye beside him as if I was his sick little baby that he had to care for. Diane, come over here and lye down. I lay perfectly still with my head resting on daddy's jacket. Tears rolled down the sides of my face as I looked at the bright stars above. My heart was beating so loud in my ears I began to moan like a woman in travail. We're going to have to get her home. Sam I know that! I've sent Lottie and Michelle for ice and water because she's burning up. Mama spoke with compassion while addressing me. Diane quit crying; what is it that hurts? Mama my head, It feels like it's gonna blow up. Mama cut her eyes at Lottie when she brought back an orange soda. Girl didn't I tell you to bring me some ice and water. Mama the park ran out of bottled water. The pain was astronomical and I couldn't take it any longer so I stood up to get some relief. As I looked up into the sky the stars that had sat perfectly still now moved. They were spinning around my head so fast they disappeared and then there was nothing left but darkness. For a moment there wasn't a sound, just darkness. I don't even remember hitting the ground. It was weird; I could hear daddy screaming my name, Xavier was yelling for me and Kayla began to cry. I was unable to move or open my eyes. I could hear the rest of my family crowding around along with other spectators, but I couldn't respond to any of their requests. Somebody call an ambulance. Diane wake up and quit breathing like that. Don't do this to me. This is your daddy; please wake up. Don't do this. A strange woman interrupted daddy and began talking. Excuse me, I'm a nurse, let me look at her. Do you know what happened? Mama was the only calm one. She said her head was hurting and then she passed out. Does she have any illnesses? She has chronic migraines and had been complaining all day of a headache. She patted my face several times. Sweetie! Sweetie! Wake up. You are going to be just fine. I wanted to tell her that I couldn't get enough air, but my mouth wouldn't move. Sweetie, I want you to take nice deep breaths. Breathe honey. That's right, breathe nice and easy. She turned my head to the side as my body began to convulse. I vomited and shortly after I was able to open my eyes. I looked around and saw a thousand eyes looking back at me. Daddy's face was stricken with panic. When he realized I was going to be okay he walked away to gather himself. The woman who helped me was really nice, but embarrassment set in and I began to push her away. Sweetie, don't get up. I need for you to lay still. The ambulance is here so please allow them to check you out. No! I'm fine. You really should go to the hospital. I don't want to go to the hospital. Mama acted as if she was embarrassed. Diane quit being so rude; she's only trying to help you. I know mama, but I'm fine and I feel one hundred percent better. The woman turned to mama and said she understood. As she walked away I thanked her for everything. Mama was upset with my response. Diane I don't know why you're so angry. Because mama, I blacked out and started shaking and stuff in front of all these people. Girl there is nothing to be ashamed of, you should be thankful you're alive. Kayla grabbed hold of me and refused to let me go. Xavier tucked his head and walked over to daddy. Mama what's wrong with him? Diane he's scared. Both of your kids were shaken up a bit. I stopped in my tracks and hugged Kayla until she gasped for air. I walked over to Xavier, pulled him into my arms and kissed his forehead. I'm okay Xavier. You don't have to worry about me because I'm fine. I sat on the bleachers next to daddy. His face was all crumbled up. Diane I think you should go to the hospital and get checked out because it's just not normal for a person to have as many headaches as you do and black out like that. Daddy I've already been checked. I have chronic migraines and that's it. It's just something that I have to deal with. Well how come they won't give you anything for it. I have been prescribed medication for the problem, but that's not to say it will always work. Daddy exhaled heavily then turned his attention to the left of me. There in the shadows stood an ambulance crew, a day late and a dollar short. Excuse me, we were told you passed out. Yes sir I did and I am fine now. Well if you don't mind we have to ask you some questions and we would like to make sure you're okay. When I couldn't answer certain questions pertaining to how long I was out, mama intervened. The paramedic was direct and bold in addressing me. Considering the fact that you have a heart murmur, asthma, and chronic migraines, it is our suggestion that you allow us to take you to the hospital. How long would I have to stay? Probably overnight. No can do, I have to go to work in three hours. Since you are refusing to go, then I have to ask you to sign this form of refusal. I signed and they were on their way. We gathered our things and walked back to the car in silence. Daddy took my keys and drove the kids and myself home while mama followed in their car. Before I could get out of the car good Xavier and Kayla gave Eddie the run down on the turn of events that occurred at the park. Are you okay baby? Yes. Why don't you stay home from work and get some rest. Eddie I'm fine. Once I passed out and vomited the sickness left me. It was like waiting for a volcano to erupt and once everything was over there was this calm that came over me. I feel a little lightheaded, but I am more than capable of handling work. Eddie stood there with a puzzled look on his face. He knew how stubborn I was, so instead of arguing he threw up his hands and accepted my decision. I really didn't want to go. Everything in me said to stay home. However, if I chose to stay home I would have had to endure my lieutenant's harsh words concerning the fact that I had taken off a few days prior. When I got out of the shower Eddie had prepared my uniform. It was pressed and creased nicely and my shoes shined like new glass. It was his night off so he did the dishes and put the kids to bed. As I was getting dressed I realized I didn't really care for the uniform and all that it represented. I didn't like the fact that it changed me into someone I didn't want to be. I headed for the door and hurriedly kissed Eddie's lips before my own turned cold. I rushed to my car and sped off as my disposition began to change. I could feel the transformation of my personality taking place instantly. No matter how much I struggled against it, the uniform and I were becoming one and by the time I opened the doors to the precinct the transformation was complete. The warm blood in my veins froze to the hard-core reality that I was no longer Diane. I had become a nameless, but mighty soldier. One who had to be strong and fearless in the face of danger. The mask I was now forced to wear protected the person inside from getting hurt. Good-bye Diane. I'll see you in 10 hours when day breaks. As I entered the door of the precinct I realized how much I hated it. The morale was low and the environment made me sick. I couldn't understand how these professional men and women could come to work everyday with no self-respect and no real intention of doing the work they were hired to do. Garbage overflowed from the trashcans onto the floors and instead of picking it up or changing the bag they would constantly throw food and paper into the corner until the cleaner came the next day to pick up after them, and sometimes it would be two or three days before we even got a cleaner. The place smelled like a sewer and the kitchen was disgusting. The unisex bathroom wasn't only filthy; the men had dug peepholes in the walls, so they could watch the women use the bathroom. It became very depressing to go to work. After briefing I received my car assignment, 121 East with Officer Samantha Jackson. It was my night to drive and Samantha's night to slump down in her seat and relax. The two of us together didn't weigh 200 lbs. and that included our equipment. We both loved our families and we both wanted to return home safely after each tour.

What time is it Samantha? Three O'clock in the A.M and we still have four more hours to go. I'm going to have to pull over for a minute. Why, is something wrong Diane? This headache is still swimming in the back of my head. Is it the same one you had earlier? Yeah girl! Diane you are crazy because I would be in my bed calling hogs if my head were hurting like that. Whatever Samantha! Well, before you pull over can you go to the corner store so I can get some hot chocolate? Before I could respond to her the dispatcher began to put out a distress call. Any car in the South sector! Any car in the South, at FernHill and Sycamore streets you have multiple shots being fired. Car crews were cutting each other off to let the radio dispatcher know they were responding. I turned on my lights and siren and headed in that direction. We are a good ways away Diane. It doesn't matter; I'm still going. I was driving at a speed of 60 mph south down Fillmore Street. My light was green and just

111

when I was about to go through it a yellow cab and a small red car crossed my path going west on Valley Drive. Quickly, I jammed on the breaks and looked up at the light. Isn't our side green? My eyes say yes, those nuts ran the light as if we were invisible. I put the pedal to the metal and jumped behind them. Samantha blew the air horn for them to stop, but they continued on and picked up speed. Radio! Radio! 121-East requires assistance. We're going west on Valley Drive behind a red vehicle bearing California registration 007FQW. I tried to stay as close to them as possible. The cab was pulling away from the red car and the red car was pulling away from us. They made a right turn onto Avery Street and then a quick left onto King Street. I was four seconds behind them. As I made a quick left turn onto King Street I pulled up directly behind the cab. The red car had stopped adjacent to the cab. I got on the loud speaker and began giving commands. In the meantime Samantha persistently radioed for help. Suddenly a black male exited the cab, pointed a .45 caliber automatic at the window of the red car, and then at the windshield of my car. In a blink of an eye Samantha and I both ducked down under the dash. I threw the gearshift into reverse and mashed down on the gas. It was only by the grace of God that I didn't hit anyone or anything. The only thing that mattered at that moment was getting out of the line of fire. When my car spun out I looked up and saw the man run up on a porch and into a house. It seemed as if eternity had passed by and help wasn't coming. Samantha continued to scream over the radio. 121-East needs back up. We have a man with a gun. We request back up; send us some help radio. Hold your horses' 121-East all of your cars are tied up on the shooting across town. I don't care where they are we just had a guy point a gun at us so if you have to send another precinct, then send them radio! I put the car in drive and pulled behind the red vehicle. The cab driver took off 90 going west. There were two men sitting in the red vehicle and they watched our every move.

Samantha, don't take your gun off those guys. I'm going up on this porch to see where that man went. I kicked at the door and gave orders for the man to come out. Diane let's get out of here, something isn't right. Be quiet Samantha and keep your gun on those men. A woman came to the door and pleaded with me not to hurt her boyfriend. I stepped in and ordered the man and the woman to the floor at gunpoint. I picked up the fully loaded .45 automatic and placed the man under arrest. We stepped out on the porch and then to the sidewalk. The man began to shake and would not take his eyes off the red car. Samantha ordered him to the ground. He wouldn't listen; his eyes were fixed on that car. Listen brother, I don't want to shoot you so get down on the ground! He complied, but kept his eyes on the car. Samantha yelled at the radio dispatcher concerning our request for help. He informed us that he notified the other dispatcher and help should be coming within seconds. The men in the red vehicle drove up into the driveway behind me. From that point on everything seemed to go in slow motion. I swung around with my gun pointed towards the individuals in the red vehicle. The black silhouettes sat perfectly still, watching me as I drew closer and closer. My heart was beating so loud I was sure they could hear it. Why weren't they moving? Why wouldn't they comply with my commands? What were they waiting for? Curiosity led me toward the back seat. One more step and I would be able to see everything in their vehicle. Then I heard sirens ringing throughout the air. I've never been happier to hear those sirens. Help was finally coming. With a mind of its own my body turned away from the car and the men in the red vehicle sped off into the night. The only thing they left behind was their tire tracks. The man on the ground began screaming with tears of joy. Thank you; you don't know what you've done. You saved my life. What are you talking about? They were gonna kill all of us. Who were they? That was the drug lord and murderer you guys have been looking for. That was "The Monster." Oh no! Samantha put that over the air right now! Police cars began pulling up on the sidewalk and everywhere. Our prisoner began questioning us as if he had the right to do so. Are you guys gonna let me go? Let you go for what! Because I could've said something while they were here and had I done that he would've killed all of us. One more step and your face would've been blown off because there was a man lying down in the back seat with an AK.47 pointed up at the window waiting for you to stick your face in. How do you know? Because when I got out of the cab he rose up and pointed it at me to kill me. That's why I pulled my gun out. I didn't mean to point it at you. I figure you owe me, so take these handcuffs off me please. I began reading the man his rights. You have the right to remain silent. He shouted, no I have the right to speak cause' you ain't no real cop anyway. You just do whatever the white man tells you to do. You ain't nothin' but a house nigga. You ain't no real sista. Be quiet and listen; anything you say will be held against you in a court of law. You have a right to an attorney. If you can't afford an attorney then one will be appointed to you by the court system. Do you understand these rights I've just read to you? I understand that you ain't givin' a brother a break; I told you I didn't mean to point that gun at you. The man continued to curse and belittle me. However, he failed to realize that it wasn't registering with me. My mind was trying to process everything that happened, but my thoughts were scattered around like a jigsaw puzzle. Hours passed and the sun began to rise in the East. It was time to go home. As I walked to my car I could feel my blood warming again. I drove slowly down the city streets as I struggled to keep my heavy eyelids from closing. My mind kept pressing the rewind button regarding those men with guns, only this time it added some things. I walked up to the red vehicle and stuck my face in the window. Shots ring throughout the night air, my screams follow and then my body falls hopelessly to the ground. Just as I pull into my driveway I snap out of it. Tears covered my face like fresh dewdrops of the morning. I sat there with the engine running to gather myself. My demeanor was changing and I could feel again. The words that came forth from the mouth of that man were now remembered. All that I do or try to do for my people and my community is never appreciated. I am still nothing but a sell out to them. To my white counterparts I'm a nigger or some worthless nothing who stole this job from an eligible white man. To my people I'm just a nappy headed sell out with a badge and no real powers. To society I'm colored and not accepted or respected as a person and in my community I've been cast out and considered the enemy. Questions rang in my mind. Who am I and how have I become this thing for everyone to hate? I turned the car off and walked into the house. My attitude began adjusting from the mentality of a warrior back to Diane. As I began to peel off the uniform the mask disappeared also. Ahhhh, I can breathe again. Welcome back Diane. I climbed into my bed and cuddled under Eddie. He threw his muscle filled arms around me making me feel protected, comforted, and loved. How was work baby? At the mere sound of his voice I broke down and cried, and then I told him how I came very close to losing my life. Eddie held me tightly in his arms and we attempted to go to sleep. I'm not going to ever let you go baby, not ever. If you want to quit, then do it. This job isn't worth me losing you. I'm sorry Eddie; I should've listened to you and stayed home. Maybe God gave me that headache to keep me home with you and even after I blacked out I still didn't listen.

Journal Insert
The Solemn Truth

I'm a woman
My skin is brown
I'm not a nigger
I'm a human figure
I'm not colored
Like an empty face with no distinction
Colored is what's done to a piece of paper
Why don't you show me some appreciation
I thought I'd only have to tell that to the white man's
Face
But I seem to have to tell it to people of my own
Black race
Why am I such a disappointment to the people I love and
Struggle for
Maybe it's the anger from the white man before
Or maybe it's the rage from doing what I have to do
Black brother   Black Sister   You're no exception
To the rule
You could never understand the words that I preach
Unless you've walked in my footsteps and faced death
At arms reach
Yes
My heart beats to the same African drum
I sometimes feel the dryness of its presence in my chest
This makes my whole body cold and numb
Who am I to those out there
A shallow figure with an empty heart
Or do they care
I've seen many faces
Most unkind, but true
I am a black woman
But you say my face is blue

SPIRITUAL CONFESSIONS
And my coming of age

Cast me out like the darkness in the sky
Hang me up to dry
For reasons I can't explain why
You say I'm not really black   Just the white man's toy
Doing whatever he asks
Just to give him joy
You say I sell myself short to get recognition
But there is a difference between selling and applying
When you have the ambition
I can't explain why
My people express such anger
Declaring war on me
Instead of war on the stranger
I'm like a pawn in distress
Without a sense of direction
Imprisoned in a world
That lacks appreciation
Stress and anger falling down on my head
From both sides of the fence
Both wanting me dead
At times I hear an unfamiliar voice trembling in my ear
It tells me to give up
His name is fear
But I'll keep on trying to make a difference
For my people and my life
For the black human race
And although my shadow lurks silently at night
My soul however remains true
Yes, I am a black woman
But you say my face is blue

Diane

15
THE CALL

Hey son, would you like to go to dinner? Eddie looked over at me and remembered his promise. I would love to dad, but I promised Diane we'd do something special before she goes to work tonight. Don't worry about it; we'll do it some other night. Eddie paused. Give me a minute dad while I check with Diane. Maybe we can still go to dinner. Eddie pulled me to the side to discuss the matter at hand. Diane I know I haven't spent a lot of time with you lately and I know I promised that we would do something special today, it's just that my dad has never asked me to go to dinner with him before. Eddie, are you trying to get out of spending time with me again? This is the last time Diane. I swear it. But Eddie you promised. Fine! I'll go to dinner with daddy some other time. I glanced over at Mr. C and he seemed different. His countenance was radiant and there was a cloud of peace about him. Eddie. Yes Diane. I've changed my mind; go to dinner with your father. No. I told you I'll go some other time. Why not? Because I don't want to hear your mouth Diane! I am serious Eddie, go on and have dinner with your dad. No, I'm going to stay with you today, just give me a minute. I would like to spend a little more time with my dad before we go.

We spent the rest of the day together and had a nice time. After our date it was soon time for me to go to that dreadful place called work. I was tired and I really didn't have it in me to work through the night. However, I went in like a good soldier. The politics of the police department disgusted me terribly, which caused me to be more vocal concerning the ills of the department. I eventually teamed up with a man whose name was Sherman. We got along fine because he was just as militant as I. Rebellion gave us a sense of empowerment and mistreatment caused us to boldly speak out against the system, which also caused our peers to hate us. We had a lot in common. We both loved the arts, music, and men. I didn't know God, but I believed He existed. Sherman, however, felt that God was a huge part of people's imagination. This kept us at odds anytime the subject about religion was brought up. As usual, we received our assignments, loaded the police cruiser with our equipment and went on our way. I became addicted to danger and sought it out purposely on every tour of duty. The principles of death fascinated me. There was something about taking life to the end and then turning back that gave me a rush. Fear wouldn't creep up on me until I was home in bed. With my eyes shut and my mind free to wonder I would see myself at work and the dangerous situations I put myself in. I asked myself, why are you doing this? The answer was simple. At least in death there was an end to the torment, but in life it continues. I was dying within and there was no one to help me. Sherman and I patrolled the dark streets looking for criminals. Finally, after countless hours we came across a car with stolen tags and the chase was on. Sherman drove at speeds of 80 mph through the city streets while I yelled out our coordinates to the dispatcher. I waited patiently for the suspects to bail out of the car. I loved running and I considered it a challenge for them to attempt to get away from me. It reminded me of my competitors on the track only these competitors were sometimes armed. Other police cars trailed us waiting for the same thing and then in a blink of an eye the suspects crashed head on into a tree. The driver and passenger both climbed out of their perspective windows. There were officers everywhere, even the ones who hated me. We were all there to help each other and make sure everyone was safe. The driver ran toward a ten-foot high fence and went over it. Several other officers and I ensued. They took one look at the fence and decided to take another route. I, on the other hand, went over it. Although the yards were dark, I could see that the suspect was directly in front of me. I was closing in on him when… "BOOM"…my ear felt as if it had exploded. I fell to the ground sucking up its dirt. I deeply inhaled as if it were my last breath. How could I have been so careless as to run through these yards blind? Was it the other suspect hiding out in the yards waiting to take a shot at me? I'm sure it wasn't the suspect I was chasing because I saw his hands and there was nothing in them. I lay there shivering and heard footsteps crunching the leaves as they drew closer to me. Fear gripped me and I couldn't move. I didn't know if I was shot or not. Tears jumped from the lids of my eyes to the ground beneath me. The footsteps drew closer and closer. I could see them, but wait! These shoes looked exactly like mine. They shined like glass. The pants that draped the top half of these shoes were blue like mine. He stopped and stood over me with his gun in his hand. I didn't know what his intentions were, so I dared not look up at him. I kept my eyes to the ground and with surety he spoke. Next time, get out of my way, and then he ran off. My feeble attempts to recognize his voice and to figure out his identity failed. After realizing I wasn't shot the fear left and anger arose. What was he trying to do, shoot through me to get to the suspect? How dare he think of me as an insignificant nothing by making me his target! If by chance I weren't in the way, who gave him the right to attempt to take the life of an unarmed man? It was all so unfair. I pulled myself up, brushed myself off and walked back to my car. I wanted to call mama and daddy to tell them what happened, but decided not to worry them with my problems. I was having trouble processing what happened. My mind was all messed up and I couldn't stop shaking. Mama and daddy have always feared that someday I'd get hurt by some ruthless criminal. However, they never considered the ruthless men in blue who I found were my worst enemies. I explained to Sherman what happened and you would've thought he'd completely lost his mind the way he was rantin' and ravin'. We drove around for hours talking about the ills of the police department and society as a whole when I received an emergency message to return to the station. Sherman drove us back on two wheels, cutting corners and leaving rubber marks in the street. The technician at the desk was waiting for me.

Diane your husband said to call him at home as soon as possible. Did he say what he wanted? No, but he sounded frantic. The telephone rang once before Eddie snatched it up. Eddie sounded as if a truck had run him over twice and he wept bitterly. Eddie what's wrong? It's my dad. What about him? He's having real bad chest pains and I think he's having a heart attack. Eddie, please stop making rash assumptions. Just hurry up and get over there. I've already called an ambulance Diane, but I just can't bear to see my daddy dying. Eddie your father is going to be okay. Immediately I thought about Mrs. C. Eddie where's your mother? She's about 45 minutes away. When I talked to her she said she'd be here shortly. Eddie quit mulling around and get up; your dad needs you. Diane I need you to be with me. Give me five minutes. How are you going to get off work? I'll have to get permission from my lieutenant and then I'll meet you at your dad's house in a few minutes. I made it there in three minutes. Eddie's truck was sitting in front of a huge red fire truck. I opened the door and entered a realm of uncertainty. There was a peace that had set in that house. The same peace that was there earlier was there again, or had it left? There were two burly firemen standing in the hallway with their hands stuffed in their pockets while one shorter fireman continued talking to Mr. C. They were rendered helpless to the silent pain my father-in-law suffered. The calm was as thick as the morning fog. Everything seemed to flow in slow motion, even the breaths from my mouth. Mr. C. stood up, wrapped himself in his wife's green housecoat, and grabbed his medication. The ambulance crew came in and asked questions and he answered softly. His left hand stay clutched to his chest. Mr. Camden is your wife on the way? Yes sir. We need to get you to the hospital as soon as possible. I'm not going anywhere until my wife gets here. Eddie pleaded with his father to allow the paramedics to take him to the hospital. Daddy, go on! I'll wait for mama. He wanted to walk out on his own, but the ambulance crew suggested against it. After pondering over it for a minute he climbed upon the gurney and they rolled him out. Mrs. C. pulled up and ran to the ambulance just as they were closing the door. Eddie sat in his truck and I talked with him through the open window. We watched from a distance through the small square window in the rear of the ambulance. We could see Mrs. C talking with her husband as the ambulance crew quickly connected tubes to him.

What are they waiting for? What's taking them so long to get to the hospital? Why don't they just leave? Eddie, please calm down. There are certain things they must do first. Tears melted his masculine exterior as he took deep breaths to calm down. Suddenly the ambulance took off and we followed. Eddie had already instructed the rest of the family, including a few aunts, to meet us at the hospital. One by one, family members came in with faces full of worry. Eddie's older sister Anna was missing among the crowd. We were having a hard time trying to reach her at the prison where she worked. Mrs. C. emerged from beyond the doors where all the doctors disguised themselves in white masks and coats. Eddie ran to his mother. Mama is daddy going to be okay?

They're working on him son. What took them so long to get him here? Your dad had a massive heat attack when they got him in the ambulance, so they had to stabilize him. That's why we were sitting outside the house for so long. Eddie would have fallen if Mrs. C. hadn't grabbed him and pulled him into her bosom. Eddie sobbed in his mother's arms for a brief moment then joined the rest of the family. There were people scattered throughout the emergency waiting area with empty faces holding empty conversations. After a while the dreadful silence in that place was broken by our laughter. We forgot about the negative possibilities and began to converse as if nothing had happened. Our bellies juggled giggles and a peace fell over us until that man in the white coat shadowed the doorway. He called for the Camden family and the laughter subsided. We were taken to a small room. It was difficult for all of us to fit into the room, so most of us stood in the doorway listening. I stood by myself in the hallway behind them all. Silence sealed our mouths and trouble touched our hearts. The doctor asked Mrs. C. to have a seat and when she refused he sat down. His medical terminology puzzled us and his demeanor scared us. Your husband and dad experienced a massive heart attack when he came in here. The vessels were clotted, cutting off the blood flow to the heart, thereby leaving the heart with no oxygen. The oxygen deprivation was very severe. We tried everything we knew. Mrs. C. interrupted the doctor's flow of words to get a better understanding of the information he was giving. What are you saying doctor? How is my husband doing? When the doctor went to answer for some reason my ears went deaf and in a split second Eddie, his brother, and sisters began screaming. They ran out of the room and out of the hospital. Bewildered, I looked to Mrs. C., but her head hung down low as if her neck refused to hold it any longer. Eddie's Aunt Rita walked up to me and hugged me. I still didn't know what was going on. Baby, why don't you go and see about your husband. I looked at her as if to say why and then walked away to look for Eddie. I searched the parking lot only to find his siblings scattered all over everywhere, lost and confused. Eddie was leaning over the hood of his truck weeping. His face lay in a puddle of tears and his hands were tightly clutched under his chest.

Eddie what's wrong? What happened? You didn't hear what the doctor said! No. Diane, my daddy is dead! I can't believe it. I was just talking to him. I felt something bad was gonna happen, but why my daddy? He asked me to take him to dinner earlier and I said, no, I'll take you tomorrow. I should have taken him because there will be no more tomorrow's with him. This was the first time he ever asked me to take him anywhere. It was as if he knew he was going to die and I put it off and told him no. I let him down. Why did my daddy have to die? Why? I wrapped my arms around Eddie and cried along with him. He was blaming himself, but in a sense I felt as if he resented me. I knew he didn't go to dinner with his dad because he'd already promised me we would spend some time together. I kept him from spending the evening with Mr. C. and now it's too late. Eddie and I shared the same pains. The shocking pain of death and guilt, which kept us both bound within. Finally, Anna had received the message to get to the hospital quickly. A friend of hers knew the dilemma and was instructed to get her to the hospital as soon as possible without giving her the bad news. We stood outside in silence with salt stained faces. A truck pulled up with Anna sitting on the passenger side. Her face was pressed hard against the window. Her eyes asked the question, what's going on and our broken faces told the story. Not daddy! No, not daddy! Please don't tell me its daddy! Mrs. C. walked up and hugged her. Yes baby, your daddy is gone. Anna's screams sent chills running down my spine and caused us all to re-live the initial shock of Mr. C's death. We went back inside and were asked to view the body to say our good-byes. Everyone marched into the room except for me. My feet wouldn't budge because I didn't want to see him that way.

The few days that passed by seemed like weeks. Family and friends from all around the globe filled the church on this dark and gloomy day while Mr. C. lay still in his coffin. Mr. C. was clean. He was dressed in a blue suit and a red shirt and Mrs. C. made sure her and her children were dressed in the same colors. I watched as people piled on top of each other when there were no more seats. I hadn't seen most of these people in a while. However, for some it was my first time meeting them. It's so uncanny how people can come together for a funeral, but don't speak to each other during the year. No telephone call; no hello, nothing! We get too caught up in our own lives that we forget the one's that are truly important to us. Eddie held my hand tightly as his eyes slid over to where his father lay, cold, hard, and still in that coffin. The reality of his father's death caused him to turn away, and the longing for this to be some big mistake gave him the courage to look again and again and again. Pastor Bradley titled his message, "Are you ready?" Those three small words made me squirm in my seat so bad I almost got splinters. I knew I wasn't ready. There was a part of me that wanted to be. I felt because I was young I had time to "Come to Jesus." I didn't want to waste my prestigious party going years in a dress and around church folk, so after the message was over I made an agreement with God. I decided that I would go to Jesus, just not right now. Call me in a few years; I should be ready by then. Besides I feel I'm a fairly good person already. Mrs. C., Eddie, and the rest of his sibling gathered around the casket one last time to say their final good-bye as the church emptied herself of everyone else. I stood a far off from people. I didn't know how to rid myself of the pain and I certainly couldn't erase Eddie's or the kids. How was I going to mend the broken pieces of their lives? While in the midst of my panic Eddie came over to me and hugged me. The questions that riddled my mind went away and I became settled within myself. After the funeral everyone fled to Mrs. C's home, supposedly to comfort those of us that were suffering the loss of Mr. C. However, it was evident that some only came for the free food. Xavier and Kayla went home with mama and daddy so we could make sure Eddie's family had a place to rest their heads. Eddie and I had at least eight other folk staying in our home. It was crowded, but we didn't mind one bit. Eddie and I took a few blankets and made our bed on the living room floor in front of the fireplace. We made a nice fire and cuddled together. Eddie, are you okay? No, and I don't know how I'm gonna get through this. We'll get through this together, one day at a time. That's easy for you to say, you still have a dad, so you can't possibly know what I'm feeling. Eddie that's not fair. Don't you know I feel everything you feel? He may not have been my natural daddy, but he was still like a dad to me. I loved him because you loved him. I'm sorry Diane. I really didn't mean it like that. I understand. It's just that I never wanted any of my parents to die before me. What are you talking about Eddie? I just didn't want to ever have to go through what I'm going through right now, so I figured it would be easier if I died first. Sweetie, eventually we're all going to die. It's a part of life and it's not up to us to choose who goes first. Eddie laid there motionless in deep thought. I love you very much Eddie. I love you too and I'm glad you're here with me. Eddie kissed me and disappeared through the doorway. A few of his uncles were waiting for him in the kitchen. Diane why don't you let us take Eddie out for a little bit to get his mind off of things. Before I could answer Eddie interjected with a big no. Diane I'm not going to leave you alone. Its okay, you can go with them. I'll be fine. Are you sure? Yes I'm sure. After Eddie left his Uncle Syn, short for Syntrell, came down the stairs like a sneaky dog claiming to be looking for the bathroom. When I looked up he was half naked and part of his private area was showing. Exasperated, I turned my head. Syn, the bathroom is straight ahead, but you are gonna have to put some clothes on in my house. When he smiled the gold tooth in the front of his mouth almost blinded me and his country slang made my skin crawl. Am sorreee. I did-ent realize my trousers were hangin' down like dat where you could see all a' my parts. I guess am gonna be on my way sweetie. I guess you will Uncle Sin. Well, good night Diane. Whatever! I lay there with my head full of thoughts. I know this old country dog didn't try that cheap country mess with me. He thinks he's nickel slick, but I got his penny change. I don't know and I don't care about the sick, twisted things they do amongst family in Mississippi, but we sure don't do it up here. And what kind of name is that for a preacher anyhow? Syn! He's full of sin alright. That name suits him just fine. If he tries anything foolish he's gonna be full of something else like bullet holes. I slid my gun up under my pillow just in case he decided to try something stupid. Hours passed and everyone had gone to sleep except for the kids in the basement playing pool. The house was as still as a winter sky. I listened attentively to the pool balls cracking against each other and the sound of fire on the hearth, shooting into the air and making a popping noise. Soon I placed all of my attention on that fire. I laid there in a daze watching those flames light up the darkness around me. Its warmth enveloped me like a blanket. I began to think about Mr. C. and how I would miss his face. Suddenly my mind began to play back the turn of events concerning his death. Mama and daddy came to mind and I imagined them in Mr. C's shoes. The inconceivable thought shredded my heart like paper. Tears flooded my eyes and my cries filled the room as I hovered over on my knees. Earnestly I prayed to a God I've never known. A God I've rejected practically my whole life. Oh God! What's going on? Why did this have to happen now? I know we can't live forever, but he wasn't that old. Why him? Why now? My mama and daddy are around the same age. It would kill me if I lost them. The thought of it hurts too badly. I'll change. I promise I'll change. Just don't take them away from me. Please! The cracking sound of the pool balls grew faint and the popping sound of the fire grew louder and louder. With my face planted in my hands I wept like a thousand seagulls beside the ocean. The fire that was cracking and popping like fireworks began to quiet down. However, the flames continued to dance upon the logs as if they were dancing to their own music. Then a voice called my name, "DIANE." It was one that I hadn't heard before. It sounded as if it were coming from behind me. This voice was so powerful it moved through my entire being, touching the very center of my soul. Out of fear I shook uncontrollably because I knew it was God and I thought He was standing over me waiting to take me out of there, so I didn't dare lift my face out of the palms of my hands. He had the voice of the wind, the rain and the seas. There was a peace in the room like none other and the fire on the hearth seemed to have gotten brighter because it was now peeking through the cracks between my fingers. The floor beneath me trembled at the sound of His voice. My mouth froze in the open state it was in, leaving saliva to run freely out of it. My eyes were the only things moving. They roamed the prison that held them captive, but were unsuccessful in their search for a way out. My fearful body remained still. I couldn't move and I couldn't say a word. Moans and groans were the only sounds coming forth from within me. The first thing to mind was, "I wasn't ready." I wasn't ready to meet Him and I knew I had been given more than enough opportunities to surrender to the Lord. Now, here I am with my filthy self, kneeling before the one and only, true and living holy God all covered in sin. It amazed me that no one had awakened to my cries. I was in awe that the pool balls stopped cracking and the popping sound from the fire ceased when God showed up. His presence was so glorious and powerful that time had to stop and worship Him. It seemed as if I was on my knees for eternity, then off in a distance I heard the pool balls crashing into one another again, the giggles and sniggles of the children and the cracking of the flames of fire on the hearth came back. Slowly, I spread my fingers and let my eyes roam the space in front of me. I gazed into the fire and was hesitant about looking behind me. The normality of my breathing still hadn't returned. Panting, I began to move my head to the side. Inch by inch I turned with my eyes as wide as life. Turning, turning, turned. He was gone and I let out a sigh of relief because I thought God was going to remove me from the face of the earth, because while in His presence His glory revealed to me how sinful I actually was. The shadows from the flames of fire danced on the wall behind me. My heart felt as if it had stopped, but now it was beating again. Something was different about it. Something was different about me. I felt a peace over me like never before and my heart was warm within me. I was still in awe, yet full of questions regarding what had just happened. I knew that God had surely visited me on this night. I laid my head down to rest with a new flame burning in my heart. It was as if someone got inside of me and turned on the lights. This flame was the beginning of my burning desire for the Lord. My pain was leaving and I was changing. The sting of death no longer plagued my mind and its heaviness was no longer a burden to my soul. Joy and peace I did find; and with the resurrection of life I've been made whole. Once I was blind, but now I see.

Journal Insert
THE DAMASCUS ROAD – SAUL'S CONVERSION

As Saul journeyed he came near Damascus, and suddenly a light shone around him from heaven. Then he fell to the ground, and heard a voice saying to him, "Saul, Saul, why are you persecuting Me?" And he said, "Who are You, Lord?" Then the Lord said, "I am Jesus, whom you are persecuting. It is hard for you to kick against the goads." So he, trembling and astonished, said, "Lord, what do You want me to do?" Then the Lord said to him, "Arise and go into the city, and you will be told what you must do."

Acts 9:3-6

Saul became Paul, boldly proclaiming the Word of God throughout the land.

16
I'LL FLY AWAY

Fried chicken and the soulful sounds of Mahalia Jackson roamed the air as grandma Jones stirred around in her kitchen like a busy bee. She always prepared us a light snack whenever we came to visit. I sat in her rusted green and white slider on the porch to keep an eye on Xavier and Kayla. The slider made a loud squeaking sound as I slid it back and forth. While gazing into my memory I searched for dreams to look at as if they were secret pictures tucked away. I smiled at the possibilities life had to offer, but frowned on the truth. My life had become a living hell. I felt I had no peace and no real sense of direction or joy. I ran everyday to relieve my stress. However, I could never catch up to what I thought I needed. I sang in nightclubs and did several recordings to fill the void in my life, but it only made me feel emptier than I had before. I went back to school and studied to prove to myself that I could be the lawyer I promised daddy I would be. Consequently, I realized that my intellect was getting me nowhere. Something was missing in my life and no matter what I did I couldn't find the solution to my problems. Depression was wearing a hole into my mind and denial kept me from getting help. I gazed upon my children and saw promise in them. There was a jubilant aura about them and a joy I used to know, until now. Somewhere along the way I have become a stranger to its sound.

Xavier and Kayla enjoyed spending time with grandma as much as I did. I watched as they played tag in front of the house. They reminded me of the days that Sam and I ran up and down this old crooked sidewalk. We would slap each other and scream you're it, and then run through grandpa's garden, trampling his green tomatoes. Our recklessness would then be covered up with dirt and rocks in hopes that our mischief would not be discovered. Laughter emerged from my belly as Xavier and Kayla trampled over the old dirt where grandpa's garden used to be. Life doesn't do anything but repeat itself from generation to generation and it amazes me to know that when one life passes on another will rise in its place. The old wooden screen door creaked and grandma's face emerged from within. Ah eeeh eeeh eeeh. Look at those silly kids runnin' around in the dirt. They are the spittin' image of you. You're absolutely right grandma. I was just sitting here thinking the same thing. Diane I want you to know I appreciate y'all spendin' so much time with me. Grandma we love you and we love being with you, besides, Xavier and Kayla don't know how to ask for anything other than, can we visit great-grandma today? She laughed whole-heartedly, making her round shiny face glow and jiggle at the same time. Well grandma I better get going. Do you have to work tonight Diane? No, I'm going out with the girls tonight. Diane you really shouldn't hang out like you do. It's not proper for a married woman to be out that time of night without her husband. Well my husband is out that time of night without his wife, so what's the difference! I'm not talkin' about Eddie. I'm talkin' about you and how you were raised to be a respectable woman. Grandma I'm not doing anything wrong. I'm just going out for a few hours to have some fun to keep my mind off things. What things? The kinds of things that make you wanna holler grandma. What's wrong Diane? Everything, but I'm fine. Diane I thought you started going back to church. I did. Well can't you have fun in church instead of hanging out in the street all the time? Not the kind of fun I want to have. God can give you everything you're looking for. I opened my mouth and grabbed a huge yawn that I found in the pit of my stomach. Whew! Look at the time. Grandma I gotta go. Grandma looked at me with pity and exhaled. Diane I'm not going to badger you. I just want you to be careful. I will grandma. I stood up, wrapped my arms around her neck and kissed her on the cheek. I love you very much grandma and I'll call you tomorrow. Okay baby. I called out to Xavier and Kayla and before we left they both gave her a big kiss.

I fixed myself up really nice and stood in the mirror gazing at the finished product. You look really nice Diane, now let's go and have some fun girl. I dropped the kids off with mama and promised to pick them up in the morning. Mama cut her eye at me, but before she had a chance to give me a piece of her mind I blew kisses at the kids and rushed out of the door. As I drove down the street I asked myself a question. Diane what is your problem? You have everything anyone could ask for yet you still feel unfulfilled. Why do you feel so lost?

Why can't you get your act together? I found myself answering myself with three words, I don't know. It's okay to talk to yourself from time to time, but when you start to answer yourself you know there's a real problem brewing underneath the surface. The club was packed and the music could be heard up the street and down. The moment I passed through the doors my mood changed. I felt as though I didn't want to be there, however, I didn't want to go home either. I was tired of being by myself and in a way I was tired of the nightlife. I headed for the dance floor and tried to dance myself in the mood, but to no avail I still felt disengaged from everyone and everything. Though my body was there, my mind was somewhere else. I went to the bar several times assuming that if I got drunk then I could have fun. My girlfriends were standing in the corner engaged in idle conversation, and although I was in their company I felt as if I stood alone. Nothing they were saying interested me. They were talking a lot about nothing. What is wrong with me? Usually I'm the life of the party. What's happening to me? I stood back watching Sam clown around on the dance floor with strange girls and decided to go and dance with him. I danced circles around Sam when this strange man tried to cut in. He looked like…let's just say, I was petrified. My eyes bucked and I gave Sam the look as if to say, don't leave me with him. Sam asked the guy to leave us alone, nevertheless he insisted on dancing with me. I nicely told him that I didn't want to dance. The man cursed me as if I was a mutt on the street. I opened my mouth to curse him back and my words turned into nerdy phrases like, you better watch your tongue with me man. I tried to curse, but couldn't. Sam looked at me as if I was crazy and helped escort the man out of the club. I stood there bewildered. Suddenly, I realized I didn't feel comfortable there anymore, yet I refused to leave. I made my way back to the bar and got another drink. I just figured I wasn't drunk enough. My girlfriends were still huddled up in the corner talking about nothing, so I went over with my drink in my hand to join them. I stood against the wall and listened to their chitter chatter. There were a thousand conversations rising to the ceiling along with the music. As I lifted my drink to my mouth the noise began to fade away and I heard a still voice moving through my soul. He asked…what are you doing here? This voice sounded familiar. It was the voice from the fireplace. The voice moved through my entire being and left me with a sense of fear. The noise resumed as if time had stopped momentarily. Frantically I looked around for the person who said it, but my girlfriends were the only people around me. I don't think anyone in there could have spoken with such authority and power as the voice that spoke to me. I tapped my girlfriend on the shoulder and asked her if she heard what I heard. She called me a drunk and ignored me. However, after several drinks I was more sober than I was before I had gotten there. I couldn't get drunk to save my life. The voice was powerful enough to stop time and grasp my attention, compassionate enough not to destroy me, yet small enough to touch the center of my heart. I pulled the drink away from my mouth and set it down. The taste for alcohol, cursing, hanging out in bars, and the destructive lifestyle I'd been leading was gone. I left it all behind; including Sam and my friends, and I went home. In the back of my mind I knew that voice belonged to the Spirit of God. I knew the question asked was more of a command and a call to come out rather than a meaningless inquiry. I didn't have the full understanding as to what was happening to me. All I knew is that it was right and so I followed. After putting down all of my bad habits I picked up the Bible. I had no understanding as to what the Bible was all about. I always felt it was a boring book, but I was now finding it to be highly interesting. I wanted to know about God and I wanted to live for Him, only I didn't know how. On Sunday I took Xavier and Kayla to church. I listened attentively to the message and afterwards Pastor Bradley had altar call. People were going up with broken faces, surrendering their lives to Jesus. I wanted to surrender. I wanted to be saved; however, I was unable to move. My hands clung to the pew before me and wouldn't let go. There was a tugging at my spirit to go up, but my feet were glued to the floor beneath me. I looked to the altar and then to the back of the church. I wanted someone to go up with me, so I wouldn't be alone. However, no one else was going. I have to do this. I want to do this. I thought about the voice questioning me in the club and the fireplace experience, so I snatched my hands loose from the grips of fear and turned to take a step. A strange voice began speaking to me. Where are you going? You know if you go up there everyone is going to be watching you and they're going to laugh at that ugly dress you have on.

People are going to see that the back of your head is as nappy as sin. Humph, a nappy head and an ugly dress, what a combination. I found myself listening to that voice and then answering it. Yeah, I guess you're right. I can't possibly go up there looking like this. I placed my hands back on that pew and gripped it tightly in case my feet decided to pull a fast one and take me up to the altar looking like raggedy Ann. I stood there and allowed the opportunity to pass me by and after service I felt terrible. Sunday after Sunday I broke empty promises to give my life over. Soon I convinced myself that as long as I was going to church then I was fine and all of that sanctification stuff really wasn't necessary. I went to church faithfully and I put down all of my bad habits, satisfied in knowing that I was a morally good person. Every time I heard the Spirit of God telling me to go and give up completely I ignored Him and drowned His voice out with conversation or thoughts. Eddie was happy with the change because I put down a lot of things he didn't like anyway. However, I was slightly confused with the way things were going. I wanted Eddie to be with me, only he didn't want to have anything to do with church. I was accustomed to having Eddie by my side during major transitions in my life, but now it seemed as if I was walking this path by myself. I needed to talk to him about what was happening to me. He didn't understand and he didn't want to. No one understood. Not my family, not mama and daddy, and not my friends. They thought I had gone crazy and kept throwing up in my face certain statements that I had made. I was the one who vowed before everyone that I wasn't going to be a hand me down church girl. I was the one who ridiculed church folk. I didn't want to have anything to do with living holy. Now I found myself being drawn to the very thing I resisted for years. How do I explain this to the people I love when I don't even have a full understanding myself? The more I read the less confusing the Bible became. The Word, which lined the pages penetrated my soul and became life within me. I couldn't deny it. The change felt good and it was getting better and better each day. Everything seemed to be going just right, until grandma, my best friend became ill.

As usual I went over to her house to take her shopping, but she said she didn't feel good. She looked sluggish and her mouth seemed to be twisted. What's wrong grandma? Oh this old pacemaker ain't actin' right. I think you need to see a doctor. Maybe, but I think I'll wait until your mama and her sisters get back from the Caribbean. Grandma if you need to go and see the doctor I can take you and then I'll call my mama and the rest of them later. I don't think it's that bad Diane, but I want you to take a look at my chest because this old thing seems as though it's gonna push through my skin. Grandma took off her shirt. A small-boxed shaped object had risen to the surface of her skin and the corner of it was pushing through. Grandma that pacemaker is not supposed to be like that. I'm taking you to the hospital right now. I tried calling daddy and he wasn't home so I left him a message. I rushed grandma to the emergency room and after her examination I was told she had a stroke and the pacemaker had busted open and needed to be taken out. The doctor said the procedure would be simple as if I had given him permission to proceed. Excuse me doctor, but I can't make those decisions; I'm only the granddaughter. My mother and the rest of her daughters are in the Caribbean. You're going to have to get in touch with someone. How is this possible? I just took my grandma to the doctor for her regular appointment last week. She was complaining about her pacemaker then. However, the doctor said it was fine. Mrs. Camden I've read her chart and I don't know what was established during her regular appointment. All I know is that we're going to admit her and her paperwork needs to be signed. I looked up and saw daddy pushing his way through the emergency doors like a soft tornado. Concern straddled the top of his brow and made it look as if he was frowning and his nostrils were spread open. Diane is everything okay with your grandma? I don't know daddy, something's wrong with her pacemaker and the doctor said she had a stroke. Oh my goodness, your mama is going to have a fit. Speaking of mama, did you get in touch with her daddy? No, they had already left the hotel. Their plane lands in four hours. That's too long daddy, a decision has to be made as soon as possible. Don't worry, we'll get it all straightened out; let's go and talk to your grandmother. I took daddy to her room and she was very glad to see him. How you doing ma'? I would be fine if they would let me loose. You're gonna have to stay and have some tests done ma, but you'll be fine. Sam I don't wanna stay in this hospital ya' here me. I wanna go home. It ain't no sense in them keepin' me. Grandma got all flustered and her southern accent smothered her words as they fell slothfully from her tongue. Grandma, please don't get upset. They have to take the tests to make sure you're okay. Diane I don't wanna be bothered, they make me nervous. Grandma rolled her eyes around in her head, sucked her teeth and began to pout. I laughed and sat back in my chair. Ma you are somethin' else. I'm going home to shower so I can get to the airport on time. Diane you stay here with your grandma until we get back. Okay daddy. The nurse came in and gave grandma something to help her relax. When she fell asleep I asked God to touch her body and take her pain away. I watched her closely. She emulated all that I knew peace and love to be. Grandma's hair was white as snow and her skin was the color of amber and cocoa mixed together. Her lips were thick and curved like my mama's. I marveled at her beauty and laid my head across her arm. I wasn't worried because I had read how Jesus Christ healed and delivered people just like my grandma. I knew grandma belonged to Him and I knew He would heal her.

Grandma had the pacemaker removed and we were all delighted that her heart was operating fine. We enjoyed seeing her home and walking around like her normal self. However, within a few weeks things began to fall apart. Grandma had become disoriented as if her mind had gone back several days and was trying to play catch up. My family called me to tell me grandma looked as if she had another stroke. I rushed over and when I walked in grandma was barely sitting up in her chair. Her head was hanging down and she couldn't lift it. She couldn't talk and she had lost control of her lip. Now the Euphrates River had lost its curves. It was just hanging from her face without form. Grandma what happened? Why can't you talk to me? She looked at me as if she wanted to say something, but the only sound that came forth was grunts. When the ambulance came to take her away I stood on the porch beside the green and white slider she used to sit in and I cried. The sirens of that ambulance rang in my mind like a thousand bells over and over again. My pain drove me to my knees. Oh God in heaven I don't understand what's going on. I know I haven't done all that you've asked of me Lord, but please don't take my grandma away from me. Please heal her. Please take her pain away and let her not suffer. I went to the hospital everyday to let grandma know that I would always be by her side. I watched over her as she lay in that bed staring at the light of the sun shining through the window. Her jubilant facial expression was lost somewhere between her home and the hospital and her words were stolen in the night. Grandma I don't know if you can hear me or not, but I want you to know that Jesus loves you. The Bible says that the Lord will never leave you nor forsake you if you believe on Him, and I know you do. He's going to heal you grandma. I know because I asked Him to. Her eyes met mine and a tear slid down her face. I knew she heard me and that made me happy. Several days later grandma slipped into a coma and my heart broke. Lord I'm confused. My grandma seems to be deteriorating instead of getting better. I just want to talk to her and I need her to talk to me, but she just lies there like she's gone already. I opened my Bible searching for some answers. I read and read until I tired out. The next day I rose early and went to the hospital to see her. When I got there I began straightening out her flowers on the windowsill, then I opened her curtain, which separated her from the person on the other side. Leave that curtain be girl and pull it close. In amazement I turned to look at grandma. My heart beat with excitement. Grandma! How do you feel? Thirsty! I laughed and got her some water. Thank you Jesus, for answering my prayer! I talked with grandma a bit and let her know how she sent the entire family through a big scare. We laughed together just like old times then I left and made a B line to mama's house to give her the news.

Mama! Mama! Girl what's the matter with you? Why have you burst through my doors like a lunatic? Grandma woke up. Diane she's always been able to open her eyes, but she's out of it. Mama I just left the hospital and grandma woke up and told me she was thirsty. We laughed and we talked for a long time. I asked her how she felt and she said fine. You mean to tell me she's talking! Yes mama, didn't I just say that. Mama threw her laundry down and called her sisters to give them the news and then the entire family met at the hospital to see God's miracle. It had been a long four weeks for all of us. We flooded grandma with kisses and hugs and filled her room with laughter and conversation. What happened to me? Ma you were out of it for quite some time. Ah eeh eeh eeeh. I don't remember a thing. That's okay, we're just glad to have you back. It's good to be back. Grandma we're going to make you a huge dinner when you get out of here. Well I hope so because I'm starvin' ah eeeh eeeh eeeh. I went home with a smile on my face and slept like a baby. I couldn't wait until the break of day so that I could see my grandma again. Early the next morning I got up and went to the store. I bought the sweetest fruit I could find so that grandma could have something to nibble on in case she got hungry. I picked up a balloon with a picture of a teddy bear plastered over the front of it from the hospital lobby. A song was singing in my spirit...Oh, how I love Jesus, no one can tear us apart, He took my broken pieces and gave me a brand new start. I wore happiness like a newly bought dress. I whistled to the song playing in my heart as I bounced all the way to grandma's room. Nevertheless, my smile ran away. Grandma's bed had been stripped and her flowers removed. Panic rose up in me and I began to sweat badly. A nurse approached me with concern. May I help you? Yes, I'm looking for my grandmother. Oh, the woman that was next to the window! Yes. I'm sorry to have to tell you this, but she went into cardiac arrest in the middle of the night and has been moved to I.C.U. on the tenth floor. The rest of your family just went upstairs a few minutes ago. I ran toward the elevators and rushed upstairs in a flash. Mama and daddy were standing in a corner talking. The rest of the family was huddled in groups with blank faces.

Diane. Yes mama. The doctor's finally figured out what the problem is with your grandma. When they took the pacemaker out, they left one of the wires in her heart. They said it was stuck and they would've had to rip it loose and they didn't want to do that, so they left it in. The wire began leaking poisons into her system, which sent an infection throughout her entire body including her brain. Why did it take them so long to figure this out? It's just not fair! Diane she still has a chance to survive. They are going to perform open-heart surgery to fix the problem. What is her chances mama? She has a 50/50 chance of survival. Where is she? She's being prepped for surgery as we speak. Diane you can wait around if you want to, but the surgery is going to be a long one. I gave the fruit to the rest of my family and walked away. Diane, are you coming back? Yeah, I'll be back in a few hours. As I walked through the parking lot the wind blew strong and tried to take my balloon up with it. I looked up, saw the teddy bear struggling against the wind and decided to hold on tight. At first I refused to let it go because I needed it to stay with me. Then I thought; what was the sense in me trying to hold onto it when it wanted to be free. I opened my hands and let it go. The balloon went up and up, fluttering in the wind like a bird in its natural habitat. I stood in the middle of the parking lot staring into the sky until I couldn't see the balloon anymore and before I knew it the teddy bear was gone for good. I walked around for hours trying to clear my mind and then returned to the waiting area where my family was. Everyone was sitting around joking and laughing. The hospital staff lined the table with chips and soda for our disposal. When the doctor came out he addressed the entire family. How is she doctor? The surgery went well; however, she's in critical condition. Her body has filled up with fluids and her heart is weak. We will be monitoring her closely to see if her heart works on its' own. Can we see her? Yes, but please, not more than three at a time. I went in with mama and Aunt Betsy. Mama placed her hand upon grandma's forehead and stroked her hair. Aunt Betsy placed grandma's cross that was connected to a beaded string on the wall beside her. Mama we're here for you. You're gonna make it through this, so just be strong. Please be strong. Aunt Betsy left the room because her words were breaking up and she didn't want to upset grandma especially if she could hear us. I looked at grandma and then looked away. Silence glued my lips together and sadness shook me as if I had the chills. I looked to my mama for strength, but she stood in a trance. As I walked away I heard mama speaking to grandma. Ma' we love you. You can make it, just hold on. Mama walked out and I looked upon grandma's face and began taking pictures of her beauty with every bat of my eye. I love you too grandma and I know you're going to be fine. Everyone decided to go home to get a good nights rest and then return in the morning to see about grandma. Twenty-four hours sure is a long time before we know whether grandma is going to live or die, but I'm not going to think on anything negative because she can't die. She can't leave me now. My mind was spinning out of control and I wasn't able to avoid the poisonous thoughts that were knocking on my skull to get in. I went home, apprised Eddie of the situation, kissed him and the children, and went to bed. Eddie held me all night long and I felt his heart beating in unison with mine until the break of day. When I opened my eyes I felt a peace and I knew everything was going to be alright. Thank you God for blessing me with a wonderful husband who truly loves me and thank you for answering my prayers and allowing me to speak with my grandma and her with me. Before I could plant my feet on the carpet the telephone was ringing. Girl where are you? Mama I just got up. I'll be there in a bit. Well hurry up and don't take all day. I hung up the telephone and began singing a song that was in my spirit. Eddie looked at me and gave me that beautiful smile that makes my heart do flips. Baby, you sure seem happy this morning, was that your mama? Yes it was. Well did she say everything was a-okay or something because you sure are dancing around here as if you just got some good news. No, she just told me to hurry up. I feel as though everything is okay and that God has answered our prayers. Before I could get into the shower the telephone rang again. Eddie if that's mama tell her I'm comin'! Diane your mama said for you to come to the hospital right now. What's her hurry? I said I was comin'! As I clothed my partially wet body Eddie attempted to comb my hair when the telephone rang again. I grabbed my shoes and quickly stuffed my feet in them. Eddie held the telephone and didn't say one word. Nothing on his body moved, not even his eyes. In silence he sat on the bed with the telephone to his ear. I assumed it was someone else and grabbed my purse. Eddie I'll see you later. I turned to rush down the stairs and out the door when Eddie hung up the telephone and called out to me. Diane! What is it Eddie, I gotta go! When Eddie's eyes fell to the floor I knew something wasn't right. Eddie what's wrong? That was your mother. They were trying to get you to the hospital so that you could say your good-byes while grandma was still alive. What do you mean, while she was still alive? Diane her heart was weakening and now it has stopped for good. I felt several bombs go off in my head. Cramps ran throughout my body, entered my mind, and distorted everything I knew to be sensible. Diane, are you going to be okay? Eddie, I did everything I knew to be right. He promised. He said in His Word that all I had to do was believe on Him and everything I asked would come to pass. I think I did that. I did do that and He still took her. Why Eddie! Why! What I didn't realize was that God does everything according to His purpose and our prayers must be prayed according to His will. Tears ran rapidly down my face, but were soon chased away by anger. Diane, stop torturing yourself like this. I can't answer those questions; I don't think anyone can. I stood in the middle of my bedroom watching the room spin around me. My mouth opened to release the tornado that was twisting around in my inner most being and produced shrieks as loud as a runaway train clamping down on the brakes. Diane, you're scaring the children and I haven't told them yet. I don't mean to. I called Mrs. Bea from next door to come and get the children. She's gonna watch them until we get back from the hospital.

I walked into the waiting area of the intensive care unit only to see Aunt Cindy and mama on separate telephones making calls to other family members. I stood in the doorway and watched as daddy and everyone else just stared out into space as if they were waiting for some miracle to fall out of the sky. Mama's eyes caught hold of mine and she lowered the earpiece of the telephone anticipating a word from me. My mouth moved, but I lost my sense of speech. Diane, do you want to go and see your grandmother? I nodded in agreement. Go on back to her room; the nurse knows you're coming. Eddie grabbed my hand and pulled me back. Are you sure you want to see her. Yes Eddie. Diane I've been back there and she doesn't look the same. Don't you want to remember her in peace? What difference does it make whether I remember her in peace or in pain? If I don't go back there I'm not going to have any peace and I'll always carry the pain. If I do go back there I'm still going to have pain and no peace. Any way you look at it they're both poison, so I choose to take the lesser of the two poisons and say good-bye face to face. As I entered the room my eyes locked onto the bright yellow curtain that hung perfectly still around her bed. My right hand covered my mouth to keep the rest of the tornado locked inside as my left hand reached out for the curtain. I pulled it back and made just enough room for me to pass through. They had her covered with several blankets and I didn't want to know why. Her stomach looked like a mountain. It was swollen so bad I couldn't see her face. When I began to hyperventilate Eddie suggested we leave. I refused. Slowly, I made my way to the head of her bed. I peered down at what used to be her face and wept. I couldn't find her eyes due to all of the inflammation. They were lost within her face. Even her nose was sinking. I placed my right hand over her forehead and caressed her cold, rubbery like skin. My words choked me and left me speechless. Eddie moaned, come on Diane let's go. I grabbed Eddie's hand and walked out. Eddie, that's not her. What do you mean Diane? That's not my grandma! If that's not her Diane, then who is it? It's the shell that kept her. She's soaring high above the heavens like a bird in the sky.

The funeral had come and gone. Everyone was going on with life except for me. I began to shy away from people. I left my politeness and my ability to communicate with people in my grandma's hospital room. I developed a hatred for everyone, especially the doctors who worked on my grandma. I hated their smiles and the vicarious ways in which they explained things. For weeks I kept to myself, hiding in my bedroom, and trying to sleep the pain away. When I wasn't sleeping I would lie there contemplating other ways I could hate. In a way I felt trapped because I didn't like the way I was feeling. Nonetheless, my broken heart wouldn't allow me to change my behavior. The family was to meet at grandma's house to pack up her stuff. I didn't want to go, but mama insisted. I walked in only to see boxes and paper everywhere. I walked through in silence, watching as they chose her things for themselves. I wanted to help mama and the rest of them clean and pack, however, it all seemed so final and I wasn't ready to close that door. Diane. Yes mama. Don't you want to take something of your grandmother's to remember her by? No. Why not? Because none of these things is gonna bring her back or make me feel like she's still here. Diane I understand that you're hurting, but no one here has forgotten her. We choose to remember her with laughter and joy in our hearts. Mama walked away and left me standing there. I gazed around the room and my eyes landed on my grandma's white china set and grandpa's wooden treasure box. They were sitting side by side in her china cabinet, watching and waiting for me to pick them up and when I left I took them home with me. Eddie can you get those things out of my car and bring them in the house. Sure baby, as long as you sit down and have dinner with the kids and me. I cooked a nice dinner for you. Not tonight. I'm not hungry and I planned on lying down for a bit. Diane I understand how you feel, but lately the only thing you've been doing is sleeping. You've stopped talking to me and you won't interact with the kids. You have to snap out of this thing. What do you mean snap out of it? Don't talk to me as if I'm some sort of looney bin. Diane I didn't mean it like that at all. It's just that the sweet Diane I once knew has decided to be mean and nasty to everyone, even me. I wanted to reach out and hug him, kiss him and tell him how much I loved him. I couldn't, my thoughts were consumed with the loss of my grandma, so I held my peace. I thought it would be a good idea to distance myself from everyone. This way I wouldn't feel the hurt and pain if God decided to take them home too. I went up to my room and tried to sleep, but the bright sun lit up the darkness under my eyelids. I heard the laughter of my children out in the backyard. Eddie was making weird sounds with his mouth while chasing them. Restless, I sat up in the bed and turned on the television. Two men and a woman were having a discussion about life and forgiveness. The conversation caught my attention. One of the men said, too often we travel through life wasting our time hating one another for reasons we can't explain. That sentence hit me in the center of my heart and caused me to move to the end of the bed to get closer to the television. The man continued to talk. We must love one another and stop blaming others for our own faults and things beyond our control...Let that anger and pride go, it isn't good for you. The camera zoomed in on his face, which brought it closer to the screen. We were looking each other face to face. He stretched out his hand and pointed his finger at me and said you must learn to forgive! Forgive all the people you have accused of doing you wrong. Forgive your friends, your family, teachers, lawyers, and doctors. I fell off the bed and onto the floor. With my face pressed on the hard floor I cried out to God. I knew He was speaking to me through this man on the television. Lord, please forgive me for the way I've been acting over the past few months. I have spent all my days and nights hating and learning new ways to hate, all because I felt I didn't get what I wanted. I've been acting out like a 2-year-old brat. I repent for my sins of omission and commission. I repent for speaking against you and for placing blame on you. Oh God, forgive me for the wickedness that roams throughout my entire being and the evil thoughts that I've allowed to make beds in my mind. I am truly sorry. Lord I forgive the doctors and the hospital staff for everything. I forgive Lord. I forgive. When I had finished praying the only thing that came forth out of my mouth were groans and the chains that kept me bound were loosed. The Lord took all my burdens and just like that I was free. The hate and anger was gone and the love of Christ reigned in me. In my ignorance I felt that because I stopped doing wrong, then God would do according to what I asked and that was to heal my grandma and let her live. When I look back I realize God answered every last one of my prayers. He woke her out of a coma and gave me a chance to speak with her when she was in the hospital. I was angry for a long time, but God healed grandma just as I asked. He washed away her tears and took her to be with Him. For that I'm grateful. God may not shower us with the blessings we think we should have, and His answers to long awaited prayers may not come when we want them or how we think they should come, but God always knows what's best and His perfect will is always going to be accomplished. Thank you Jesus for everything you have done for me, the things that you are doing for me right now and for all the things you will do for me.

Early Sunday morning I gladly gave my life to Christ and the following week I was baptized. Here I am Lord. I thank you Father for being a friend and loving enough to redeem me and set me free by sacrificing your Son Jesus Christ. You are holy and worthy to be praised. Lord, please have mercy on my soul. Forgive me for my sins. I want to live holy, but I need you to show me how. Teach me the things that I don't understand. Clean me up and make me whole. Renew in me a clean and righteous spirit. I need you and I can't do anything without you. Teach me how to walk right. Teach me how to talk right. I want to stand upright and perfect before you. I love you Lord. I want you to come into my life Lord. Come into my heart and live in me and through me. You created me, and I give you praise. My soul loves you Jesus. Anoint me to obey you. I give you my life for the rest of my life. Amen.

Journal Insert

As I travel through the passages of my mind
I can see a beautiful dove floating in the peaceful blue skies.
He stretched his wings out and circled around a hill
Full of broken dandelions unknown and in the middle stands one daffodil.
All covered in spores from its weedy environment,
Drenched in dew from silent tears of abandonment.
Oh what a precious flower so innocent and pure
Tainted by vehement shadows; abstinence is the only cure.
There will come a time when it seems it will lose its beauty,
Wilting in strife to fulfill its duty
But the dove swoops down grabbing it up in his beak,
Ripping it from the ground that appeared unstable and weak.
He flew to the seas that pushed up against the hill.
A battle between the clean and unclean,
and the saving of a dying daffodil.
He opened his beak and let the flower fall endlessly onto the blue seas,
releasing it of its guilt and pain
Erasing all of its iniquities.
The daffodil washed ashore on new but solid ground.
It took root and stood tall with no evil and destruction around.
The dipping into the water and the drowning of its sin
Produced a new life born, possessing the innocence of a newborn once again.

Diane

17
PAPA WAS A ROLLING STONE

I opened my eyes to a beautiful morning. The birds were singing praises
to God and the sun was peeking through the open spaces in my curtains.
Eddie's head was plastered under my arm and his heart gave me love
taps against my side. I kissed his forehead and his slumber filled eyes
opened. Good morning baby and happy mother's day. Thank you. No,
thank you. I couldn't have asked for a better wife and mother to our
children. His kind words made me blush. Are you ready for your gifts?
I already have my gift; he's lying next to me. I mean the gifts the kids
and I have for you. Sure. Okay, get up and come downstairs with me.
Eddie placed his soft hands over my eyes and walked me down the stairs.
When he removed them I stood before my dining room table lined with
roses he bought and cards the kids made. There were three suit bags
lying on the couch with several boxes of shoes stacked up in the corner.
The kids kissed me and screamed, Happy Mother's Day Mommy. Thank
you very much for everything, but I don't need, nor do I deserve all of
this. Eddie wrapped his arms around my waist and held me tightly. My
wife deserves this and more. I love you and I just want to take care of
you. Thank you Eddie, I love you too. Well if you love me then you'll
try on these outfits that your lovely husband bought you. Okay, but I
have to hurry or else I'll be late for church. Diane, are we still going out
to dinner with your crazy family? Yes we're going to dinner, but my
family isn't crazy. Who's all going? Mama and daddy will be attending.
Sam, Michelle, Lottie and her husband are going. Uncle George and
Aunt Cindy said they would go. Of course, Chole is going along with all
of us if you don't procrastinate. I'll go as long as your crazy family
promises not to compete with each other as to who can pass gas the
loudest. My family doesn't do that and once again, they aren't crazy.
Oh yes they are. You just don't know it yet. Xavier and Kayla laughed
as I chased Eddie around the house with a pillow. I tripped and fell to
the floor and Eddie took advantage of the situation. He sat on me and
tickled me to death. I begged him not to; however, laughter held my

words prisoner and my ribs felt like they caved in as I lost my breath. Okay Eddie I give. I have to go to church. Do you really give? Yes, I give. Is your family crazy? Yes, they are truly nut cases. Now will you please stop tickling me? Xavier and Kayla joined in and helped Eddie tickle me for a few more seconds. By the time I got to church I had a permanent smile on my face and laughter in my belly. After service we met at mama and daddy's house then drove all the way to the lake to a restaurant Chole chose. The scenery was beautiful. Water lined roads led the way as we followed mama and daddy. Tree limbs stretched forth toward the heavens as the sun kissed their branches. When we arrived at the restaurant we were all starving. This is a nice restaurant Chole, is the food good? Thank you Diane, and yes the food is wonderful. The menus were filled with tasty dishes as well as exotic prices. We passed the bread around the table swiftly as if that was all the food we were going to get. Finally our waitress came over to take our orders and the majority of the orders consisted of steak and chicken except for Uncle George and Aunt Cindy. Aunt Cindy scanned the menu carefully before ordering for Chole, herself and Uncle George. I'll have two of your two for one Lobster and steak dinners with the soup and shrimp scampi. The waitress took the orders and disappeared into the back. Daddy looked over his glasses across the table at Aunt Cindy and smirked. Cindy what do you plan on doing with all that food? Man that was a bargain I couldn't refuse. They are giving us dinner for two for just one price and if we don't eat it all we'll have enough to take home. I'm sure you're right, eh heh eh heh hehehe. As daddy laughed bread flew out of the space between his teeth. Eddie and I placed our hands over our salads to keep all unwanted saliva and chewed up food out of our plates, but daddy didn't seem to care. He just kept on laughing and spitting as if it was okay. Lottie was at the other end of the table blabbing about nothing to her husband, Sam, Michelle, and Chole. Xavier and Kayla sat still as they sucked up all of their apple juice. Mama and Aunt Cindy debated over some song when daddy stepped up to add his two cents. What's the problem with the song? Mama looked confused before answering daddy. I'm not sure I understand what Cindy is actually saying? If you all would listen to what I'm saying then you would get it. Daddy chuckled before speaking. Well go on Mrs. Cindy, we want to hear what you have to say. Aunt Cindy perked up when she realized she had the floor. Do y'all remember that old song Papa was a rolling stone, wherever he laid his hat was his home; and when he died all he left us was alone? We all agreed that we remembered. Well, I was just wandering how much money he actually got for them and if they had to pay it back. Uncle George, already drunk from the last holiday, continued to chomp down on his salad and only added in blurbs of you've got to be kidding me. Everyone looked at Aunt Cindy as if she was crazy. There was a moment of silence and then at the same time everyone burst into tears. We laughed so hard that no sound came forth, just tears. Mama tried to hide her face under the table as it became difficult to hold her food in her mouth. Michelle was puzzled because she didn't know what was so funny and Sam made sure everyone heard his loud mouth. Finally, daddy gained his composure and spoke. Woman what in the world are you talking about. Papa didn't get them a bank l-o-a-n. He left them "alone." Mama said, alone as in by themselves! Laughter rang out and people began to stare. Aunt Cindy began explaining. You all don't understand, papa was so busy hanging out in the streets and spending his money on alcohol and women that when he died he had to get a loan because he didn't have any money to leave his family. Mama yelled out, where did he get the loan from? Aunt Cindy exclaimed that the loan came from a loan shark. Mama almost fell out of her chair. Soon Eddie joined in. Loan Shark, did you forget the man is dead? I sat in silence and after carefully weighing the situation I kind of understood both sides and decided to speak on it. Wait a minute mama. I think Aunt Cindy has a point. Uncle George looked up and said you've gotta be kidding me, and then went back to eating. All I'm saying is that I understand both sides. If papa did throw all his money away in the streets, then he probably did receive money from loan sharks and when he died he left his family in debt. Oh Diane, please! What are y'all drinking besides soda? Eddie, be quiet! I told you that I could see both sides because in death its possible papa left them by themselves, a-l-o-n-e, and it's also possible that he left them in debt with all of his loans. Mama agreed with Eddie. Diane you sound just as crazy as your Aunt Cindy. Where do you get your rationale? Ech eeee eeee eeee ha ha ha ha hahahahaha. Mama if you laugh any harder you are going to burst a blood vessel.

147

The waitress brought out several dishes of food, but they were all for Aunt Cindy, Uncle George, and Chole. They had so much food they began passing around some of their dishes for all of us to taste. Gee Eddie, maybe we should've ordered the same thing. I know that's right, that stuff looks good. Ten minutes later the waitress was coming back with several more dishes. Daddy began to murmur. I know this has got to be our food by now. However, the dishes were placed in front of Aunt Cindy, Uncle George, and Chole once again. Uncle George had a big sinister smile on his face. Don't weep about it now; you should've looked at the menu closely. Next time pay attention. Sam calmly interjected. Where was that at on the menu and how much did it cost? Uncle George said, Cindy, go on and point it out to the ignant boy who don't know how to read a simple menu. Aunt Cindy smiled. It was on the back and it was only $75.00 for two. While they were sharing ah's and ooh's I began to search the menu. After reading their selected item three times I tapped mama on the hand. What do you want girl? Mama they think this is two dinners for one price, but it simply says two entrees for one price of $75.00, and they have had at least six entrees, which is a total of $225.00. Mama placed her hand over her mouth and buried her face into daddy's shoulder and I planted my face within my arms on the table. The air was ringing with the same question; what's wrong with them? Mama and I were laughing uncontrollably. I looked up to tell everybody what we were laughing at, only I looked right into uncle Georges' face and fell flat on mine. He was chewing like a camel. His lips curved around his fork and made slurping sounds when he pulled it out of his mouth. Finally, mama told the entire table of Aunt Cindy's mistake, and as we laughed she sat in silence. Uncle George sighed, you've gotta be kidding me. Cindy didn't you read the thing before you ordered this stuff? Yes I did! There must be some mistake. The sinister smile slid off Uncle Georges' face, his eyebrows ran into each other, and he stopped chewing like a camel. He stood up to make a very important statement. Every last one of you ate some of this food, so by right you all should contribute. Daddy sat erect in his chair. Man how are you going to ask somebody to pay for something you offered. Uncle George looked like a dusty brown egg in a country wicker basket, but after counting their money they didn't have enough cash on hand, so everyone offered to help them pay for their meal. However, Aunt Cindy pulled out her plastic and paid the bill in full. On the way home Eddie and I talked about the turn of events and had a good laugh. We hadn't planned on having such a wonderful time especially since this was the first Mother's Day dinner without grandma, but we enjoyed ourselves. Xavier and Kayla slept in the back seat while music lightly tapped on their ears. It warmed my heart to watch them sleep so peacefully. They reminded me of myself when I was a child. Daddy would be singing and mama would be talking and peeking back at us. It was so easy for us to fall asleep in the back seat when daddy was driving because we knew we were safe and we knew he would always get us from one place to the next without a problem. All we had to do was close our eyes and trust him. When I look at Xavier and Kayla I'm amazed at their willingness to trust so deeply, but confused as to how I lost my ability to trust like that as I grew older. What happened and how did I stray away so far? I don't exactly remember when I stopped trusting. All I know is that at some point in my life I stopped. It seemed easier that way, but now I know different. As we drove along the winding road, up the bridges and down, through the rain and rough terrain, their slender bodies just went along with the motions of the car. They offered no resistance because they knew their father was in control. I turned toward Eddie and smiled. He grabbed hold of my hand and began singing to me in his own special way just like daddy used to do mama. I've come to realize that life doesn't do anything but repeat itself. Now some 20 years later Eddie and I have become our parents and our children have taken our places. Time sure finds a way to get away from you. Again, I glanced back at my children as my mother did with me. Kayla opened her eyes while still asleep then very slowly they closed again. Her big brown eyes were so beautiful and clear you could almost see through them. I was captivated by the innocent flames that lit up her eyes. I did a visual search over their bodies, making sure their shirts were moving up and down. When I was absolutely sure they were still breathing I exhaled with a sigh. While watching them I realized I'd been missing something all these years. I'd failed to see the world through the eyes of a child. Somewhere along the way I'd stopped listening, feeling, and loving life. Somewhere along the way I'd stopped living. I slid down in my seat and listened to my thoughts as the wind wrapped around my face. I want to get back to the place where I can see the world and people the way a child does. That's how God would have us all to be, like little children viewing the world through the eyes of innocence, captivated by the love of God. Lord, thank you for my children; my miracle and my divine inspiration. Thank you for taking the time to use them to teach me about you.

18
<u>DIPPED IN GOD'S GLORY</u>

I began to study God's Word diligently, at home, work, and in my car. It shed light on the dark areas in my life and gave me an understanding of both natural and spiritual matters. My heart literally flipped every time I read about the miraculous works of Jesus and His Apostles. I sojourned from the Old Testament to the New Testament, learning about God and how much He truly loves and cares for me. Certain Scriptures stuck with me such as, John 3:16. It says, "For God so loved the world, He gave His only begotten Son." It blew my mind to know that Jesus died for raggedy old me. He gave up His life and took on my sins just to save me. Who am I that I should be blessed to receive such a wonderful and sacrificial gift of love?

The church was studying about the baptism of the Holy Spirit on Wednesday evenings after prayer. We roamed the pages of the book of Acts feverishly. My hunger for the Lord grew and I wanted to know more about the filling of the Holy Spirit. A touch was no longer enough. I wanted to be baptized in the Spirit and I wanted to please God more than anything in the world. I really wanted to know the power of His resurrection, so I went before the Lord with expectancy in my heart each day. Fill me Lord. I want to walk in your way. I want to worship you Lord. I want to give you all the praise, so please remove anything in me that's not like you. Touch my mind, my body and my spirit so that I may be free to receive from you Lord. Baptize me with fire from on high and dip me in your Glory. Lord I'm going to break my plate until you bless me. I'm going to stay before you until you bless me. I was determined to receive the filling God had for me. I ate only fruits, vegetables, and The Word of God; and the only liquid I allowed myself was water. Eddie didn't understand, he thought I was starving myself to death for no reason. However, I was far from starving. God sustained me through the fast where my concentration was on Him instead of on the food. I spent wonderful days and evenings with the Lord. The Holy Spirit would speak to my spirit on some days and then there would be a period of weeks where He wouldn't say anything. Months had passed by and still no baptism. I didn't want to question God, but doubt began to get the best of me. I began to wonder if all this was worth it. I'd sacrificed everything. I spent the majority of my time with the Lord. I went to bed late and rose early for prayer and meditation on The Word of God. Eddie watched me with a scornful eye and complained that I wasn't spending enough time with him and the kids although he was never home to spend any time with us. He thought I was a lunatic church groupie that just followed the pack. I knew nothing he said was true because God helped me to balance my life and family, but still, Eddie and I began to drift further apart. We no longer talked about the same things, nor were we interested in the same things, however, I didn't withhold anything from Eddie. I loved him and I used each day as another opportunity to prove that to him. I was different and that upset him because he lacked understanding regarding the change. My desires changed, my language and my disposition changed and that put us at odds because he saw my relationship with the Lord as betrayal to him.

I had been fasting for just about a year when it came time for the church to travel to North Carolina to the National Prayer Clinic. I felt in my heart that I was going and that God would indeed bless me with the filling of the Holy Spirit while on this trip, after all, I'd been fasting for a year. Unfortunately, the opportunity did not present itself for me to travel with the church to North Carolina, so I stayed back. Frustrated, I ended my fast when the church came back home. I hadn't tasted real food in so long I forgot what it tasted like. The only thing I was sure of is that I missed it and I felt as though I deserved it. After weeks of indulging myself in all types of cuisine the Spirit of the Lord spoke to me while I was at work. It was so cold the wind felt like it cut right through my clothing. The city was quiet, so Eddie and I patrolled our sector making sure it stayed that way. The cold weather acted as a better crime deterrent than the police. Eddie and I listened closely to the police radio for emergency calls when I heard the Spirit of the Lord speaking to me over the voice of the radio dispatcher. "Sanctify Ye A Fast." I began communing with the Lord from within. Lord, what do you mean when you say sanctify ye a fast? I have been fasting for over a year and I don't know what else you want me to do. I waited for a response from the

Lord, but there was none. I thought about what the Spirit of the Lord said and I was persuaded to commit myself to fasting again. However, the Spirit of the Lord continued to speak to me on several occasions saying, "Sanctify Ye a Fast." What is it that I'm missing Lord? What is it that I'm not getting? The hours at work were long and since I spent the majority of my time outdoors I was more susceptible to catching colds. I felt my body weakening from flu-like symptoms, but I refused to take a day off. I had one week left to complete an entire year without taking a sick day and the incentive for that was a one thousand dollar bonus check.

Diane, you need to eat something like a bowl of hot grits. I guess you're right Eddie. If I can get something hot in my system then I would probably feel much better. Why don't you take a few days off; you can barely lift your head up, your eyes are weak and you can't talk. You know you need your voice in order to work. Eddie, thank you for your concern, but as long as I can whisper I am going to work. Nothing is going to stop me from receiving that one thousand dollar check. Then, once again I heard the Spirit of the Lord say, "Sanctify Ye a Fast." By the time I got home my head felt as if it were fifty pounds. My throat felt like brand new sandpaper and my voice had just about left me. My chest and my face ached. My head and stomach hurt; and there was a ringing sound in my ears like the ringing sound on the emergency broadcast system. To sum it up, I felt like someone ran me over with a tractor twice. I went straight to my room and crawled up under the blanket. Eddie fixed me a nice hot bowl of soup and massaged my aching body. Diane how do you feel now? Terrible, but I'm going to work in the morning. I don't think you should, but you do what you feel is right. Eddie didn't want to cuddle with me for fear of catching my germs, so we slept with pillows between us. The alarm clock went off at 5 A.M sharp. I lifted my head off the pillow with ease and sat up in my bed. To my surprise the headache was gone. My face was still stuffed up, but I felt good. I felt well enough to go to work. I turned toward Eddie and opened my mouth to tell him to wake up, however, nothing came out. I couldn't even whisper. I jumped out of bed, turned on the light and ran to the mirror. I opened my mouth wide and peered in. I examined the contents of my mouth as if I were going to find my voice hiding behind my tonsils or something. What's wrong Diane? I motioned to him that I couldn't talk. He laughed wholeheartedly. Well I guess you gotta stay home after all. Realizing I just kissed my one thousand dollars good-bye I grew angry. The kids went to school and Eddie left for work without me. I thought, well Lord it's only you and I. Before I could think on another syllable the Spirit of the Lord said, "Sanctify Ye a Fast." His voice held me still in my tracks. Lord you keep saying this to me and I've done all that you've asked. When the Spirit of the Lord began to speak again I fell to my knees. He spoke in a gentle manner. I needed you to separate yourself from people, work, and your family. I needed you by yourself. After He finished speaking I prayed and asked for forgiveness. I cried after realizing God just wanted to spend time alone with me where I could enter into intimate fellowship with Him. Laughter quickly entered my belly when I thought about my sudden laryngitis and the statement I made, as long as I can whisper I'm going to work. Who says that God doesn't have a sense of humor? I stayed before the Lord constantly. The more time I spent with Him, the more I wanted to be with Him. While the house was empty my days were filled with studying and meditating on God's Word. After preparing dinner and spending time with my family, the rest of my evenings were consumed with prayer, worship, and songs of Zion in praise to God; so by the time I was ready for bed the Lord tucked me in and cradled me through the night. Several days passed and I was feeling real good in my spirit. As usual, I got up and saw Eddie and the kids to the door. Once they were gone I ran and grabbed my Bible with excitement in my heart. I prayed and meditated for most of the morning and then I made myself breakfast, but for some reason this morning I just couldn't seem to get enough of the Word. My spirit was hungry and no matter what I did I just couldn't seem to curve the craving. After breakfast I grabbed a stack of Christian videotapes and plugged in one after the next. I watched two sermons, which added to my spiritual high. I decided to watch one more tape and then take a nap. The minister's title to his sermon was, "The Alabaster Box." I sat on the couch and listened intensely. Every word that flowed out of his mouth touched my heart. He read from Luke 7:36-50 and expounded on the sinful woman and her love and devotion for Jesus. He impressed upon me that real love and devotion toward Jesus must come from a deep awareness of our sin. She expressed to God what was in her heart and offered all that she had to him, "The Alabaster Box." I began clapping and shouting Amen. Then he stood still. A look of seriousness came over him and as he talked I knew he was talking to me. Someone in here has an Alabaster Box. Someone in here has been hiding something and God says give it to Him! Suddenly, my secret thoughts I thought were hidden began to come to the forefront of my mind. I shook my head violently to get rid of them, but they didn't budge. The minister kept saying give it up, give it up; give Him all you got. I knew without a doubt he was talking to me, however, I couldn't let God know my secret. Softly, I said no, I can't. Then it felt as if someone was standing right behind me. I knew it was the Spirit of the Lord. His presence was so evident and breathtaking I didn't dare turn my head. Suddenly, it was as if He leaned over the couch to whisper in my ear. I felt His face next to mine and He said, "You might as well give it up because I already know what it is." Not even a second later the minister on the television said, you might as well give it up because the Lord knows what it is anyway. Shame faced I threw myself to the floor and wept bitterly. Lord I'm sorry for the ugly secrets I've kept. Nothing is hidden from you for you are God Almighty. I opened my Alabaster Box and poured its contents before the Lord, confessing everything that I should have confessed a long time ago. Instead, I tucked my sins away in a room in my mind, locked the door, and threw away the key. In the midst of my weeping God's glory fell over me and His power encircled me. I was truly in Him and He was in and all around me. Every time I would attempt to move to the left or the right I would get another touch of His glory and my skin felt as if it turned inside out. When I attempted to stand I felt Him touch my legs and I would fall back to the floor. His holy presence and power were awesome. I felt like I was being made all over again. My mouth was filled with His praises as I knelt on the floor. I lifted my hands and my head toward the heavens and opened my eyes to see many birds descending. There were rows and rows of people bending before a man who was standing on a rock. He stood over them with His arms stretched out. Clouds billowed beneath them. The skies behind Him were a beautiful lavender color, none like I had ever seen before. When I closed my eyes and opened them again there was nothing there but the ceiling. I don't know how long I was in the Lord's presence, but it seemed like eternity. When I got up the Spirit of the Lord said, "Now that I've filled you go and get your family." I didn't understand fully what the Lord meant. I felt as if I was still in the heavens and I didn't want to come down, but to some extent I did know they needed me. I knew the devil had been busy in my home while I was on the mountaintop with Jesus. I just didn't realize the extent of the damage that he'd caused while I was gone. I went to bed with the love of God in my heart. I now had His stamp of approval, the Baptism of the Holy Spirit. The Lord humbled me and He blessed me with this wonderful gift in spite of me and I will be forever grateful.

<u>Journal Insert</u>

I asked the Lord a question
What must I do to receive?
And the only answer I got
Was pray diligently and believe.
I thought, believe on what!
I need someone to tell me,
And take the blinders off my eyes
So I can really see.
I do kneel down and pray.
I do lift my hands high.
So why haven't I received?
Why Lord? Why?
I cried a thousand tears,
But I just didn't understand.
I was leaning on my reasoning,
And how I thought I should stand.
I traveled through the days
On five and ten minute prayers
Expecting the Lord to help me shed
My flesh and sinful layers.
I asked Him once more
What must I do to receive?
And the Lord replied again
Pray diligently and believe.
So after waddling in my mess,
And being dragged through muck and mud
I began to thank Him for His fullness
That's when the seed began to bud.
I fasted and I prayed.
I expected to receive,
But when it didn't happen
Doubt grieved what I believed.
I was restless in my spirit,
My mind and body too.

My intellect got me nowhere with God.
What was I going to do?
I wanted to get close to Him
So there would be no more me.
I wanted to feel His presence.
That's where I wanted to be.
I grew tired of just a touch.
I thirsted for the Word.
I wanted to receive
All I could from the Lord.
I got up early in the morn'
Before the sun shone on my face
Stayed upon my wretched knees;
I was determined to win this spiritual race.
After dropping the things I enjoyed
And fasting for most of the year
The Lord said, "Sanctify Ye a Fast"
But yet, I had my career.
I fasted, prayed, and worked.
I refused to separate.
It took for me to get sick
For the Lord to operate!
For seven days I stayed in.
For seven days I prayed with diligence.
And that's when He showed me
Something I had not confessed.
I had an Alabaster Box
Containing a secret locked in my mind.
The Lord said, "Turn it over"
And put it far behind.
The very moment I did that
With repentance...sincere sorrow
The Spirit came over me like a flood,
Baptizing me for the morrows.
I saw the heavens open up
And many birds descending.

SPIRITUAL CONFESSIONS
And my coming of age

A form of a man with His arms stretched out
Over rows of people bending.
A lot of things confuse me
And there are still some things I don't understand,
But I've learned to wait upon the Lord.
He's my rock on which I firmly stand.

Diane

When the Lord showed up, it wasn't because of anything I had done.
It wasn't because I had fasted.
It was because He chose to honor my obedience in His time.

19
<u>SHATTERED DREAMS</u>

Much had changed between Eddie and I after the Lord chose me unto Himself. It seemed as if I had gone away on an extended vacation and when I got back I came home to a complete stranger. It was as if we no longer knew each other. I wonder if we ever did because our line of communication had not only rusted, it had been severed. Basically, we lacked the ability to meet one another's needs. The Lord's command stuck in my mind, "Now that I've filled you go and get your family." At the time He said it I didn't understand what He meant, but with each passing day the definition became clearer. Like sheep my family had gone astray and I knew bringing them back wasn't going to be easy. Eddie began looking at me as if I had just fallen from a cloud in the sky. I felt as if I'd lost him forever. He went his way and I went mine, so in order to save my marriage I had to act fast. In my haste I arranged a trip to the Bahamas so that we could spend some quality time together. The flight was long and the conversation fell to the floor. We pranced around each other as if we were on a blind date. Our words tripped over our tongues and the nervousness was evident. Side by side we sat as friction separated us. My mind searched for a subject to share with him, but failed to touch on anything interesting, so I communed with the Lord while Eddie slept. Silence accompanied us to our destination. After we landed I looked up at the sky and found it to be a picture of beauty. Purple, orange, and blue streaks stretched across its face as the sun sank into the waters beneath.

Well Diane, we're here. What do you want to do first? I have a romantic dinner planned for the two of us, which I believe we're late for. I'm tired and I don't know if I feel up to dinner right now. Do we have to go? Yes we do! Besides, it's already been paid for. We took our bags to the room and headed downstairs to the restaurant. I watched Eddie crumple up his face while on the elevator. I reached out to hold his hand, but instead of embracing the romantic gesture he stepped away. When the doors opened he rushed off the elevator as if I did something wrong. Instead of walking with me he walked ahead of me. Eddie was acting as if I'd twisted his arm and forced him to come on this trip and I was beginning to regret the whole thing. During dinner Eddie's obvious animosity toward me began to subside as he settled down. Empty belts of laughter forced its way through our stale conversation as we filled our bellies with shrimp and lobster tails. I smiled at the beautiful man sitting across from me and remembered why I loved him so much. However, when our eyes met I saw a stranger. Lord, where's my husband? Where did he go?

Eddie, are you enjoying yourself? Yeah, but I could've done the same thing at home without spending any money. I'm not concerned about the money Eddie. I did this for us. I know you did and I appreciate it, but you also know I don't like surprises. Eddie why is it that you always have to take something good and turn it into something awful? All I'm saying is that I wish you would've consulted me about a trip I don't care to be on before you went ahead and planned a vacation. Eddie's words were covered in ice as they came forth from his mouth. I listened attentively and weighed every word as if my life depended on it. His contempt for me was evident in his conversation and the look on his face will be embedded in my mind forever. Noticing my hurt and disappointment he ended his sentence by saying, regardless, I'm sure we'll have a nice time. I began to question myself regarding this entire situation. I couldn't figure out how someone could be so ungrateful and evil when all you want to do is show them love, especially when that someone is your husband. Diane, don't look like that. Look like what Eddie! Don't give me that look like you're about to cry. Well what do you expect me to do after you just spit on everything I've done? That's not what I'm doing. Yes you are! Okay, I'll tell you what; forget about what I said and let's enjoy the vacation. I agreed and finished my meal.

By the time we got back to the hotel room exhaustion put us both to sleep. Before I knew it I'd entered another world, a place where dreams flood your entire being. Suddenly, darkness surrounded me. Eddie and I were working. We had our guns drawn as we carefully searched someone's backyard. There were a few officers assisting us. I don't know what we were looking for; nonetheless, we searched intensely and without fail. As I climbed to the top of a wooden stockade fence Eddie stirred around behind my back. I turned to find him hovering over a cardboard box, which was sitting on top of a garbage can. The box contained several cans that were fuchsia in color. They were very bright and beautiful. Eddie picked up some of the cans and walked away with them. He ignored me and began walking down the dark street with the cans. I called out to him, but he answered not a word. I ran after him to catch up with him and I ended up at a dry desolate field where there were many lions blocking the way. Eddie passed right through them as I stood there in fear. I was afraid of the lions and that fear kept me from going through. They looked at me and roared loudly. However, something was wrong with them, they appeared to be lame. Some were limping while a few had only three legs. There was one in the midst of them and he was lying on top of a mound that was covered with a black velvet blanket. This one was really sick. When I looked up Eddie was far away. He was leaving me, so I prayed to God to give me the strength to pass through the lions and for them not to hurt me. I closed my eyes and ran through. When I opened them I was right behind Eddie. I got down on my knees and began praying. When I opened my eyes I was looking up into the heavens. There was a man in a cloud and He held a beautiful rose up to His nose. I knew He represented the Lord. Eddie was looking up at the man also, but his back was to me. The man reached through the cloud to give me the rose and I stretched my hand forward to receive it, however when the rose came through the cloud it became a beautiful chrome sword. As I humbly held it in my hands I realized I had been draped with a white robe. I turned toward Eddie and I said, Eddie look what the Lord gave me. Eddie was on one knee as he bowed down to the ground. When he looked up there was a reflection of God's light shining upon his face. Tears flooded his eyes and one ran across his cheekbone. I then took the sword and girded it about my waist. When I woke up I was puzzled by the dream. It was so real it stuck with me night and day. I wrote it down in my journal, went into prayer, and asked the Lord to give me the revelation knowledge concerning the dream.

Every morning I watched the sun rise out of the crystal clear water. Our first few days were spent struggling to be romantic. Eddie caught some type of virus, which made him really sick, so he spent a lot of time in bed. I walked the beach alone while couples whizzed past me, drenched in love and laughter. Occasionally they would look over at me with pity. I thought, is my loneliness that obvious? Their stares made me feel uncomfortable and so my attention would quickly turn to my notepad where I would sit down and pour out my inner most feelings. In between thought and reason I glanced back at the walkway hoping Eddie would show up. Any hope that I had regarding romance quickly diminished in the crowd of strange faces. My idea of romance and intimacy was overshadowed by Eddie's illness and rude behavior. When I wasn't alone I spent hours trying to nurse him back to health. He said he felt bad because he thought he ruined the vacation, but as the days passed on it got better. I was just happy we were able to be together. On the fourth day Eddie was really sick and he moaned constantly, insisting I take him home. He yelled over and over, I don't want to die here, please take me home. Sweat poured from his body as he shook violently in the bed. I phoned the hotel nurse and she urged me to bring him down for an examination. The office was small and cold. Behind the small white desk sat a black woman in the whitest nurse's uniform I ever saw. She spoke with a Bahamian accent, which made it very difficult to understand her. She soon grew tired of us interrupting her with excuse me and pardon me, and quickly silenced us with her sarcasm. I didn't know whether to thank her or to be offended and Eddie was too sick to care. After her two-minute examination she came up with a diagnosis. Ah, I know wat da problem iz. He jes' got da' flu. Within seconds she gave him some type of home remedy that consisted of a mixture of lemons, honey, and hot sauce along with chewable vitamin C tablets. The day before our departure his illness began to subside, allowing us to spend a little time together. The next day Eddie felt like himself again and we headed home. We didn't really want to return to work right after our vacation so we took additional time off and when we finally returned to duty we were well rested and ready to go.

Eddie and I left the station house early and went on patrol. We wanted to get a head start before we had to pick up our rookie-trainee for the day. Eddie drove and I had my head in my Bible. He circled the blocks of Stoneridge, Brock, and Hampshire over and over again. What do you see Eddie? Oh nothing, we don't really patrol this area over here, so I'm just doing a little routine patrol. I put my head back in my Bible but quickly looked up when Eddie began screaming. There's Katrina, the report technician that works downtown. Eddie I remember her; I went to school with her. Do you want to give her a ride Diane? I don't care. Katrina got in our patrol car and smiled at me. Although we shared a few words the conversation seemed to flow quite nicely between her and Eddie. After noticing it, I gave him the eye and went back to reading the Word of God. We dropped her off and rushed back to our side of town to pick up our trainee. Officer Downing was waiting in the corridor of the precinct with an ambiguous smile on his face. Hello Officer's Camden and Camden. I'm Officer Downing your new trainee. Eddie shook his hand and said good morning as I introduced myself as his senior officer and advisor. Officer Camden is there anything I need to do before we head out? Eddie stepped forward just as bold and blunt as he could be. Go and clean out the car and make sure we have all of the supplies we need. Of course, but when are we going on the street to do some police work? We'll go after we've had our breakfast! The food was cold and greasy, but the emptiness in my stomach said it didn't care. Eddie and I sat side by side while Officer Downing sat across from us. His brand new badge glistened under the lights and his eagerness to do what he considered real police work was sickening. Our conversation consisted mainly of instructions and procedures we insisted he follow. He sucked it all up like a kid with a plate full of spaghetti.

Now that we've taught you the basics it's time to take you to the jungle. The jungle! What's the jungle? It's a gang and drug infested area. Who named it the jungle? The drug boys gave it that name because they consider themselves to be as wild as animals and their habitat as that of a jungle. They don't care anything about you, your family, or your life. I sat back and listened to Eddie and Officer Downing talk as we made our way to the jungle. We knew they would spot us before we could spot them because of their posted lookouts, but that never stopped us from catching them. Slowly, we turned the corner. Up ahead were eight guys wearing baggy jeans and t-shirts standing on the street corner in front of a small store. The outside of the store was hand painted with many colors. Pictures of beer bottles, lottery tickets, and half naked black women plastered the face of the store. Quickly, their heads turned our way and they scattered like roaches when the light comes on. We circled the block for 20 minutes to let them know we were there to stay. We stopped at the intersection and across the street on a porch were two guys.

Diane, do you see what I see? Yes, that's Marcus Freeman, the drug dealer. Officer Downing, look across the street. Do you see the guy with the black jacket on? Yes sir, I do. Diane and I just locked him up last month with 78 bags of marijuana. Really! Do you think he's still up to something because he won't take his eyes off you guys? Good observation Officer Downing. I watched intensely and noticed Marcus Freeman stuffing what appeared to be a weapon into his pocket. Everyone be careful; he's stuffing something in his pocket and I can't see what it is exactly. Eddie concurred and then quickly gave out instructions. Okay, just get ready. I'm going to step on the gas and when we get close enough, jump out and grab him. When Eddie roared our engine Marcus jumped up and ran into the hallway of an abandoned house. Of course, we followed suit. Diane, watch the other guy on the porch. No! The rookie can watch him. Officer Downing, do not let this guy out of your sight. I understand Officer Camden; you can count on me. With our guns drawn Eddie and I went up the stairs and into the house. Every step was crucial because we didn't know what this guy had or where he was in the house. Eddie entered the upstairs apartment, hid behind the doorway and said he could see the guy hiding something in the back room. I trailed slightly behind Eddie as we entered the living room. When we arrived at the first bedroom we saw Marcus Freeman crouching down in the corner. Let me see your hands! Let me see your hands! Eddie gave voice commands until Marcus followed the instructions. My gun didn't move off my target until after Eddie handcuffed him. Eddie stay with the prisoner while I search the remainder of the room for whatever it was that he was hiding. Wow! This is really fun. Eddie and I turned around to see our Gomer Pile wannabe trainee standing there with a stupid smile on his face. He shook his head up and down in amazement while his hands rested on his hips. I was trying to hold my tongue, but I couldn't. Excuse me Officer Downing, but where is the guy I told you to watch? Oh, he said he had something really important to do, so I let him go. What do you mean you let him go! If I told you to detain him then I meant it! I'm sorry. It won't happen again. That's okay just come with me and help me search this room. Why, what's in it? Eddie saw the guy stuffing something in there. Eddie handcuffed the prisoner and sat him in a chair in the kitchen for our safety. Officer Downing and I came across a closet where the suspect had thrown several bullets. I yelled out to Eddie to let him know of our discovery. What's up Diane? We found a lot of ammo. Eddie turned and looked back at the prisoner. Hey Marcus, where there's ammo there's guns, so why don't you tell us where you put the gun. Sweat poured down the sides of the prisoners face as we continued our search. Eddie was like a kid bugging his parents on a road trip. Did you find it yet? How long is it going to take you? Do you think it's over here or over there? Eddie! Are you watching the prisoner or are you watching us? Go back in there with him and let us finish our search. Well hurry up and get to the bathroom because he ran in there also. Okay Eddie, go back into the kitchen before I have to pull rank. Eddie mulled around in the hallway talking to the prisoner and eventually made his way into the bathroom. Hey Diane! Look what I found. I poked my head around the corner and Eddie was standing there holding a .45 cal automatic. Then I heard heavy footsteps pounding the floor and then the stairs. Eddie and I stepped into the kitchen to see where the noise was coming from only to find an empty chair and a missing prisoner. Eddie where is the prisoner? Eddie had a dumb look on his face and then took off like superman through the house. I dropped everything and followed Eddie. Officer Downing followed behind me, which made us look like the three stooges in police uniform. There was no time to take the stairs one by one, so I took eight and then 10. When I hit the landing I felt my left knee pop out of its joint as if a huge rubber band had broken. Eddie ran onto the porch and looked to the right to see where the prisoner had gone. There was a crowd standing outside and they were all looking to the left and laughing. Our eyes followed theirs and we saw the prisoner running down the middle of the street with his hands cuffed behind his back. Eddie jumped into the police cruiser and attempted to cut the prisoner off on the next street. Officer Downing and I chased the prisoner on foot. Remembering my old track days I took off like Wilma Rudolph. I had the prisoner in sight and was gaining ground when the lower part of my left leg decided to separate from my knee and go its own way. The pain was out of this world and my screams let everyone know exactly how I felt. I looked down and the lower part of my leg was swinging back and forth, then finally, it locked back into its place. I hobbled after the prisoner into someone's backyard. He was in front of a stockade fence jumping up and down, attempting to throw his body over the fence. This was the most hilarious thing I had ever seen because he had no hands to propel him, they were cuffed behind his back. I limped over to him with my gun drawn, but couldn't tell him to stop because I was laughing too hard.

What are you, stupid or something? Do you think if you bounce up and down a little harder you'll bounce right over that eight-foot fence without any hands? I think I did better than you guys; you let me get away. What are your names: Officer's Dumb, Dumb, and Dumber? The prisoner laughed hysterically. Oh you think that's funny. Let's see if you laugh at this. You have the right to remain silent. Anything you say will be held against you in a court of law. Now let your face kiss the ground. I'm sorry officer, but I'm not getting on that dirty ground! Man, don't let me have to tell you twice. As he hit the ground I holstered my weapon and tightened his handcuffs. I looked up to find Officer Downing standing over me with his weapon pointed at the prisoner. Officer Downing is your finger by any chance on that trigger? No, it sure is not. I'm just making sure because you have that gun pointed in my direction. Better yet, you can put it away now; the situation is under control. I heard Eddie screeching the tires on the street behind me while screaming over the radio. Diane where are you? Radio I can't find my partner. Every time I attempted to tell him I was okay he'd cut me off, so I decided to exit the backyard and meet him on the street. Officer Downing can you help me escort this gentleman out of this yard; I can barely walk? I most certainly will. Officer Camden I would just like to tell you that you can really run fast, I didn't think you had it in you. I appreciate that, but you see where it got me. Yeah, that limp doesn't look too good. When the other officers realized where we were they all came and offered their assistance, including Eddie. Diane, are you okay? Yes Eddie, but my leg feels like it's broken. I think you better go to the hospital and get it checked out. Maybe later, I just don't think it's all that bad. The other patrolmen including my lieutenant flooded me with the same questions until Lt. Ellis finally gave me a direct order to go to the emergency room. I was treated, ordered off duty, and placed on leave with a serious injury to my left knee. The doctor said my ACL and cartilage were torn. He gave me a set of crutches and referred me to see a specialist. I went to see Dr. Morgan a few days later. He had a trustworthy face that said I know what I'm doing. He sat down calmly in the chair across from the table where I lay. Diane, I think you're going to be out of work for a while. Really! Yes, really. From what I can see you've damaged your ligament and cartilage, but there's just too much swelling to tell. When will you know for sure Dr. Morgan? When I go inside and take a good look around. I lowered my head when he began to discuss the surgical procedure involved. Diane I know you're nervous, but don't be. I can do this type of surgery with my eyes closed; believe me, It isn't as bad as you think. Dr. Morgan was right. The surgery was quick and simple, but my ACL was torn and I would need addition surgery. I went through physical therapy for almost a year in an attempt to strengthen that knee. I wanted to avoid surgery at all costs. However, it only worsened. The condition of my left knee was beginning to deteriorate and more surgery was inevitable. Dr. Morgan wanted to convince me to use donor tissue because he said my own were like rubber bands and he didn't want to take the chance in using it to repair my knee. Daddy was highly against using someone else's tissue. He said it wasn't safe and he didn't want me to go through that. Eddie and I talked about it in great detail. However, in the end I decided to do what the Lord said, and that was to trust him and use my own tissue to repair my knee. Dr. Morgan cut my patella tendon in half and used it to replace my ACL. The knee was stable, but the surgery left me with limited usage of that leg. I wasn't able to bend my knee beyond a thirty-degree angle. Dr. Morgan said my options were slim and with my left leg now crippled I began to get a little frustrated.

20
WHY ME......WHY THIS.......WHY NOW!

As the Lord cradled me in His arms I sang songs of Zion, praising Him throughout the morning. The words to a lovely song stuck with me, For the many times I've fallen, yet you forgave me, thank you, I thank you Lord...Thank you for letting me know that I'm not alone and even though weapons may form; thank you Jesus, they won't prosper...No, they won't prosper...For He shall hide me in His secret place, the Lord shall hide me in the midst of trouble; He shall hide me.. I played that track over and over again. With my head phones clung to my ears and my pillow fastened around my head I watched the eyes of my love search my mind and my soul. In the midst of the song our eyes met where I saw pain and agony in his, a man off in a distant land, struggling to find his way back. I wondered if he could see the presence of the Lord in my eyes because I sure felt Him all over and around me, thank you Jesus. With each word that song began to minister to my soul, lifting me higher and higher, equipping me for a battle unknown. The song began to spew out of my mouth, rolling off my tongue like Jell-O, so smooth and so sweet. My love wrapped his arms around me. I threw him a smile and kept on singing. I wanted to let him know that I was somewhere else. I was there in the physical, but spiritually I was with Jesus. When I got up to get a drink of water my Headphones went with me. As I stood in the kitchen the Spirit of the Lord spoke to my spirit and said, "It's so easy to get a divorce, but how easy is it to stay in it?" I thought, okay Lord I here you, but you didn't tell me or show me who this word was for. Immediately I thought about a girlfriend who I had spoken to several weeks before about her divorcing her husband. I was trying to convince her that divorce was the easy way out and easy wasn't always best. I remembered telling her that sometimes God takes us the long and difficult way just so that we would appreciate the blessing once we got it. Many of us take the things that God has given us for granted and don't realize the beauty of those blessings until they are taken away. I drank my water and then climbed the stairs to my room. I lay back down in my spot next to my love. I lay down in the palms of God's hands. The Spirit of the Lord spoke to my spirit and once again He said, "It's so easy to get a divorce, but how easy is it to stay in it?" I went into prayer asking the Lord to reveal to me the person He would have me to deliver this message to and then I quietly fell asleep. When I awoke I could still hear that song singing in my spirit. I laid my CD player aside and picked up my remote control. As I switched back and forth from channel to channel my love opened his eyes and sat up in bed to watch television with me. We began watching a movie about a woman that was involved with a married man and how this stranger who was also married fell in love with her after trying to help her rid herself of that unhealthy relationship. After watching this movie for over an hour I began to think about my own marriage and the problems we were having. I couldn't figure it out. Eddie and I had loved each other practically our whole lives, so why was there this distant feeling between us? Why haven't we been able to at least communicate to each other for the last year and a half? We have always talked about any and everything, except now it was different. He didn't want to hear what I had to say and I grew tired of being ignored, so silence crept into our marriage and we became as two strangers on the street. Eddie wasn't just my husband or lover, he was my best friend and confidant, so it hurt really bad to lose this. In the midst of my thoughts I felt as though I was being separated from myself. It was as if I could feel the Lord wrapping His arms around me, rocking me from side to side, sprinkling me with His grace. I began to feel my mouth moving and the words that came out of it were not my own. I was fully aware that the Lord wasn't just in the room, He was in control.

Eddie, look at me. What is it Diane? You have been quiet for the last few days and I can feel that there is something wrong here. Diane once again, you don't know what you're talking about. Eddie just be honest and tell me what you have been trying to spit out. I don't have anything to say, if I did then I would tell you, but I don't. Eddie why don't you tell me what or who has caused us to become strangers? I don't know what you're talking about Diane. Is it another woman? Why is it that every time we have problems you contribute it to being another woman? Eddie why do you keep answering my questions with a question? Because you can't handle the truth! Whatever you feel you have to tell me Eddie, I can handle it and I will understand. No you won't, so leave it alone! I really don't want to talk about it anymore. Eddie, since you're insisting on being evasive then I'll tell you what the problem is. The Lord continued to rock me back and forth, cradling me in His arms. I could see myself, but I couldn't feel myself. Each word I spoke was weighted in God's grace. Eddie tried to ignore me, he focused his attention onto the television and my attention was focused on the Lord. Eddie the problem came about when I began to seek the Lord for myself. I spent a lot of time with Jesus and you became jealous. You couldn't figure out why I changed or why I was different. You didn't and you still don't understand why I give my all where Jesus is concerned. You feel as though I don't understand you anymore so you abandoned me because our conversation was no longer the same. You've met someone that you think you're in love with. You have tried to fill your life with her to forget about me, but you can't. You've been with her sexually, consummating an unlawful marriage, something you said you would never do. You've thought seriously about leaving me because you felt I was no longer the person you married and that our marriage was too far gone to be saved, and now the scars from infidelity stare you in the face every time you look in the mirror. You feel as though you are no good to anyone, not even yourself. Now you feel broken and torn physically, mentally, and spiritually. You've tried to tell me, but the words never made it past your lips and you told yourself over and over again that I would never understand because you don't even understand. After the last word slid off my tongue I slowly lifted my head. When I glanced over at Eddie his innocent baby face was now stained with guilt and soaked with tears. That's when I knew the words that flowed out of my mouth spoke truth. The truth came from his heart by the Spirit of the Lord. There was this peace over me that I can't describe. I searched my soul for a man named anger, but I couldn't find him. I saw what was happening and I heard what was said, but I was not in control; the Lord was. Eddie looked at me, placed his head in my lap and wept. Diane I am so sorry. I never meant to hurt you. I love you and I want my wife back. Please forgive me and don't walk away from me. I didn't really pay Eddie too much attention while he was speaking because I was still in awe with the way in which God moved. Not only was I in awe, but somewhat in shock. Eddie continued to apologize, but I couldn't respond. The Holy Spirit was my protector and my shield. The entire conversation bounced off me like bulletproof glass repelling the bullet. Soon after, my mind began to fill with questions of who, what, when, where, and why. Who it was turned out to be someone I knew and worked with, Katrina was her name. The act of infidelity was the what. The answer to when happened before I could've ever imagined and also during the times I was with my Father. The where was never mentioned and the why said, because I decided to pick up my cross to follow Jesus.

I left the room and proceeded down the stairs to my living room couch where I stretched out my fragile body. Eddie followed begging for my forgiveness. I just lay there staring into the ceiling as if I was going to see directly into the throne room of God. Diane I wish you would talk to me. Eddie, right now I can't even say that I like you so please leave me alone. Can you ever forgive me? Can you promise to stay away from her and be faithful to me? Eddie sat there looking dumbfounded. Diane I can't make that promise. Why not! Because I fell in love with her and although it's over between us I would still like to keep her as a friend. Then you've lost me as your wife. Diane, please don't say that. What do you want from me Eddie? I want you to forgive me. Well I want you to leave! Diane I can tell you that if I find that I'm not going to be faithful then I will leave, but please give me another chance. I tuned Eddie out and closed my eyes. I needed some time to myself, so he left and for the remainder of the day I laid in silence making several attempts to gain some type of understanding from this entire situation. Several hours passed by and the anointing began to subside. I began to feel the after effects of the dagger that was shoved into my back that I didn't feel initially. I cried out to my Savior for His mercy and His help. Lord, please don't leave me now. I can't do this by myself. I can't handle this. Help me Lord! Please help me. The pain was real. Anger, hatred, confusion, and contempt numbed my brain. Tears swelled in my eyes and the beats of my heart felt as if they were punching holes into my chest. Beads of sweat were popping up all over my body. Thunder rumbled in my stomach up to my mouth, releasing murderous screams. I felt as if the walls were caving in on me. My only thought was divorce. According to God's Word, because of Eddie's adultery I was free to leave this unequally yoked marriage. I saw it as a way to erase all the pain he caused me. How could he? Why would he do this to us? Every time I thought about how much I loved and cared for him the thoughts of rejection and humiliation pounced on my head. I screamed out in agony. What difference does it make, you love to be hurt and you hurt to be loved; I'm going to hurt if I stay and I'm going to hurt if I leave, so what do I do? Then I heard the Spirit of the Lord say, "It's so easy to get a divorce, but how easy is it to stay in it?" Oh my God! The Word you gave me this morning was for me? I found myself questioning the Lord. Father why did you let this happen? I gave you my life. I have done all that you have asked of me. How could this have happened? Why me Lord? Why, Why, Why! Now I was really confused because that thing that I wanted to do, I could not do, and that thing that I felt I could not bring myself to do, I had to do. I thought about picking up a gun and killing them both. I often wondered how a person could get so enraged to cause harm to another individual and now here I am faced with my own dilemma. Thoughts of them together tormented my mind and pretty soon I couldn't take it anymore. My whole world had been snatched away from me. I was stripped of my life, my love, and everything that had to do with me. I found myself slowly climbing the stairs to my room with hate in my heart. Things were beginning to make sense. The reason why Eddie was so sick and mean spirited while we were in the Bahamas was due to his sin. His heart wasn't right and his eyes were darkened with the image of another woman. I remembered the time he circled that block while we were working and we picked her up and took her to work. I now felt like an idiot. He had the nerve to pick up his girlfriend with his wife in the car. I began thinking about the times I left town and the uneasy feelings I had concerning Eddie when I returned. I always felt that some woman was involved some how and now I know why. Had she been in my bed also? Things were beginning to come together. I thought back on the time I caught him riding her in our Corvette with the top down. They were laughing and having a good time. When I stopped him he said he saw her on the bus stop and picked her up to take her home. I knew then that something wasn't right, but I had the kids in the car and that's the only reason I held my peace. Lord, please help me, this pain is real and I feel like the bottom just fell from under me. When I entered my bedroom my eyes rested on the place where I kept my 9 mm automatic weapon. I picked it up and held it in my hand. I thought about how I could go to her home, quickly pull the trigger and wipe her and Eddie from existence. However, the love of God quickly rose up in me and I tossed the gun aside and wept. I went into my office that I used as my prayer closet. I pleaded with the Lord to give me direction and after a short time a soft still voice moved throughout my soul. It was the Lord. He said, "Forgive." I was so startled by what He said I actually stopped crying for a moment. When it finally registered as to what He was asking of me I was thrown into a rage. My weeps turned into screams and eventually my screams melted into silent tears. Lord I know what you've asked of me and because I love you I will obey you. Lord you know that I could never hurt anyone. Why is it that no one cares about me? Why is it that people have done nothing but hurt me all of my little insignificant life? All I want to do is love like you love Lord. I could never hurt that woman and I most certainly couldn't hurt Eddie. I love him, but I don't know if I am strong enough to get through all of this. I don't know if I can live with the fact that he cheated on me. I don't know if I want to. I cried so much that my face swelled twice its normal size. My eyes were weary and my body was weakened as if I had been in a battle for quite some time. I laid down hoping that I would awake and realize that this was all just an ugly dream. I closed my eyes and that song began to minister to my spirit all over again. For the many times I've fallen, yet you forgave me, thank you. Lord I thank you.

I heard sounds of laughter off in the distance. I thought I was dreaming, but I wasn't, it was my children, Xavier and Kayla. They were laughing and joking with their father. As I slowly opened my swollen eyes I gazed around the room trying to figure out where I was. I didn't understand why I felt so worn out and weak. Before I could plant my feet on the ground my mind played an instant replay concerning the turn of events from that morning and instantly my thoughts were disfigured and the hole in my heart widened. The pain crippled me and I fell to the floor weeping in silence. Lord I know what you are telling me to do, but I need you to help me with this one. Why would you have me to stay with this man? Do you know what he has done to me? Do you know what he has done to our family? He has ruined everything. I needed to get out because I couldn't be around him. I didn't want to look at him, but then I thought about my children. I knew that they would suspect something right away and I didn't want them to be effected by this nonsense. I tried to clear my face so that I could at least make my presence known to them. I proceeded down the stairs to the kitchen where they all were assembled. Immediately, the kids looked at me as if I were an alien that fell out of space. If I looked anything like I was feeling I am sure they knew that there was a problem. Eddie attempted several times to talk to me as if nothing had happened, however, I couldn't speak. The pain and anger inside of me had silenced me. Every time I looked at him I wanted to vomit. After a while I just couldn't take it anymore, so I went back to my four-cornered room where I didn't have to look at the problem. This was where I spent most of my days and as each day crept by my pain grew worse. Eddie and I slept in separate rooms and held no conversation. I stayed home from work for weeks because the rumor concerning Eddie's infidelity quickly spread throughout the department, which left me looking like the stupid-naïve wife. We worked together in the same precinct as partners while Katrina worked in headquarters. I had always kept my personal life private, now I was left humiliated and shamed before the entire police department. Now I felt my perfect marriage was not so perfect and I became an easy target for ridicule and scorn. I didn't want to show my face to anyone and I hadn't made my mind up as to what I was going to do with my marriage. If my marriage ended, then so did our partnership and relationship at work? I had a lot to think about and I needed to be alone without the eyes of my ex-love peering into my soul that used to be connected to his. I spent some of my days searching for Katrina at her office, but I couldn't locate her. I drove down her street desperately searching for her home for which I had no address. I wanted her to face me to see the damage that her and Eddie caused by their foolish and selfish acts. I needed to let her know how I felt. The Spirit of the Lord was telling me to forgive and my flesh was telling me to break every bone in her body. Needless to say, I leaned more towards following the leading of my flesh. I took a lot of long drives alone and made excuses to get out of the house to get away from Eddie. I drove around for hours and was on my way home until I remembered I needed some milk. I stopped at the market not too far from my home. When I came out a strange man was standing next to my car as I was trying to get in. Excuse me Ms., but are you Eddie's wife? Yes I am. Can I talk to you? About what! Slowly, he lowered his head and I knew in my spirit who he was. My name is Frank, Minister Frank and I need to tell you about your husband, but there's something I don't understand. What's that? You are too beautiful to receive such treatment from him. I stood in silence trying to figure this man out. Your husband has hurt me badly and you need to know what kind of man you're married to. I stopped him in the midst of his conversation and questioned him. Are you Katrina's husband? His eyes bulged with a surprised look on his face. You know! Yes I know all about the affair. I realized he was trying to hurt Eddie by springing this on me, and I was angered by his lack of concern for my feelings in all of this. However, at his request I prayed with him and we went our separate ways. When he told me he was a minister I knew this was an attack straight from the pit of hell on the both of us. When I got home I thought about his ill intentions and prayed for him.

I had gotten over the shock, although the pain was still very real and the scars on my heart felt as if they would be there for all eternity. I felt as though I was walking down the street one morning enjoying the scenery without a care in the world, then all of a sudden I stepped into a hole and landed dead smack in the middle of hell. I went into prayer asking the Lord to show me or tell me what to do because I could no longer live the way I was living. Lord, I don't know how to live with this thing hanging over my head. I really don't think I can do this. I could feel my spirit and my soul weeping within me. My heart wept even more. Then the Spirit of the Lord spoke to me and said, "Yes you can do this." Lord I can't. I have tried, but I can't. Then the Spirit of the Lord spoke again, but this time He had my full attention. Yes you can do this, when I chose you for salvation you weren't perfect either. Whether you are guilty of infidelity, gluttony, or murder, sin is sin. What he has done is no different than the sinful things you did when you were in the world because sin is sin. Eddie has called out to me and I forgave him just as I forgave you. You say that you want to be like me, but you have not forgiven when I told you to forgive, so just as I forgave you, you have to forgive him and then go to the woman in question and forgive her. I was humbled by the voice and presence of the Lord. I sat there with my mouth hung wide open because not only did I have to embrace my bleeding heart, I had to embrace the woman who stole the love of my life. I knew that this request was of the Lord because the only thought I had concerning her was something bad. Forgiveness wasn't included, but there was no way I would disobey the Lord again. I realize now that I hadn't obeyed God in the first place. I was not capable of doing this by myself and I wasn't ready. I asked the Lord to prepare me to do this, to take the anger from my heart, and prepare her heart to receive what I had to say so that when the time came I would respond in a godly way and not in a way that Diane would handle it. I no longer asked the questions regarding how because I knew that if the Lord requested me to do this, then it was for a reason and it was going to work out for my good because He was going to help me. With each passing day it seemed as though the road I had to take grew longer and longer. It became an uphill battle for me because now I had to deal with me. It was no longer Eddie or what he had done. I realized that I hadn't really forgiven him although I spoke it several times. I only forgave with words because I knew that's what the Lord would have me to do, but real forgiveness comes from the heart and not from the lip. Lord I don't know where this road is taking me, nevertheless, I just want to hold unto you and your promises and be as a blind woman trusting you to guide me through this unfamiliar territory. Lord I thank you for my husband whom I love dearly. Thank you for these rough and terrible times because I know that through them I will grow stronger in you and I know that in all of this there is a blessing waiting for me.

The months flew by like paper in the wind. It wasn't easy, but Eddie and I had begun to work on a new marriage together. To repair the old was too much like throwing something over the debris of our marriage where the evidence of what took place would always be there peeking out at us from time to time. Therefore, we had to start out fresh if our marriage was going to work. It was a little rough in the beginning because he didn't want to offend me and I didn't trust him. I wondered if I could ever trust again. I didn't want to live with doubt knocking on the back of my head every time Eddie left the house or was out a little late. I didn't want to worry about him cheating on me again. Consequently, worry had gotten the best of me. I had made my own prison. I put up walls where nobody and nothing could ever get in to hurt me again. I became cynical and I was beginning to hate myself. The Spirit of the Lord had told me that if I trusted in Him, then I wouldn't have to worry about Eddie. I believed Him although some days were more difficult than others. I even convinced myself that I was ready to talk to Katrina face to face, until the Lord granted me my wish. I got up early one Saturday morning to pay my bills and get some pop-tarts for my snack. I was full of giggles because everything seemed to be working out just fine for me, or at least fine enough to cope with my life. My marriage was finally getting back on track. My heart had begun to heal and Katrina was far from my mind, but I had this weird feeling I was going to bump into her. I quickly dismissed that feeling since I hadn't seen her even after desperately seeking her. As I pulled into the parking lot of the plaza I smiled as the sun shined in my eyes. I sat and listened to the last two minutes of the song playing on the CD player and then blew a kiss to Jesus and told Him thank you. I gathered my bills and exited my vehicle still bouncing and humming the tunes I had just heard. I greeted an elderly woman on the way into the store with a smile. She reminded me of my grandmother, so sweet and fragile. The smile had stretched clear across my face and as the doors slid open my eyes met another pair of eyes. It was her, Katrina and her five children. The smile raced off my face and quickly grabbed a frown along with his cousin called hate. Then came anger and the anger manifested itself into rage. Only this time I could hear the afflicted woman screaming on the inside of me instead of without. My heart burned like fire. I stood there frozen as my mind replayed everything I thought I had buried. Shame flushed her face and she immediately turned her attention to the cashier as she checked out. Everything in me told me to go and give her a piece of my mind. I could no longer hear the Spirit speaking truth to me because I chose to listen to my flesh, which was screaming for me to hurt her. I took one step in her direction and her little girl looked up at me, gave me this inquisitive look and then smiled. The Word of God flashed in my mind, "If anyone offend these little ones, then it would be better for them if a milestone were hung around his neck." I stopped in my tracks and I saw pain in that child's eyes, a pain similar to mine. I chose to stay with my husband, but Katrina's husband left her after she admitted her infidelity. So it wasn't difficult to imagine what those children might be going through. Though my heart was filled with anger I chose walk away. I stormed through the isles, attempting to calm myself by mulling around in the rear of the store. I struggled to fight back tears and the hate that was chewing at my heart. I wanted enough time to pass for her to leave the store so I wouldn't have to look at her face again. After a short time I grabbed a gallon of milk and went to the check out line only to find her still there. How is it possible that she is still here? Who in the world takes this long to check out a small cart of groceries? It just doesn't make any sense. My eyes stared her down to let her know how much I hated her. I didn't want to do that, but my eyes somewhat acted on their own. Katrina wouldn't look at me. She couldn't. When she realized I was standing in the line beside her she hurriedly grabbed her children and her groceries and exited the store. Suddenly I heard the Spirit of the Lord say, "You still aren't ready." I felt terrible. I rushed to my car, laid my head across the seat and cried crocodile tears. Lord I'm sorry. I've messed up again. I thought I was ready to do what you asked of me, but this raggedy flesh keeps getting in the way. I want to forgive, but I need help in doing so. I don't like feeling like this. All of this anger is beginning to affect my walk with you. How can I be an effective witness if I can't complete a simple task as this? Since this happened I haven't been able to pray or think right, so Lord I am asking for your help. Please give me another chance. Lord, please don't leave me. After soaking my seats with saliva and mucus I drove off feeling like the worst person on earth.

Soon the Lord blessed me with His grace and I was able to really forgive Eddie. One year had passed by and I really felt as if I was getting back on track with my life. The sun was shining bright and I decided to take a nice drive by myself. I drove down Main Street and found that the traffic was really congested so I decided to take the side streets. As I turned the corner I saw Katrina standing on a corner waiting for her children to get off the school bus. This time there was no anger, nor was there any contempt for her. I pulled up and beckoned for her to come to my car window. At first she was hesitant in approaching, but she came anyway. I told her that I forgave her and she thanked me. When I drove off I felt as if a huge weight had fallen off my shoulders. At that very moment I was released from the prison I had created for myself. I was free and it was all because I obeyed God. Forgive me Father for taking so long in doing this small thing for you. I know my steps are ordered and I thank you for allowing me to see that I couldn't do this on my own. I know without a doubt that it was by your grace and your mercy that I was able to forgive according to your time and perfect will.

21
9 1 1

I climbed out of my bed early to get all of my chores done. I didn't want time to catch up with me because this was the day that Sharon and I were going to drive to Canada to eat at this really nice restaurant called Mandarins for her birthday and I didn't want to hear her yap at me about always being late. After finishing my cleaning I ran some errands and paid my bills. On the way home I drove by my dad's upholstery shop where, as usual, he was sitting in the window at his sewing machine. I blew and he lifted up his head and waved. I traveled around the corner, drove by mama and daddy's house and blew so that mama would know I came through. Once I got home I showered, got dressed and called my mama. I wanted to make sure I told her to have a safe trip before she left for the Caribbean Festival in Toronto, but I was too late. She had already left. The road was long and the scenery was so beautiful I couldn't have imagined a more perfect picture. As the music softly played in my ear I wondered about life and my place in it. I thought about the love of God, where He has brought me from, and what He's brought me through. I've learned that as long as I keep my mind stayed on Jesus I can't fail. I now know what it really means to love as Jesus loves, that unwavering, uncompromising love, to love in spite of, the true love of Jesus. After all, God loved us so much that He gave His only begotten Son and in spite of our constant failures and short comings the Lord still loves us, so how dare we love any less than that. Are we greater than God that we can't open up our hearts to forgive and love as He has loved? No. We are as little nothings and without God we can do nothing. I glanced at the cars in the front of us and in the rear hopelessly looking for a familiar face. My mother and my Aunt Cindy were somewhere on the Q.E.W., 30 minutes from where I was headed. I knew they were nearby because they only had about a 20-minute jump on me and they drive like turtles. Sam was also on his way to Toronto. However, I don't know when he left or who he was with, but anxiously I peered into every car that passed by me, searching for their faces to throw them a wave, a smile, or even a simple blow of my horn to let them know that I'm always happy to see them. It felt good to be able to get away from everything, the hustle and bustle of life even if it was just for a day. Everyone thought we were crazy to drive a few hours to Canada for dinner, but the both of us needed a change of scenery so it wouldn't have mattered if we had to drive four hours, we were still going. Sharon was singing along with the gospel tunes that had filled my car. The song soothed my mind and before I knew it the words to the song was rolling off my tongue. Our hearts were filled with music while our bellies roared with laughter all the way to Canada and on into the restaurant. There we sat peeling jumbo shrimp while reminiscing about our past, God's continuous blessings over our lives, and marriage. We found that our experiences in growing up were quite similar and that our mothers had to have grown up in the same household. We agreed, while you're yet young you really don't understand most of the decisions your parents make concerning you. You fight and push against everything they say and do because you don't feel they hear you or understand anything about you, not realizing that they have been there, did that, and done that. Now that I'm all grown up and have a family of my own I understand why they did the things they did. Raising a child isn't easy, so you do the best you can with what you have and pray that child doesn't stray. I can now say I appreciate the way my parents raised me. I'm glad they were strict because had they not been, who knows where I'd be today.

I pushed away from the table to get my dessert and Sharon, of course, had something to say. Girl you know you needn't get anymore food! I knew it was impossible for me to squeeze any more food into my stomach because I had already unsnapped my pants in a desperate attempt to allow myself to breathe. I needed an excuse to go and let the waitress know it was Sharon's birthday so they could sing Happy Birthday to her. When the time came several people approached our table clapping hands and singing as if they were in a parade of some sort. They placed a lobster hat on top of her head and gave her a piece of cake and some Jell-O. I couldn't stop laughing because she was so embarrassed her face turned red. On the way back we shared the words to more songs and laughed when we didn't know them, but made up words in their place. You know how you get into a song and the next thing you know you are on stage in front of a million people tearing the song up, but then it comes to a part you don't really know, so you say something that sounds like it; well that's what we did. I was about twenty minutes from entering back into the U.S.A when my pager went off. My home number appeared with a 911 message. What's wrong Diane? Oh nothing. Eddie always pages me 911 when he wants me to return the page immediately. Well do you want to use my telephone when you drop me off at home? No, it will only take me 10 minutes to get home from your house, so I'll wait. We continued singing and talking when my pager went off again 555-1234...911...911...911. It went off three more times all with the same message so I put the pedal to the metal in an attempt to get home. While Sharon was singing I was pretending not to be worried and began talking to the Lord. Father I know my mother and Aunt Cindy left for Toronto by themselves, I pray that they haven't been in an accident. Lord I know you are watching over all of us, so I know everything is just fine. Thank you for everything. The urge to call home grew stronger and stronger in my heart so I quickly got off at the exit to take Sharon home, but before I made it to her house I pulled over on Main St. near a pay phone. As I dialed the number I continued to thank the Lord. Hello Xavier is daddy paging me? No mommy. Daddy left and he said he'd be back in a minute. Well who's paging me? I am. Is everything alright? I don't know mama; Officer Joe was knocking on our door looking for you or daddy. What did he want? I don't know, I told him that you left town for the day and that daddy wasn't here, but he said it was an emergency and that he needed to get in touch with you as soon as possible. Well did he say why? No mommy that's why I paged you. I paged daddy too because Officer Joe had tears in his eyes. My hands began to shake and I tried desperately not to worry. Okay, I'll call Officer Joe at the station. Is everything okay mommy? Of course, everything is fine. I am sure of it. I'll be home soon. After hanging up the telephone I began to look for another quarter. It's probably not even an emergency. Lord which one of my family members got into trouble this time. I'm tired of bailing people out of jail. The telephone rang and the report technician answered. Hello Mickey is Officer Joe in the station house? She fumbled with her words before answering me. Yes, hold on a second. I looked back at the car and Sharon was still singing, bopping her head back and forth, and then I remembered the good time we had. I began to wonder where Eddie was. I missed him and I couldn't wait to see him. Hello, this is Officer Joe how can I help you? Joe this is Diane and I'm calling to find out what the emergency is. My kids said that you were at my house. Yes I was. Well what's the problem? Silence answered me. Joe can you hear me? Yes Diane I can hear you. Well what kind of emergency warrants you to go to my house looking for me and upsetting my kids? I apologize for that, but I needed to ask a question. What is it? Do you have a father named Sam Saint James Sr.? Yes. And does he live at 162 Park Place Blvd. Yes he does. Well I'm sorry to have to tell you this Diane, but your father is dead, he had a heart attack. Dead! What do you mean dead! I didn't take him serious at all. I even smirked when I said you must have the wrong person, I just saw my dad and my dad wasn't ill, so I know you've got the wrong person. Well that's the identification he had in his wallet including your Brother Sam's emergency contact numbers. Just then my thoughts began to spin uncontrollably. All of a sudden people and things around me didn't seem all that important. Hallow screams emanated from the pits of my stomach and bolts of pain ran throughout my entire body exasperating my lungs and draining the strength from my legs, which were already crippled. The next thing I knew I was on the ground. From that point on everything went in slow motion. I saw Sharon exit the car running toward me, with a look of bewilderment. Officer Joe was screaming through the receiver. Diane where are you so I can come and get you? Sharon attempted to pick me up off the ground, but she couldn't lift me. Diane what's wrong? My-my-my dad. What's wrong with your dad? He's de----. I couldn't force the words out of my mouth. I choked off mucus and tears. I couldn't speak so I screamed. Oh Lord, say it ain't so. Please Lord, say it ain't so. Please don't let my daddy be dead. Come on Diane get up. I couldn't move. I didn't want to move and then I heard Eddie's voice off in a distance calling me. I thought I was losing my mind. I heard Eddie's voice, but how can that be? I needed him to hold me and I needed him to make everything okay, but it had to be in my head. Then suddenly his hands wrapped around my waist and picked me up off the ground and I knew he was real. I thought...how did you find me and where did you come from Eddie? Tears fell from Sharon's face as Eddie carried me away and placed me in his truck. I pounded the dashboard with my fists as I fought desperately to make myself wake up from this terrible nightmare. When my hands began to swell and throb with pain I realized that I couldn't make this thing go away. I wasn't dreaming. This was reality, but how and why? Oh God why my dad? Please give him another chance. Please, let him live. I attempted to settle myself so I could pray. Dear God I know I haven't done all that you've required of me and I know I'm not always obedient, so Lord I'm asking for forgiveness for all of my sins. I truly repent. If there is anything in me that isn't like you Lord I pray that you take it out of me right now. I love you with my whole heart and soul and I'm going to praise you even in this trouble. Nothing can separate me from you Oh God. So I pray to you dear Lord, please bring my father back. I'm not sure if he accepted you as Lord over his life, however, that's between you and him. If it's Your will let this all be a mistake. Only you can do it. You hold the power of life and death in your hands. I don't care what the doctors say and I don't care what it looks like. My faith in you is greater than any problem and I believe you for a miracle, but Lord I'm going to pray that your perfect will be done and not mine. When I lifted my head my clothes were soaked from the outpour of tears that flooded my entire being. As Sharon drove off in my car Eddie wiped his face clean and jumped in the truck. Eddie attempted to console me although my mind was completely numb. I continued to pray inwardly as Eddie slowly turned the corners. He drove very delicately so he wouldn't shake or rattle me as if I was this glass figurine sitting on the hood of the truck. I had convinced myself that everything was going to be okay and this was all some sort of mistake. I believed God was going to show up and baffle the minds of the doctors and everyone around.

Eddie how did you find me? How did you know I was on Main St.? I didn't, it was just a coincidence. I was at the Pier down the street having a drink and talking with a few people about what happened. I just found out not too long ago and I was trying to make some sense out of all of this. I was trying to figure out how I was going to tell you. I was on my way home when I saw the car and then I looked around and saw you on the ground. Eddie how did you find out? Xavier kept paging me and when I called him back he told me that Officer Joe was looking for us. I called Officer Joe at the station and he told me, but I don't understand how you found out. The same way you did. Officer Joe told you over the telephone! Yes. I told him not to tell you! Why would he do something like that? I turned my head toward the side and cried. We drove the rest of the way in silence. As we pulled into the parking lot I could feel the peace of the Lord all over me. Eddie grabbed hold of my hand and walked me into the hospital. The security guards stopped us at the door, inquired as to what our business at the hospital was and then demanded us to move our vehicle. Eddie quietly offered an explanation to the guard. I'm a police officer and my wife just lost her father and after I walk her in I will move my vehicle. The guard squared his shoulders, grabbed hold of his belt, and began raising his voice. I don't care what you're doing; you will move your vehicle right now! Eddie burst into a rage like a cage-less lion and before I knew it they were screaming at each other. Eddie I really don't need this right now. Eddie swallowed his pride and stepped away from the guard and the guard opened the door for us. Eddie took me to a small room while he searched for a nurse. Lord I know you're here with me. Thank you for answering my prayers, and I thank you for your love. Thank you for your grace and your mercy and your tender care. When the doctor walked in a nurse was with him. I managed to crank out a smile at the familiar faces that stood before me. They sat down and asked me to join them. I refused and did not move from the place where my feet had been planted. Dr. James had tears in his eyes as he began to speak. Diane, you are the first family member to show up and the only other family member we were able to contact was Sam Jr. He's on his way, but I realize he was just about in Toronto when he received the call, so we need you to identify the body. I stood there watching as each word rolled off his tongue. It all seemed so strange. I was accustomed to coming into the hospital while on duty and working with these same people on cases just like my own only this time I was on the opposite side of the fence. I was there when people received bad news about the death of a loved one, but now I'm on the receiving end and it doesn't seem right. The peace that was over me began to lift, not of its own doing, but of my own. Anger filled my heart and I could hear myself screaming inwardly…What do you mean identify the body? I didn't come here for that. I came expecting a miracle! Tears burned tracks across my face as I stared through those familiar faces sitting before me. I asked what happened. Dr. James lowered his head and began to explain. Your father came into the emergency room for a bad toothache. We called dentistry down here to check him out, gave penicillin, and a referral to see the dentist. He left and passed out beyond the doors from an apparent heart attack. I questioned if they were sure his death was caused by a heart attack and they felt 100% sure of his cause of death. They left to give me a few minutes to myself before I was called to identify the body. Eddie stood outside the room when a strange woman walked up demanding that we listen to her story, insisting that the doctor was lying. Don't believe them because they are lying to cover their tracks, I saw what happened. I didn't want to hear anything she had to say. I thought she was crazy, nonetheless, she continued with her story. I saw the man when he walked out and he was fine. A few minutes later I went to smoke a cigarette and I saw the man slumped over the wheel of his car. When I went back inside I told the nurse at the desk that there was a man slumped over the wheel of his car and she said okay, but didn't do anything about it. Shortly after, I was called to a room to be seen by the doctor. I was examined and about an hour and a half later I was released. When I got outside I noticed that the man was still slumped over the wheel. At first I thought he might have been drunk or asleep, but it just didn't feel right so again I told the nurse at the desk. This time I demanded they do something and I quickly got their attention. They went out and checked on him. The key was in the ignition; however, he never got a chance to start the car up. They dragged him from the car to the doors of the emergency room and tried to work on him, but the man was dead. Eddie took her name and telephone number and the woman walked away. I didn't want to hear it. It was much more acceptable for me to believe that my daddy died of natural causes than fowl play or someone's carelessness. I stood there in the same spot trying to gather my thoughts and then I heard someone walking through the hall. The clunking of the shoes echoed throughout the entire hallway. They were hard, heavy, and loud. I wondered who it could be. As the echo grew closer I affixed my eyes to the frame of the doorway, peering into the hall. It was Sam. As a child, whenever Sam was upset his nostrils would spread open as if two holes were dug out where his nose used to be just like my dads. As he passed by I noticed the two holes were so wide they had joined together. His eyes were red from the tears he'd shed on the way to the hospital, but to save face he wiped them away and stood up straight to walk in strong like the man that once was, who is now lying on the table dead. He looked so much like daddy that the mere sight of him paralyzed me with fear. I thought he would say something. I thought we would fall into each other's arms and cry, but pain had crushed his face. Not a word was spoken between us, not a gesture, nor tear. He passed by, viewed the body and left. The time it took for him to pass by the doorway and the meeting of our eyes is all we did to embrace each other on that terrible night.

The nurse called me in and I entered the room very slowly. I stood over him as if I had never seen him before and I washed his face with my tears. I kissed his forehead and as my lips touched his skin I cried heavily because I couldn't remember the last time I kissed my dad and it hurt me to my heart. As I wiped his face dry I laid my hands on him and began to pray. The rubbery surface of his face was as cold as ice. My dad was gone. It was evident that he was no longer in the body that lay before me so still and lifeless. I touched his chest, hopelessly scanning for a pulse, only it wasn't so soft anymore. It had hardened from the sting of death. My legs were hurting me terribly and I hated the fact that I was indeed handicapped. As my strength gave way I sat down in the chair beside him, placed my head between my legs and wept ever so sadly. Dad I love you. I can't remember the last time I told you that besides writing it on a birthday or Father's day card, but I really love you. Forgive me Lord for taking my father for granted. Forgive me for the times I gave him a hard time and forgive me for being so difficult. Dad I know I've caused you to have headaches at times, but I appreciate the way you and mom kept me. I respect you for the man you were, the father you will always be, and most of all I respect you for the values you instilled in me. I wouldn't be where I am today had it been any different. Yes, I fought against you and mom once I reached a certain age, but now that I'm older with children of my own I know it was all for my good. I'm really going to miss not having you around. I sat in silence for a while staring at the floor, wondering how I was going to form the words to tell my mother who was almost three hours away that her husband, my dad was dead. How could I explain this? She shouldn't be told over the telephone, nor should she have to go through this. What am I going to do? Sam's gone and now I have to bear this responsibility all on my own. Realizing what had to be accomplished, I let go of my anger, wiped away my tears and stood up. Dad you always told me because I was the oldest I had to take responsibility for my brother and sisters. I will not let you down. I will take care of all of them, especially mom. I rubbed my hand across his gray and white hair that I was responsible for giving him, kissed him one last time and left. When I opened the door I could hear the voices of family and friends chattering and murmuring throughout the hallway. I wanted to avoid them all, but as I attempted to walk by unnoticed the brace on my leg seemed to be clicking louder than usual and everyone turned my way. Aunt Betsy burst into tears and grabbed me. She wrapped her arms around my neck, choked the air out of me and spread mucus all up the sides of my face as she attempted to console me. I hugged her and let her go only to be bombarded with more hugs and tears which began to rip through the shield I thought I put up when I left my dad's side. I felt my strength going and more tears arising. I had to get out. I needed to get away, but my mother-in-law grabbed hold of me and would not let me go. Aunts, Uncles, and cousins surrounded me like buzzards circling over the dead. I searched over the faces for my sisters, Lottie and Michelle, but they weren't there. Eddie had gone to get them and had not yet returned. I came to the conclusion that I really needed my mother more than ever. I pulled away from everyone only to hear, don't go far, we are here for you and we don't want you to be alone. I'm not going anywhere; I just need some air. When they turned their backs I saw the opportunity to escape. I rushed out the doors and I went back into the hospital on the opposite side of them. When I slid in a corner near the pay phones I heard them questioning as to my whereabouts. They ran by me not realizing where I was. Finally I exhaled. I lifted the telephone to make the phone calls I dreaded. My grandma and Uncle Ted had to be told; only I didn't want to tell grandma on the telephone. She was old and I wanted someone with her. Slowly I dialed the number. Hello grandma, how are you?

I'm fine baby, how's everyone? My lip quivered but I managed to push out a few words without spilling them. We are all just fine. She mumbled the words emm humph. How's your daddy doing with his business? He has been doing real good grandma, but I called because I need Uncle Teddy's telephone number. Why, what's wrong? Oh nothing. What makes you think that there is something wrong? I can hear it in your voice. Really grandma, everything is fine. I just need to ask Uncle Teddy something. Okay, its 555- wait a minute. Oh shoot! Now why can't I ever remember that number? It's 555-2212. Naw, that can't be it. While she searched her memory for the number I prayed for her to hurry up because I couldn't fight the tears back any longer. My nose was running badly, but I didn't want to risk blowing my nose or sniffling because then she would know that I was crying. I got it! The number is 555-6423. Thanks grandma. Do you need anything else? No grandma that's it. Well all right, you make sure you tell your mama and daddy I said hello. The word daddy nearly knocked the telephone out of my hand. My mind was screaming daddy; I aint got no daddy no more! Although my thoughts rebelled, my lips complied with what was right. I will definitely tell them. Okay baby you take care. Good-bye grandma I'll talk to you soon. Okay baby. I love you grandma. I love you too baby. Hurriedly, I hung up the telephone, took a deep breath and dialed the number grandma had given me. After explaining everything to Uncle Teddy he broke down and we cried together. Uncle Teddy can you go over and tell grandma what happened. I didn't think it would be good for her health to tell her on the telephone. She is already curious because I had to ask her for your telephone number. Yes, I'll tell her just as soon as I get my head together. My baby brother, oh my God, why my brother? He paused and then words just slid off his lips. Where is your mother? She's in Toronto and we haven't been able to reach her yet. You mean to tell me she doesn't know! No not yet. Can you give me the area code and telephone number to the hospital so I can find out what happened? After I gave him the telephone number we said good-bye. As I hung up the telephone I began thinking about my mother. We had left several messages at the hotel for her to call us immediately, but she hadn't returned to her room. I saw her face so vivid and full of life, glowing as her laughter rang throughout my mind. Then I heard a woman's cry, shattering the solemn vision of my mother, bringing me back to reality. It was Lottie. Eddie had finally found her. I folded my arms, took a deep breath and went to her side. I watched as family and others crowded her as they did me. Wailing arms surrounded her and then stretched over to me. Once again I escaped. I limped to the ramp leading to the emergency room and found myself hobbling down to the lower level. As I walked across the parking lot pain ran through my legs forcing me to find a place to sit. I came to a small tree standing alone in the midst of chaos. It was there that I found shelter and peace. I began to gather my thoughts in an attempt to make some sense out of everything that had transpired in the last four hours of my life. When I left home that afternoon before my dinner trip everything was fine. Who knew that when I waved to my dad as I drove by that it would be the last time I would see him alive. I should've stopped and talked. If I hadn't gone to dinner I could've been here for him. If I had gone to the hospital with him he'd probably still be alive. Why did this have to happen? Why him? Why now? Violently I stabbed holes in the dirt with a small branch that had fallen from the tree. I made a small grave in the dirt up under the lonely tree where I sat and buried my broken, battered, and bruised heart. It was there that I completed the wall around me to protect me and keep me separated from everyone else. I thought that as long as I kept my heart buried in that dirt, then no one and nothing could ever hurt me again. I saw my spiritual mother, Sister Bradley, approaching. When I saw her I actually smiled. Her face glowed like an angel in heaven. She was my peace in the midst of the storm. Sister Bradley sat down beside me in silence as I continued to bury my heart. She placed her hand over mine to keep me from stabbing holes into the dirt. Sister Diane I need to know if you're okay and I want you to know if you need anything I'm always here for you. I couldn't lift my head; however, I found enough strength to respond. I'm fine. I don't know how you found out so fast, but I thank you for coming. Diane I can feel your pain and I just want you to know that God loves you. He won't leave you nor will He forsake you, so although you feel alone right now He's with you. God does everything for a reason. Well, why did this have to happen? Why my dad? Did I do something wrong? No Diane. Well then what is the problem? I'm losing one family member after the next, my marriage is falling apart, my legs are crippled, and now my dad is gone. One minute he was there, and then "poof" he was gone. Don't torment yourself with questions that may never be answered just trust Him because all things are done for your good to accomplish God's perfect will for your life. Sister Bradley talked with me a while, told me to be encouraged, and then she got up and left. She gave me exactly what I needed, a word of encouragement. She didn't beat me up or flood me with tears, but she gave me her love and reminded me who I was in Christ. I was able to lift my head now and when I did I saw Eddie staggering across the parking lot weeping. He fell at my side and embraced me. Diane I'm glad I found you; believe me when I say I know how you feel. I'm here for you, so please don't shut me out now. I moved my mouth to speak, but my words left me some time ago, disabling my use for conversation. I came down here to tell you that I can't reach Michelle by telephone, so if you know exactly what building she's working in I'll go and pick her up. I looked at him and retrieved the words, I'll go with you. We rode the entire way in silence. I kept going over in my mind how I was going to tell my baby sister that our father was dead. How would I make her understand when I don't even understand? We entered the juvenile detention complex where she worked and finally found the building where she was stationed. Diane I know this is hard for you, so if you want me to go in and tell her, I will? No. This is something I have to do. Eddie rang the bell and a young white guy peeped through the small window and hesitated in opening the door. Can I help you with something? Yes I am the sister of Michelle Saint James and we have a family emergency. What kind of emergency do you have because we don't have anyone to replace her tonight? Eddie stepped up to the window to talk with the man. Listen sir! Michelle's dad just passed away and she needs to come to the hospital right away, so I personally don't care about you finding a replacement for her or not! Just hold on a second buddy, I'll go and get her, but I'm not opening the door. Eddie and I stood outside of the door peeking through the window, watching Michelle stroll down the hallway toward us. Her face looked puzzled as she searched her thoughts to figure out who was at the door for her at that time of night. As she got closer our eyes met and the instant she saw me fear colored her face pale. Her stare pierced my heart and I looked away as tears began to surface in my eyes again. As she fumbled for the key to open the door she questioned me over and over again. What's wrong Diane? When I lowered my eyes and didn't answer she wept at my silence. Diane is mama okay? Did she get hurt on the way to Toronto? No Michelle, it's not mama. It's daddy. When the tears rolled down my face she screamed and ran down the hallway to her office. Eddie and I chased her and found her on the floor under her desk. Her co-workers were attempting to console her and the man who answered the door was standing over her telling her to be quiet because she was upsetting the residents. I wanted to punch him for being so inconsiderate, but decided to leave instead. Eddie picked Michelle up off the floor and walked her out. I grabbed her purse and left. Eddie drove away with a face of steel and I sat with my head hung low. In between her moans and groans Michelle let out loud chaotic sounds mixed with questions all the way to the hospital.

Lottie and I walked Michelle into the room where our father lay. Silently we stood over him refusing to look each other in the eye. It was too painful. Lottie stroked his hair continuously. Michelle angered, set her hand on his chest as I sat in the chair beside him. We weren't in there five minutes before I was called away by family to talk to my mother on the telephone. Everyone piled behind me as I grabbed the telephone as if I was the only one capable of completing this task. I heard her sniffling before I said hello, which made it difficult for me to hold my composure. Hello mama. What in the world happened Diane? I began to whine and whimper as a child would. I don't know mama. The doctor's said he had a heart attack. A heart attack! Yes mama, I didn't want you to find out like this. Who told you? Chole called not too long ago. I scanned the faces of the family and found hers. I could have strangled her, but quickly turned away. Diane It's gonna take me a few hours. Nevertheless, I will be there as soon as possible. Please tell the doctors not to move him. Okay mama, but please drive carefully. I did exactly what mama told me to do. I went to the nurse and asked them to wait before transporting my daddy to the morgue. Mrs. Camden we can't wait that long it's ten o'clock and it's already been a few hours. Please wait just a little while longer, my mother will be here soon. It took us a while to get in touch with her. This is her husband we're talking about, so please don't take him away until she's gotten a chance to see him. The nurse lowered her head and with compassion she agreed. Okay, just inform us of her arrival. Shortly after one o'clock in the morning mama walked into the doors of the hospital with Aunt Cindy. Her sisters crowded her and even when they began to cry, she wouldn't. Everyone followed her into the room, all twenty of us. Mama sat in the chair beside the place where my father lay with her eyes affixed on the floor. When she lifted her head and stood up she placed her hand upon his face and buckled at her own screams. Aunt Betsy wrapped her arms around mama's waist and sat her back in the chair. Mama's face didn't crack until she saw daddy lying on the table still and cold. Each of us bowed our heads as mama wept bitterly. The clergyman on call came into the room to talk with us. After his words of wisdom we joined hands and bowed our heads as he prayed for us. Everyone left the room except mama. She wanted some time alone with daddy and afterwards mama gathered everyone together. Aunt Betsy didn't want mama to be alone, but mama didn't want anyone with her. Michelle grabbed mama's hand and decided to go home with her. As I walked out with Eddie mama called out to me. Diane. Yes mama. Are you okay? After clearing my throat I whispered, yes mama. Are you sure? Yes mama, I'll be okay. Mama knew I wasn't necessarily okay, but I was glad she asked. We parted our ways and I got in my vehicle. As Eddie pulled off, he reminded me that we hadn't told the kids. Diane, if you don't want to be the one to tell them, then I'll do it. Thank you Eddie, I just can't handle that right now. I understand, but they already know that something isn't right because people have called our house left and right leaving all kinds of messages on the answering machine. How do you know? Xavier told me the telephone was ringing off the hook when I called to check on him and Kayla. Why would people do that? Well I guess it's not their fault. When we got home Eddie woke up the kids and gave them the news. We all cried together and then went to bed.

22
<u>TROUBLED TIMES</u>

My spirit had quieted and my mind was as still as the pictures on the wall. Eddie had done all the necessary housework, including preparing breakfast. I didn't feel like entertaining any conversation and I didn't want to see anyone. As I made my way down the stairs Xavier and Kayla greeted me with hugs and kisses to let me know how much they loved me. I made my way to the front porch in a t-shirt and pajama pants. I pulled two quarters from my pajama pants pocket and twirled it around in my hand. These quarters were part of my daddy's belongings. It was in his pants pocket. I sat there gazing into the beautiful summer sky, attempting to gather my thoughts so that I could settle my mind. The sun was shining brightly within my eyes, warming the coldness that I allowed to shield my entire being. I thought, gee – my daddy died one year after his daddy. My family had begun to disappear, one after the next. I remember when my grandpa took ill; my daddy gathered up everyone and headed down to Ohio to see about him. The first stroke crippled his right side. The second stroke came and left, but took part of his ability to speak with it. He could no longer preach God's Word, but that didn't stop him from praising God from behind the pulpit where he sat. I remember standing in front of his church preparing myself to sing a song. I sang to the top of my lungs that mornin' and afterward we all went to the church hall for dinner. I walked over to grandpa and was happy to tell him that the Lord saved me. He looked at me, but I don't know if he even heard a word I said. Grandma was mashing up his food, helping him to eat. Food dribbled from his mouth and plastered the sides of his face when he misdirected his fork. Grandma faithfully wiped his face clean. It was then that I realized my grandpa was deteriorating. The ride home was long and quiet. Everyone's head was filled with everyone else's thoughts. Several months later grandpa suffered a third stroke which landed him in a nursing facility and bed ridden. The fourth stroke took him home. I felt as though he gave up on life because we all knew he didn't want to live like that, my grandpa was a prideful man. It was hard for me to see him in that capacity, suffering as he did. Now I struggle with my own thoughts on how my daddy suffered. As I continued to twirl my daddy's quarters in my hand I couldn't help but to imagine him in the car alone.

The heel of his shoes hit the ground – pump, pump, pump, like the beats of a drum in the night. His footprints mark the ground, but as he draws closer to his vehicle, slowly they begin to fade away. Keys jingle as they are pulled from the right pocket. A few quarters escape, jumping to the ground, but he catches them and places them back in their proper place. One push of a button and the doors unlock. He eases the right foot in, but hesitates as sirens approach. He glances over his shoulder, only to see that its and ambulance. He ducks his head and climbs into the car. The keys jingle as they fall to the floor. He blindly searches for them with his right hand as the left hand grips the steering wheel. As he bends his heart begins to race, a cough and then a gasp for air. He picks up the keys and slides the car key into the ignition. Suddenly, there is no more air. He struggles to inhale, but nothing goes in and the air within his lungs is trapped inside. The brain sends messages to his mouth to scream for help, but there is no voice because there is no air. The thoughts of a dying man fill the car. What in the world did those people do to me? God please help me. Please don't let me die. Give me another chance. I want you to know that I'm sorry for all the wrong I've done and I'm sorry for the times I disobeyed you. Oh God, my wife. Ohhh, my kids! Help me! Somebody please help me. His eyes frantically search the parking lot for help. His body leans forward and his head rests upon the steering wheel as his strength leaves his body. A woman appears and stands near the door smoking a cigarette, only he can't scream out for help. Out the corner of his eye he watches her and questions. She's looking right at me, but why is she just standing there? Why won't she help me? Pump pump   pump pump   pump pump. The beats of his heart grow louder and louder as if it will explode. Pump pump   pump. I can't breathe. God please don't let me die. Pump. God please help me! Pump. Oh God! P   U   M   P. Hours pass and finally help arrives, but now it's too late. They pull his cold, hard body from the car onto the ground. Two quarters freely roll from his pocket once again. They stop beside his body and spin in unison. Somewhat like the body and the spirit intertwining together. Exasperated one spins out and falls to the ground as the other spins on forever until they're picked up and carried off.

Lord, although it seems as if my daddy was in that car alone when he died, I know better. I know that you were right there with him and I'm grateful. I opened my hand, took a good look at those quarters and clinched them tightly in my fist. I laughed because my daddy used the quarter to describe just about everything...That ain't worth a quarter, you ain't worth a quarter, or life ain't worth a quarter. Daddy I sure wish I could tell you that life is worth more than a quarter. Its price tag was so high that only one man could pay the price and His name is Jesus. I smiled then I put the quarters back in their proper place. Peace fell upon me and I began to feel strong enough to offer help to my mother, so I got dressed and went over to her house. I parked on the wrong side of the street because family and friends from all over the map flooded the street with their cars. The younger children were playing on the front lawn, something my father never allowed us to do. Sam, his buddies, and family filled the driveway and front porch with beer bottles and laughter. I wondered how they could be so senseless. I didn't expect them to hold a pity party, though I did expect them to conduct themselves appropriately and not make a mockery out of my daddy's death. Sam saw the disappointment in my eyes as I passed by. He twisted his lips to the side as he sarcastically turned the beer bottle upside down. His lips were intimately intertwined with the mouth of the bottle and made a loud kissing sound as he pulled the bottle away. His sidekick, Joe approached me with his phony suave act. Hey Diane, how do you feel? Fine! Why don't you stay out here with us? Sam quickly responded for me as he rolled his drunken eyes. Naw, she ain't gonna stay out here with us. She's a chuch' girl and chuch' folk can't be bothered with us kinda folk. Frustration wanted me to respond. Instead, I turned away and went into the house to see mama. The house was packed with family and friends. They all sat around as the deacons from my church were preparing to leave. My church family was very supportive. They prayed with us and made most of the arrangements for the funeral. They extended themselves toward the family and exemplified what genuine love really was. We were showered in a love like no other and I knew it was the love of God. The funeral was only a day away and people were in and out of mama's home day and night as if it were Grand Central Station. Lottie, Michelle, and I cleaned and assisted mama with everything she needed along with the things she didn't need. We didn't want her to have to worry about anything. All of us, in our own way, wanted to take her pain away, even Sam. We knew he was having a very difficult time and in his attempts to drown out his problems with alcohol, he became obnoxious to everyone except mama. We didn't ask him to do anything because we knew it would break him and we didn't want to see him hurt any more than he already was. Mama was exhausted. Her pasted on smile could not camouflage her broken spirit. Sorrow followed her everywhere she went. It slowed her walk and made her drag along. It showed up in her lack of conversation and stole the warmth from her hands. Soon Michelle went home and Lottie joined Sam on the porch. I went out to ask them to quiet down when I saw my mother-in-law and Sister Whitehead walking across the street like two angels dressed in white. They were coming from the church anniversary dinner. It all seemed so strange. It was as if I was suffering from dejavu.

Diane we have been here for fifteen minutes and you have been wiping that table in the same spot, why don't you come and sit down with your mama baby. No. I'm fine Sister Whitehead. I refused to look up at them. I didn't want anyone looking in my eyes. I was afraid of what they might see, so I just kept wiping the table. Wipe, wipe, wipe as if there was some huge stain on the surface that needed to be scrubbed out. With compassion my mother-in-law spoke. Come now child, you are making me dizzy, prancing around in that kitchen like a little busy body. You need to rest your nerves for a minute. My hand stopped wiping and I looked up into mama's face. The lost look on her face let me know that I couldn't stop. I had to be there for her. I had to make sure everything was right for her, my mother. I refused to let her down, so I continued to wipe, wipe, and wipe that table as if my life depended on it. Diane! Yes mama. Sit down a while. I will mama just as soon as I'm finished. There is nothing left to do. Yes it is mama. Just let me finish. They began to talk, but kept their eyes on me. I felt like I was being probed for some sort of scientific experiment. They talked about the tragic incident surrounding daddy's death and it angered me because it was like reliving it all over again. My tears were resurrected and I fought to keep them buried as I wiped that old table. When they left mama sat down and exhaled while I quietly put the dishes away. It was late and the party on the porch grew. They became louder and louder. Mama cringed to their laughter. Diane. Yes mama. Would you please tell Sam to take his party somewhere else? I'm tired and I don't want to hear the noise. Yes mama. I went out into the driveway where cases of beer bottles were stacked on top of each other. I didn't want to, but I had to practically yell in order for Sam to hear me over the noise. Sam! What do you want Diane? Mama said that she would like for your company to go now because she's tired. Oh shut up Diane, you don't know what you're talking about. This is my dad's house; who do you think you are? You can't make us go nowhere! Sam why don't you stop showing off and listen for a chance! I'm only doing what mama asked me to do. If you asked me, common sense would tell you to stop being so selfish. How inconsiderate can you be? Have you considered mama's feelings? No! All you think about is Sam. Well, let me be the first to inform you, you are not the only one hurting so grow up and quit acting like a child. Hey Sam, why are you allowing your sister to talk to you like that? She acts as if you're her child or something. Why don't you knock her uppity butt on the ground? Sam you better tell your friends to watch who they're talking to. Shut up Diane, I'm not going to tell them nothin'. I really wanted to knock Sam off his high and mighty stoop. However, instead of responding I exhaled and began to walk away when a car pulled up. It was Pastor and Sister Bradley. Sam, Lottie, and all the rest of the pigeons who were with them didn't know who they were, so they continued to curse and drink until Pastor Bradley had gotten close enough for them to see his collar. All of a sudden they began kicking bottles under the car and hiding some of them under their arms. Pastor Bradley looked at them with a sorrowful eye while speaking to them; an eye full of compassion and concern as one would have for a lost child. Pastor and Sister Bradley came to minister to our spiritual needs as well as our physical needs. They gave us instructions for the following day pertaining to the funeral, then left after we gathered in prayer. Mama soon grew tired of the loud party on her porch so she went outside and asked them all to leave. I stood by with my arms crossed as they picked up their trash and left.

I didn't want to go to the funeral. I wasn't ready to close the book on my daddy's life. I had planned on watching him grow old and I wanted to see his business prosper. I would miss the proud look on his face when his grandchildren graduated from college, or when they got their first job. I would miss the opportunity to get him that stank-in' Lincan' he's been wanting for a lifetime. Besides, who was going to walk Michelle down the isle? Reality set in and I was forced to acknowledge the fact that I'll never see him again, at least not in this lifetime. When I get to heaven I'm going to embrace him and the rest of my loved ones. What a glorious time it will be, I can't wait. As we stood in line to view the body strange and familiar eyes searched our beings, puzzled concerning our mindsets, and pained by what they thought we were feeling. Grandma let out a loud whining sound and then cried out to the Lord, questioning Him as to why He took her baby boy. Her cries shattered my face and the tears that I endeavored not to shed came forth like new water. When it came time for me to view my daddy's body Eddie grabbed hold of my hand to let me know he was there for me. I barely got a look at his face before my eyes decided to close. Before I knew it my body turned and my feet swiftly escorted me to my seat. I looked to my brother, my mother, and my sisters to make sure they were okay. If someone were to take our pictures they would say our faces had been carved out of stone; pale, hard, and stiff, with no particular expression. I could tell that we were all hoping for the same thing; that this whole ordeal would hurry up and be over. Before Pastor Bradley proceeded with the eulogy Xavier got up to sing a song for his grandfather, my daddy. Now a teenager, Xavier had become a handsome young man. He walked to the front of the church, bowed his head and opened his mouth. Sweet angelic notes came forth and suddenly disappeared. The entire church waited with anticipation as Xavier fought desperately to force out more notes. Sorrow choked his airways and pain froze him still. I wanted to grab him and hug him until he felt better like I did when he was a baby, but I couldn't move. It was as if I could hear everyone's thoughts and feel their pain, which really burdened me, so I lowered my eyes and wept. Sam got up, wrapped his arms around

Xavier and escorted him back to his seat. The funeral wasn't long, but the drive to the cemetery seemed like eternity. Conversation and laughter dueled against crying tears except I remained silent. I peered out the window of the limousine and saw people standing alongside the road watching the cars in the long procession, wondering who died. In the midst of my daydreaming I saw a white car approaching from a distance. It looked just like my daddy's car and with great expectation I looked long and hard at the individual driving, hoping to throw a wave at him, my dad. A smile stretched across my face but soon slid away like a faded memory when I realized there was no possible way I'd see him driving by. I had totally dismissed the fact that my dad was dead. Quickly, I snatched my hand down before anyone had the opportunity to ask who it was I was getting ready to wave at. I sat in silence the rest of the way and tried to prepare myself for the last part of the funeral, to say good-bye to a man I've loved my whole life.

Journal Insert

Lord a few months ago you troubled my sleep with a series of dreams that you allowed to fill my head. I now know that these dreams had much to do with what's going on in my life. I did a play at church, of which, my mama and sisters did attend. Shortly after, my daddy died and the women of the church were at mama's side. They prepared all kinds of food for the family and made themselves available to us during this terrible time. My daddy wasn't in the dreams and he's not here now. I also realize that I have to be a constant light to my family and help lead them to Jesus Christ. I remember these dreams so clearly. I was sitting across the banister on my grandma's porch and mama was sitting in the rocker with Sister Whitehead. Sister Whitehead was holding mama's hand telling her that everything was going to be okay. I turned and looked at mama and asked; are you coming to see the play? Mama nodded her head to say yes. The next night I dreamed I was in a white room. Sister Whitehead and another woman from the church were dressed in all white with white aprons on. They were serving soup and asked me to taste it. As I was putting the spoon up to my mouth mama walked in with a group of women from the church. They were all around her. When they began to sing I was puzzled because I knew mama didn't know any church songs, but to my surprise mama was clapping her hands and singing along with the women. I smiled and then woke up. A few days later I had a vision…I saw Sister Whitehead and my mother-in-law dressed in all white. It was dark and they parked their car across the street from mama's house, then they got out and walked towards me as I stood in mama's driveway. The night after that I dreamed mama and the entire family; brothers, sisters, aunts, and uncles were all together in this white room. There was food lined up on the table, but everyone was standing around mama as she sat in a kitchen chair with two smaller children on her lap. My daddy was nowhere in the picture. Suddenly, we were standing outside at a train crossing and on the other side of the tracks was an evil being with wings. I turned to my family and gave them instructions. Holy ground is on the other side. In order for us to reach it we will have to get past that demon. Follow me and don't stop running until you reach Holy ground. I grabbed hold of two and said come on. We ran as fast as we could. After passing the demon he began to chase us. His wings were flapping and he was gaining ground. Nevertheless, we reached Holy ground and he couldn't step on it, so he turned around and went back. I also went back to get more family and each time the demon chased us. The last time it was so close it reached out to grab me, but I ducked only to land on Holy ground. After I had gotten my family safely to Holy ground the demon stood across the street telling me he knew of a shorter way we could take. I looked up and the demon was pointing to a bridge. I yelled to my family to follow me so that we could take the shortcut. We stepped off Holy ground and proceeded up the bridge. The demon began to chase us once again, laughing because we were no longer on Holy ground. I led my family back to Holy ground safely. This time the demon stepped onto Holy ground with us and stood there. We kneeled in prayer and I asked the Lord to save this demon and to make it Holy. The demon stretched out his hand, but when I looked up it was the hand of a man. Then I heard him say, I want to be Holy, but I can't. Then he slowly walked away. The Lord was showing me in these dreams that my daddy's time was up. My mother-in-law and Sister Whitehead came to my mother's home all dressed in white to comfort my mama just like it was in the dream. Afterwards I would lead my family to holy ground, but it wasn't going to be easy. The enemy would be there to try and stop me. Regarding the demon turning into human form and grabbing hold to my hand gives me the impression that the attack and hindrance will come in a way unexpected or by someone I love and am very close to. The Lord has shown me in this dream that He would be there with me and for me, and through the good and troubled times. There are no shortcuts into heaven. Jesus is the way, the truth, and the light and the only way to the Father is through Him. Therefore, I can't allow myself to be distracted by anything or anyone. I have a mission and that's to lead my family to Christ.

23
<u>YOU HAVE NOT BECAUSE YOU ASK NOT</u>

I didn't know how difficult it would be to go to mama's house without daddy being there until Labor Day came around. The family picnic was at mama's house. I watched her from the patio doors. She was standing over daddy's grill trying to cook his famous barbeque ribs. She wrapped her slender hands around the fork to flip the ribs over, but didn't have the strength that daddy had to smoothly flip them with one toss. She wrestled with the ribs, lift, half turn, pull, half turn, until she finally got them over on the other side. The mere sight of it tugged at my heart. When the rest of the family arrived we set up tables and chairs all over the yard. The tables were lined with potato salad, assorted salads, green beans, baked beans, and corn on the cob, hot dogs, chicken, hamburgers, chips, and dip. We sat around staring at each other as if we didn't know what to say. It wasn't the same without daddy. I don't know why we have to have this picnic anyway, it's only been 30 days since the funeral and I don't feel like a picnic. Why do we have to pretend that everything is okay when it really isn't? I lost my daddy and he's not here anymore. My mind began to shout out things in my head that I really didn't care to hear, so I got up out of my chair and began to walk around the yard. Mama put the last dish on the table. It was the ribs my daddy made; I mean to say the ribs mama made. She called everyone to the table to eat and in a twitch of an eye they all piled around the table like hungry cats at a smorgasbord. Forks were clinging as arms were slinging and slapping food on the plates. No one waited for the grace to be said, they just chomped down on the food like cannibals, smackin' and sloppin' with their lips steadily poppin. I bit into the ribs hoping mama made the sauce just like my daddy's. They were good, but not like his. No one could hold a candle to his sauce. He hadn't written it down, nor would he tell anyone. I used to watch him make it, but he made me promise not to give anyone the recipe. As time went on my frustration only seemed to grow. I couldn't blame it all on daddy's death. Part of it was due to me being angry over my legs deteriorating and I had to see the surgeon the next day regarding more surgery. As much as I believed God was going to heal me, somewhere in the back of my mind doubt prodded at my brain. No one really knew how much it bothered me. My left leg was now extremely smaller than the right leg and my muscles were diminishing due to the injury and lack of use. My left knee was also swollen and severely scarred from previous surgeries. Pride kept me from asking for help when I needed it. Pride also gave me a sense of false hope making me believe that I could still do the same things I used to be able to do before the accident. The sun began to subside and the dishes that were once filled with food were now empty. Everyone sat back in their chairs, some involved in conversation and others were not. I looked up at the spot where my basketball hoop used to be and I remembered when daddy stood out here with me to teach me how to shoot his famous hook shot. I don't think he ever missed.

Aw man! I missed again. Diane I told you to treat the basketball like it's your best friend. Don't pound it like you hate it. Let the tips of your fingers gently bounce it, controlling its movements with a gentle touch. Left, then right, now back and forth. Soon the ball fell under my command and I was defying the very essence of gravity. As small as I was I was soaring over daddy's head. S-W-I-S-H. In your face daddy! That's my girl. I think you got the hang of it, now I'm going to teach you my famous hook shot. From this point on daddy I'm not letting you get another hook shot on me. Daddy went to the middle of the yard, which we called mid-court. He threw the ball at me so hard it almost knocked me down. Daddy yelled check. I threw the ball back at him and bent over with my arms stretched out like Magic Johnson on the prowl. Daddy turned his back to me and bullied me with his size as he bounced the ball up and down, up and down. I put my left hand on his waist and with my right hand I attempted to strip the ball from him. Daddy pushed off on me, lifted his right hand and threw a hook shot over his head. I ran beneath the basket hoping he would miss when the net wrapped around the ball and spit it out. Daddy stood at mid-court laughing at me. The gap in his teeth looked like a black hole. His laughter echoed in my head and his smile shined in my eyes as I twitched my mouth to the side and proudly showed daddy that I could do a hook shot too. Daddy you cheated. Naw I didn't, you just can't play. The chatter of everyone's conversation grew louder in my ears as the memory of my daddy faded away, then a tear surfaced in my eye as it rested on the place where my hoop used to be.

I got up early the next morning to prepare to see Dr. Morgan. I went into prayer to meet with the Lord. Good morning Lord. Thank you for waking me. Thank you for the breath of life that you've given me. Please forgive me Lord for my inconsistencies and for all the times I've disobeyed you. I don't want to doubt you because I know too much about you. I've read from Genesis to Revelation about your delivering and healing power, your righteous standards for my life, and your holy expectations. I know you're with me. I just ask that you increase my faith and strengthen me where I am weak. Please touch me and bless me with your presence, so that no matter what Dr. Morgan has to say this morning about these crippled legs, I want your perfect will to be done. Thank you Lord Jesus for healing me, saving me, sanctifying me, and setting me free. Thank you for filling me with your precious Holy Spirit and for justifying me. I love you always. You are truly a wonderful, faithful, and loving God. For you I live and for you I'll die. After prayer I went straight to the doctor's office. I sat still on the table and waited patiently for Dr. Morgan to enter. My crutches stood proud beside the table where I sat. Small bumps ran up my naked arms, a combination of cold air and nerves. I looked down at my legs and began to wonder why they wouldn't work right. I wanted to be able to prove to Dr. Morgan that I had indeed made some progress, so I attempted to bend my left leg. After a brief struggle I made it to what looked like a 40-degree angle. I fought to bend it further and at one point it felt as though everything in my knee would break. Pain fought back and eventually won. Softly, I let my leg down and didn't dare bother the other one. I opened a magazine to pass the time away only to find most of the pages were filled with athletes and advertisements for sneakers and other sports wear. I wondered if doctors thought about how these magazines might play on the psyche of those who are handicapped who were once athletes. After a brief knock at the door Dr. Morgan entered with my chart in hand, sat at the end of my table, and exhaled. Good morning Diane, how do you feel? I feel fine Dr. Morgan. He stood over me and began to take the brace off my leg for the examination. How are the knees feeling Diane? Truthfully doctor they hurt, but I think I'm making some progress. According to my records there is no progress Diane. What do you mean doc? It's been just about two years and the surgeries seemed to have crippled you. If you don't mind doc, don't use the word cripple. It sounds so permanent. Diane sooner or later you are going to have to face the truth. I have faced the truth! Have you talked with someone concerning retiring from the force? No sir. Well I think you better. Your left knee won't bend past a 30 degree angle. The limp you have is permanent and your right knee is weakening because it's being over worked. Diane you have severe scaring in that knee along with other problems and I thought physical therapy would help, but it hasn't. I really don't want to open up both knees at the same time, but your knees are deteriorating and you are too young for the implants. Well, what are you going to do doc? I'm going to schedule you for the surgery on both knees because neither one is strong enough to support the other. My skin quivered and anger flushed over my face. As I tried desperately to fight back the tears Dr. Morgan sadly watched, then he patted my knees and said that I will be fine. Dr. Morgan, will this surgery fix the problems? I really don't know. I expected you to be walking by now. I can't promise you anything and believe me when I say; I never expected any of this to happen. Well at least tell me what my chances are. Diane there is a 50 percent chance you'll get better and there is a 50 percent chance you'll get worse. However, I don't want you worrying because you're young enough to start a new career. So when is the surgery Doc? I can make it as early as next week. I don't think so. I'm going on a trip with my church in a few weeks; so make it after that. Diane I don't know if you should go on this trip. I will be fine Dr. Morgan, I promise. Okay, I'll set you up for your pre-surgery visit two days after your return, but I really don't want you putting any pressure on your legs. That means no walking! Well how in the world am I supposed to get around Dr. Morgan? Use your crutches to swing both legs or use a wheelchair. Absolutely not! I'd rather use the crutches. I trust you'll do whatever you feel is best Diane. I know you won't jeopardize the surgery. No sir, I wouldn't do that. Dr. Morgan attempted to put the brace back on my leg when I stopped him. I'll do it myself, thank you. Okay Diane, but before I forget please do not take off this brace. Yes doc. When Dr. Morgan left the room I grabbed my brace and those wretched crutches and threw them across the room. It wasn't until I attempted to get off the table that I realized I had done a stupid thing. I needed the brace to hold my knee in place and the crutches to hold me up. Firmly, I gripped the table and stood up on my legs. The left knee wobbled as I attempted to gain control and the right knee buckled with pain. I made it over to the chair and fell to the floor. As much as I hated the crutches I needed them, so I swallowed my pride and put the brace back on my leg. I pulled myself up on the chair, picked up the crutches and hobbled out of the room. I was supposed to go right into physical therapy, but I figured what was the use. Why put myself through more pain when the outcome would still be the same. Anger slowly filled my entire being. I hated my crutches and I hated my squeaky brace. I hated the fact that people looked at me as if I had purple polka dots on my face. I hated the possibility of being crippled for life. I hated that it always took me forever to get up and down the stairs and I was really incensed when it took me almost 20 minutes to get from the door of the doctor's office to my car because I didn't have a handicap sticker to park in the handicap spaces! Even if I did have a sticker there are inconsiderate people who aren't handicapped and always take these parking spaces for themselves. After making it to my car I sat there staring into the clouded sky. My anger turned towards myself because I realized I used to be one of those people who took those spaces from those who needed them. I hung my head low and with a broken heart I began talking to the Lord. Jesus I used to be able to walk, run, and jump with no problem, but now it seems as though I'll never have that again. I am really trying not to doubt you Lord. If it is your will for me to have more surgery, then there is nothing left for me to say. My prayer is, Your will be done, but prepare my heart to receive it. I wept uncontrollably and I didn't care who saw me. I drove away with a particular destination in mind. I didn't want to go home. I just wanted to disappear for a little while. I went to church to see my pastor and as usual he welcomed me. I sat down in the huge chair in front of his desk as my mind made drastic attempts to unscramble the mixed up questions in my head. What can I do for you

Sis'? I just left the doctor's office and I was told I needed more surgery, and this time on both knees. There's a 50/50 chance that I'll be able to get back to normal and there's a 50/50 chance I'll be worse off than I am now. Pastor Bradley's eyebrows rose. Sis' you do know that God uses doctors and heals through medicine and surgery if need be. Yes sir, I do. Well then what's the problem? The problem is, I've read my Bible and have marveled at the miracles Jesus and His Apostles have performed. He made the blind to see, the lame to walk, and the dead got up. Surely He can do this for me. Pastor Bradley sat back in his chair and chuckled whole-heartedly. You are absolutely right, so what is it that you want. I don't want any more surgeries. I want the Lord to touch me and heal me Himself. Have you asked Him to do this particular thing? Somewhat! Sister Diane you have to be straight with the Lord. Go to Him and let your requests be made known. Ask and you shall receive, seek and ye shall find, knock and the door shall be opened. Pastor Bradley continued to talk and I listened. Soon the burden was lifted. I smiled, grabbed my crutches, and stood up. Thank you Pastor Bradley, you have been a real help. Pastor I know we will all be leaving for the prayer clinic soon, but you want to know something, I have purposed in my heart that I am not coming back the same; I receive my healing right now. Sis' you are going to be fine. I went right home and into prayer.

Lord here I am again. I am making my request made known to you. I know that you work through medicine, people, doctors, and whomever or whatever you choose. I appreciate that and I thank you, but the fact of the matter is; I don't want to have any more surgeries. I don't want the doctor to heal me. I want you to touch me. I want you to give me your divine healing. I want you to get the glory Lord. I believe by faith that this is already done. You've done too much for me and performed so many miracles in my life already; I would have to be crazy not to believe you now. I also know that the amount of pressure placed on me now will be measured by the anointing that will come out of me later. Thank you for choosing me for this test and thank you for giving me everything I need to pass this test for you. Amen.

24
<u>HEALING VIRTUE</u>

Eddie wasn't too keen on me going all the way to North Carolina to attend the Prayer Clinic. He said he didn't mind, but his demeanor said something I wouldn't dare repeat. My girlfriend, Sharon got her mother to take us to the airport and as usual she was on time. Eddie loaded the car with my bags and then wrapped his muscle filled arms around me. He gently kissed my lips and then escorted me to the car. The airport was filled with people rushing up and down the corridor, pulling and pushing their bags across the freshly polished floors. I was puzzled as to how I would make the long journey from the check-in to the gate of departure, but suddenly an attendant pulled up on a motorized cart and helped me aboard. I was happy to see that help had arrived, but saddened because of the indifference between myself and everyone else. It wasn't just shame that kept me bound; it was also the attention I attracted. Attention I could have done without. I stood out like a black spot on a white suit and the only thing people saw was my handicap. Diane was slowly disappearing, only to be identified with what was wrong with her. I hobbled onto the plane with a bag slung across my back. As I approached my seat a sweet old woman smiled at me and stood up to help me. Sweetie do you need any help? No Ma'am. I think I can make it. She ignored me and beckoned for the young man across from me to help me. The handsome young man placed my bag in the overhead compartment along with my crutches. I smiled and thanked him. The old woman grabbed hold of my arm and assisted me in sitting down then she sat right behind me. Honey don't you be so stubborn. If you need help ask for it. Ain't a thing wrong with askin' somebody for help! Thank you very much. You're welcome sweetie. What's your name anyhow? My name is Diane. Well you can call me Miss Winnie. I've come all the way from Louisiana and I'm bout' tired now. That's a long way Miss Winnie. Yeah, but I don't mind, where are you headed Diane? I'm going to North Carolina to the Prayer Clinic. It sure is a small world. That's where I'm going; Oh bless Jesus. Are you with all those folk that boarded the plane? Yes Ma'am. Where are you all coming from? Detroit. Diane have you ever been to the prayer clinic before? No Ma'am. I've always wanted to go, but never made it. Well I think you'll enjoy it. I'm going to do more than that. I'm going to receive my blessing because I'm not going back home the same way. God is going to heal these crippled legs. Oh honey, don't get me started, now you talkin' my language. I smiled as Miss Winnie kicked back in her seat laughing and talking to the Lord out loud as I stretched my legs out and attempted to make myself comfortable. My eyes quickly closed with a carousel of child-like thoughts floating around my head in all hopes that by sleeping I would get to North Carolina quicker. The plane landed softly, like a snowflake to the ground. The man across from me kindly handed me my escorts, suffering and sorrow. I slipped them under my arm and hobbled toward the door of the plane. Miss Winnie yelled out to me and when I turned around she gave me a bear hug and kissed me on my cheek. I turned back toward the door where a man and a wheelchair stood waiting for me. Is that thing for me? Yes, Ma'am it certainly is. Well I don't need it. I can make it just fine without a wheelchair. Ma'am this is courtesy of the airlines. Pastor Bradley and all of my friends urged me to except the help. Frustrated, I plopped down in the wheelchair and laid my crutches across my lap. The attendant whistled and happily pushed me through the long corridors as if I was an old woman in need of some sort of entertainment. I wanted to tell him that I'm not old, but I am a vibrant thirty-three year old woman and I will walk again. The attendant stopped pushing me and made a bold statement. End of the road Ma'am! I wanted to ask him; what do you mean end of the road? This is where you get off Ma'am. I growled, fine! Ma'am your bags will be coming around the gurney in a few minutes. Sarcastically, I stared him down until he turned and walked away. What was I supposed to do put my luggage on my back and hop on these crutches at the same time or did he forget that I CAN BARELY WALK! I stood helpless in the middle of the floor as people candidly waltzed by me. If at all possible, they would have walked right through me. Frustration brought about anger, and anger welcomed tears. Pastor Bradley and the bunch were approaching from afar. Hurriedly, I dried my eyes and found a seat near the car rentals desk. Are you okay Sister Diane? Yes Pastor, I'm fine. Do you guys have a ride to your hotel?

Yes sir. Just as soon as everyone gets situated we're going to pick up our rental and drive to the hotel. Well I just wanted to make sure you all are fine before I leave because my ride is here.

The humidity in North Carolina was ridiculous. The sun was beating down on us with rods of fire, transforming my silky brown skin into a burnt orange complexion. I cooled my tongue with ice-cold lemonade as I sat by the pool and watched people splash around in the water with laughter. Then a familiar voice called out to me. It was one of the women from my church. Diane why don't you join us in the pool? Maybe later, I don't want to mess up my hair. The woman looked up at me and a look of compassion fell over her. Oh I'm sorry, can you swim with your leg? Yes, I can swim. I'm not supposed to put any pressure on my leg by standing or walking, but I can swim. All I have to do is take the brace off and put the crutches down because swimming is actually a wonderful exercise for my muscles. I'm sorry. I didn't mean to ask. Don't be I'm having fun watching all of you have fun. We all laughed and they went back to splashing around in the pool. I threw my head back and let the sun beat heavily upon my face. I thought about life. I thought about my healing, and I thought about the wonderful works of God.

The church was huge and the ceilings were as high as the heavens. The rich red carpet flowed throughout the entire building like fresh blood. The pews were neatly lined up in rows, filled with people and dreams. Sharon, Zelda, and I sat like three peas in a pod; listening attentively as the men of God spoke, one after the next. At the end of the teaching session everyone greeted one another with love as we received packets containing literature and blessed oil. Everyone was really nice, not like those snobbish religious folk that walk on water on Sunday, but dance in the pit of hell Monday through Saturday. We attended services day after day with persistence, but still no healing. I began to question whether or not I would be healed. After all, God does use doctors and medicine to work miracles too. Maybe it's meant for me to have more surgery when I get back or maybe my legs are supposed to be like this. I counted the days I had left before it was time to return home and I only had two. My frustration was evident. Everyone saw it; however, no one admired it. I became silent and withdrawn. I knew I needed to deal with me, because along with frustration and anger I allowed doubt to creep in. I was trying to deal with these particular issues on top of the pain in my legs and I didn't feel I could hold myself up anymore. My hands and arms were numbed with pain from carrying the entire weight of my body. I had over done it and had come to a point where I needed someone to either carry me or push me in a wheelchair. Diane we're gonna take a break from service today. Oh yeah what are we gonna do? We thought it would be nice to go shopping at the mall and then have a nice sit down dinner. When Sharon mentioned the mall my face almost fell off because we had been there just about every day and I realized I couldn't keep up with them. They had two legs and I had none. They didn't realize how bad I suffered through the night after moving around all day, but because I didn't want to be left out of anything I went along as if everything was okay. Diane you know you don't have to go if you don't feel up to it. I know, but I think I can make it. Sharon and Zelda grabbed their purses and I snatched up my companions and slid them under my arms as usual. As we pulled into the parking lot of the mall Sharon wanted to let me out at the door while she parked, but I refused. I let them know that I could make it along with them. We didn't get through the first corridor good before the pain began ripping through my arms and legs. I suggested that we eat first in order to rest my body. I couldn't let them know what was going on with me. I didn't want to spoil the good time they were having. We found a very nice southern restaurant where we sat down and ate. I was glad because I was able to get off my feet. I had black-eyed peas and rice, cornbread, chicken, green beans, macaroni and cheese, and cherry Jell-O topped with whipped cream. We lined our table with just about everything on the buffet. Sharon and Zelda rattled on about nothing, chewing and talking at the same time. I didn't respond too well to the jokes and idle conversation being passed around the table. It's very difficult to laugh when you want to cry, so I smiled and chewed my food instead. We ate so much that our zippers unzipped themselves to allow our stomachs to stretch forth. I could hear feet shufflin' and bags rustlin' in the hallway of the mall. People began to crowd the restaurant, which quickly reminded us of our sole purpose for being there, shop till' you drop. I pulled myself up out of the chair with the help of those crutches only to find that the pain was still there. Finally Zelda confronted me. Diane why don't you let us get you a wheelchair, everyone can see that you're having a hard time. Absolutely not! Why not? Because I don't need a wheelchair! Leave it alone Zelda, Diane is just being difficult. No I'm not! If it gets to the point where I feel I need a wheelchair, then I'll go and get one myself. We walked on as if the conversation never took place. After stopping a thousand times I felt as if I couldn't move another inch. Reality set in and I decided to go and get the wheelchair. You guys go on. I'm going to go and see if I can get a wheelchair. Do you want us to go with you? No, I can do this by myself. Sharon whispered; you need to swallow all of that pride and let someone help you. I rolled my eyes at them both and threw my favorite word in their faces, "whatever." I hobbled away and reassured them that I was fine and would catch up with them later. For a healthy person the customer service desk was only a skip, hop, and jump away, but for me it was like walking that last mile to death row. Sweat moistened the calluses on the palms of my hands causing my grip to slip on the rubbery-like pads. My wrists were cracking and my strength was lacking as I made my way through the noisy crowd. When I reached the counter I saw an older white woman standing behind it. Her blue eyes were as calm as the blue seas and her smile was really nice. Excuse me Miss. How can I help you dear? I need to rent a wheelchair because I just can't make it on these crutches any longer. Oh that's not a problem, but I will need to see your driver's license and I will also need a $5.00 deposit. I gave her everything she asked for and in return I got a wheelchair. I didn't hesitate; I fell into that chair as if I had been waiting forever. The seat was nice and cushy and it also had a bag to store my items. I leaned on the counter toward the white woman behind it. Is it possible for me to leave my crutches with you? Of course you can. I'll place them right under the counter with your name on them. Thank you very much for all of your help. The woman smiled and went on to help someone else. I pushed off with every intention to find Sharon and Zelda, but after receiving many awkward stares and whispers I decided to shop on my own. It's weird, because one minute you're standing tall above everything and able to conquer anything, then suddenly you become invisible and your handicap becomes larger than life. You become so small that everyone walks over you. People were in such a hurry they walked right into my wheelchair and then got upset because they deemed me to be in the way. I smiled as a small child with his parents came toward me. The little boy pointed at the brace and bandages, which covered my legs. Mommy, look at that lady's legs. Why does she have those things on them? They gave me an odd look. The parents began to answer him as if I wasn't there or as if I couldn't hear them discussing me as they passed by. Tears flooded my face as I turned off into a toy store to get away. I didn't realize how difficult it would be to maneuver a wheelchair, so at first I kept going around in a circle until I gained control of the wheels. I came across a toy with red fur and a huge smile. I really needed a good laugh right about now. He looked happy and when I pushed his belly he laughed. I laughed with him and pretty soon the tears disappeared. I purchased him and named him happy. I placed him in my bag and he rode away with me. A familiar voice called out to me. It was Sharon and Zelda. Hey girl where have you been? I decided to do a little shopping before I caught up with you two. Did you two find some good stuff? Yes we did. Sharon what did you get? I bought some shirts that were on sale for $3.00 a piece. Oh yeah; Zelda did you find what you were looking for? Not really, but I did find some bargains. You're the one with all the bags Diane, what did you get? I opened up some of my bags to show them what I had gotten, but when I showed Zelda my new friend Happy she crossed her arms, opened her mouth and tongue lashed me. You are a grown woman. I could see if you were buying that for Kayla, but you bought it for yourself, which leads me to believe that there is something seriously wrong with you. Why don't you act your age? I grew so angry I could literally hear a time bomb ticking away in my head. This was my sister in Christ judging me for something she knew nothing about. She didn't bother to ask what Happy signified and she didn't care. I realized my plate was full. I was still trying to get over my husband's infidelity in order to repair my marriage, the loss of my father and the lack of use of my legs. Everything in me was broken, my life, my hope, my dreams and expectations, and now my spirit. I just looked at her, forced a smile across my broken face and rolled away. Sharon grabbed hold of the handlebars and began pushing me. I snatched at the wheels to get her to stop, but she continued especially when I couldn't make it up the ramp to the elevator. Humiliation and embarrassment teamed up on me and beat me down. I remained silent for the rest of the evening especially back at the hotel. I got undressed, climbed in my bed, grabbed my journal and placed my headphones over my ears. I blasted my music so that I wouldn't have to communicate with anyone, but God. He was the only one who could help me. Sharon and Zelda sat on their bed chit-chatting. My mind was flustered and I couldn't concentrate, so I threw on a top and a pair of pajama pants and hobbled out to the balcony without the crutches, defying all that I knew to be right. My knees could have buckled out at any time making my situation worse, but I didn't care. As I walked to the door I threw a few words at Sharon and Zelda. I'll be back. Where are you going? I need some air. I walked out of the room refusing to do anymore explaining. There was a small lounge type sofa in the corner of the balcony. I sat there staring out into the still of the night with no words, just tears. I didn't want to think that this trip was beginning to be a waste of my time, but I had no control over my thoughts. My mind was saying things I knew weren't true and there was a voice that kept telling me God wasn't going to heal me. I fought hard to empty my mind of those thoughts I knew weren't mine. Pretty soon the mist from my tears blinded me. I couldn't see nor think clearly. I stood up on my legs and sadly looked out at the world. Lord I have been here nearly four days with only a few days left and I haven't been healed yet. I don't want to go home the same way I came. Lord I need you to tell me what to do. I stood there waiting for a response and in the still of the night I heard nothing. At that moment I felt as if I was all alone. I hobbled back to my room, not only with broken legs, but also a broken face. My presence interrupted Sharon and Zelda's conversation. I could feel their eyes on me; nevertheless, I refused to acknowledge them. Slowly I climbed into my bed, returned the earphones to their original place and turned my face to the wall. I closed my eyes and attempted to rest when I heard a small voice squeaking like a little mouse. It was Zelda. I heard her calling my name, but I ignored her purposely. Then after taking a deep breath she called my name again, only this time it felt like the walls shook. I snatched my earphones off and slowly sat up in my bed. Already angered and broken in spirit I turned to her and Sharon with contempt in my heart. What do you want Zelda and why are you calling my name like you're crazy? Diane I just wanted to tell you while you're lying over there sulking, God wouldn't have you to be like this. There's something you're not doing. What are you talking about Zelda? I have done everything I could possibly do. I've asked God for a healing, I've prayed and consecrated myself onto Him and basically I'm tired. You are missing the point Diane! I opened my mouth to give her a piece of my mind, but nothing came out, so I was forced to listen. Why don't you take a good look at yourself! Examine yourself. You get upset and blame everybody and everything for your condition, but in all actuality it's you. What are you doing that's blocking your blessing or what haven't you done? You need to pick yourself up, stop holding a pity party for yourself and let God heal you. If you really believe that He's going to do it, then act like it. I lowered my head as my face began to fill with tears. Sharon and Zelda got up and put their shoes on. We'll be back in a minute Diane. We're going downstairs to get some coffee. I acknowledged them with a nod as they left the room. I knew what she said was true and I also knew the enemy was trying to keep me from receiving that word by keeping my mind on the things she said to me in error at the mall. I snatched the blanket off my legs and sat there looking at them. Lord is it true? Could I possibly be responsible for not believing? He didn't say anything, but I knew it was true. I doubted Him because it didn't happen when I thought it should. I sobbed like a baby after recognizing the truth. I remembered the packet that we were given at the first service, which contained information sheets as well as blessed oil. I reached down on the side of my bed into that bag and pulled out the blessed oil. I held it in my hand and opened it. I could still hear the old woman saying, here you go baby, we prayed over this oil night and day. I poured the oil into my hands and anointed my knees. Lord, forgive me for doubting you. I believe Lord. I believe. Thank you for my healing. I cupped my face within my hands as I lay across my bed. I moaned like a woman in travail as mucus covered my pillow. I didn't run for tissue, nor did I attempt to dry my eyes. I laid there like a wounded duck waddling around in my own mess. I dozed off to sleep with one thought in mind, Lord I'm sorry.

I woke up with a new purpose. I decided to wait on God and keep my mind still. We didn't go to the morning service; instead, for the first time during our trip we decided to go to the evening service. I showered and went to the pool for a swim to give my legs some exercise. Sharon sat on the side of the pool reading and Zelda flopped into the pool, mascara and all. When she came up out of the water it looked as if she was crying black tears. I shook my head, took my brace off my leg and eased into the lukewarm water. Zelda and I splashed around in the pool as if we were children on summer break. In the water I felt power and strength because I could move my legs in ways I couldn't move them on dry land. My body floated upon the water with grace as the sun hid its face from me in the thick gray clouds above. An hour or so passed by when Sharon began tapping on her watch. Y'all better come on because it's time to get dressed. What time is it Sharon? Its 3:00 and we only have three hours before service begins and Diane you know it takes you an hour to do your hair. Candidly I replied, "Whatever!" Sharon stood there as if to say, right now! I sucked my teeth before speaking. I'll be up in a minute. Zelda shouted, yeah me too! You and Diane better hurry up, I would like to get there early enough to get a good seat. While Sharon waltzed up the stairs I took one more lap around the pool, then Zelda helped me out.

The parking lot of the hotel was buzzing with all kinds of folk leaving for church. People were scattered all over the place with their Bibles in one hand and coffee in the next. We kindly made our way through the crowd, jumped in our car and left. As many people as there were we didn't think we would get a parking space close to the doors of the church, but God supplied one just for us. When we entered the church I automatically sensed that the atmosphere was much different than what I had experienced during the day services. People were on their knees in prayer moaning and calling out to God. As we searched for a place to sit I could feel someone on my heels. It was fear. He followed me into the pews and sat in my lap as I slid my crutches under the pew in front of me. I lowered my head to pray, but he kept lifting it up causing frustration to smack me in the face. Doubt joined in and began telling me that there was one day left and I wasn't healed and wouldn't be, then a minister from Ohio began praying openly for everyone with power. I began thanking the Lord over and over again for my healing. I was determined to press my way through. However, when frustration and fear left they failed to take doubt with them. Doubt attempted to hold onto me, but praise entered the room and pushed him out of his seat. The Holy Spirit lit a fire up under the minister and led the entire church into a spirit of worship. The minister's proclamations were heart wrenching. God has a blessing for you and your deliverance is in the room...Your breakthrough is in the room and your healing is in the room...Broken marriages and relationships; be ye healed and restored...Messed up finances, Satan loose your hold...The Holy Spirit is in the room...Whatever you need and whatever you asked God for you better reach out and grab it...Now stand and give the Lord His praise. The entire church was on their feet. His words penetrated my heart and as I received it into my spirit I lifted my head toward the heavens and when I opened my eyes I was somewhere else. It was as if I was watching a movie about me. I saw myself murmuring and complaining about my injuries, constantly petitioning the heavens with a basket full of questions labeled why. I saw that I had the-me, me, me, I, I, I syndrome. The Lord showed me being rude to people who wanted to help me and angry because I couldn't walk or do the things I used to do. Then I saw myself in the mall with my haughty and proud self. I treated my friends like enemies all because I couldn't walk and I hated the fact that I needed a wheelchair. I hated the fact that I needed help. When I saw myself and all I had become tears fell from my eyes. Then, I heard a voice, soft but stern. It moved throughout my entire being. It was the Holy and righteous voice of God. WHO DO YOU THINK YOU ARE? YOU HAVE BUILT YOURSELF UP ON A MOUNTAIN OF PRIDE. YOU SAID YOU BELIEVED I WOULD HEAL YOU, BUT IN THE BACK OF YOUR MIND YOU DOUBTED ME. As He spoke He flashed the last two years of my life before me. I wept bitterly and my heart broke because I realized I was stained with sin and guilt, and I had become undone before Him. I felt I'd truly disappointed Him, not realizing I couldn't possibly disappoint God. My God I'm sorry. Please forgive me; I have been selfish and rude and for that I repent. Lord if you don't ever heal me I still love you and thank you for what you've already done for me. I'm going to praise you anyway. I entered a mode of worship, not of my own doing, but of the Holy Spirit. Suddenly, I felt the hand of God touch my legs. They began to tingle from my toes to my hip, strengthening them like never before. My tears of sorrow and repentance turned into tears of joy. I jumped up and down and worshipped my God, something I hadn't been able to do since I got hurt. I thanked Him and praised Him to the top of my lungs. When I opened my eyes again I was back in the church. God has truly shown me His mercy and healed me. He gave me new legs, a new walk, and a new tongue to talk. I felt His glory all around me, but puzzled as to why He did this for me with my messed up self. I was so humbled by His acts of kindness, grace and mercy that I could not speak. As he wrapped His arms around me, comforting me in His bosom, I stood in awe because of the love He showered upon me. I wasn't worthy to receive such a gift of love, yet God saw fit to bless me. A woman from my church was standing to my left. She tapped me on my shoulder to get my attention. As I turned to her she spoke. I know God healed you because He told me so. I nodded my head in agreement and let the tears flow. When the service had ended people were greeting one another in preparation for our departure. I still could not find the words to speak. I picked up my crutches and out of habit I slid them up under my arms, but quickly realized that I had no use for them. I stood there looking at them when Sister Bradley approached me smiling. Sister Diane, God did something for you didn't He? I smiled and shook my head in agreement. Every time I tried to open my mouth I got all choked up and started crying. I felt as though my skin had been turned inside out, which left me feeling exposed and sensitive to everything. That's okay Diane; you don't have to say anything. I already know the answer. Sister Bradley turned and walked away. I dragged the crutches behind me as I walked out of the church. Sharon was in the car waiting for Zelda and myself. I got in, sat quietly in the back seat and remained that way for quite some time. I'll be right back Diane. I'm going to go and look for Zelda or else we'll never make it out of here. I waited for her to disappear into the crowd before trying to open my mouth again. Lord I know you healed me. I can still feel your hand on me and I thank you. Now Lord I need you to tell me what to do. The doctor wants me off my legs and on these crutches all braced up. I know I am to be obedient regarding the instructions given to me by my doctor, so Lord tell me what do I do with this brace and these crutches? Oh Lord, why would I need these things when my legs have been healed? Also Father, please tell me what I am to do concerning my job. I was being prepared to retire with this disability. If I accept it, then I'm saying I'm retiring with an injury that I no longer have and in a sense I would be denying your healing. If I go back to work, then I'm going back 100% and totally healed. Then I heard the Spirit of the Lord say, "Exactly!" I smiled and blew a kiss to my Lord and Savior Jesus Christ. Sharon and Zelda jumped into the car bubbling with joy. Zelda turned and looked at me with a big kool-aid smile on her face. Girl you might as well take that brace and those crutches off because God said He healed you. I wept with joy, filling the car with thanksgiving and praise because not only did God heal me, but He also answered me. As we rode back to the hotel I blew another kiss to my Lord and Savior Jesus Christ and watched the stars twinkle brightly in the sky. This night I will sleep without pain. Instead, I will sleep with God's angels.

I arose early to prepare myself for the last service. I couldn't wait to share my testimony with the entire church. This was the day we were all to wear white and take communion. It was too late to have breakfast so we headed to the lobby for coffee and bagels. On the way down the elevator I felt a small pain in my right knee. Instantly, I rebuked it. The elevator stopped and the doors opened. The lobby was full of people. A woman walked up to the three of us and began talking to us. She had a southern accent and an inquisitive eye. There's somethin' about you girls that I can't quite put my finger on. I've seen ya' in this lobby just about everyday and I know somethin' is different. You all are glowin' like the sun. I began telling her how God had truly blessed me at the evening service when Sharon began praising God for healing me. I couldn't stop smiling because God was smiling all inside me. The woman drew close to me and as we came face to face she said you're the one that was all braced up and on them crutches aren't ya'? Yes Ma'am I was. Tears flooded her eyes as she hugged all three of us. Quickly the word spread throughout the lobby and eyes examined me as if I was a lab rat of some sort. Another small pain shot through my knee as we sat at the table chatting. Puzzled, I voiced my concern to Sharon and Zelda. I know what God did for me and I will never forget it, but there is a tiny pain that keeps popping up in my knee. With boldness Zelda interrupted me. Girl that ain't nothin' but the Devil, rebuke it and then let it go. We joined hands and Sharon prayed. They both laid hands on my knees and then we got up and went to church. The sanctuary was packed with men and women from all over. What a beautiful sight it was to see the saints together all dressed in the purest white I'd ever seen. I stood up on brand new legs and testified what the Lord had done for me. I was happy to tell it and everyone was delighted to hear it. As we went up for communion I bumped into Miss Winnie. She grabbed my hands and stood back to look at me. I embraced her and kissed her face. Baby you have been given a miracle. Isn't God wonderful? Yes He is Miss Winnie! Yes He is! His glory is shining all about you. I can't wait to get back to Louisiana and tell my church all about you and what God did for you. Thank you Miss Winnie, I'll hold you in my prayers and I will never forget you. Miss Winnie began telling everyone in her pew about how she met me and how crippled I was. As I walked away I felt the power of God surge throughout my entire being and my legs felt stronger than they had before the injury. During the entire plane ride home I wondered how Eddie and everyone else would handle my good news. Would they actually believe God placed His hands on me and healed me? How will they take it? Will they think I'm crazy? At this point I really didn't care. I wasn't the same. I'd been changed and given the opportunity to return home a different woman. When I got off the plane Zelda's husband and children were waiting for her at the gate. They hugged and kissed her, flooding her with tears of joy. My eyes searched for Eddie, but I really didn't expect him to be there since we argued over the telephone for over an hour during my layover in Atlanta. I realize that after God moves mightily in a person's life the enemy isn't too far behind. However, I fell right into his trap because it takes two to create an argument. Pastor and Sister Bradley along with Sharon and Zelda knew that my conversation with Eddie wasn't a pleasant one and after standing alone by the conveyer belt I guess everyone sort of felt I wouldn't have a ride home either since I received several offers from each of them. Then I felt Eddie's strong arms wrap around me. He kissed me as if the argument never took place. I thought you weren't coming. Diane, please! You may get on my last nerve at times, but I will always love you. I love you too Eddie and I apologize for yelling at you over the telephone. I walked over to grab my bags and crutches off the conveyer belt when Eddie noticed I was walking without help. Diane why don't you have on your brace and why were your crutches up under the plane instead of up under your arms? Eddie God healed me. Yeah right! Girl, grab those crutches and quit playing around. No Eddie! I'm not kidding. God touched me and made me whole. When Eddie looked me in the face he realized I was serious. I told him the whole story on the way home. He listened, received it, and believed it. The next thing I knew he was giving my testimony to everyone he knew. I didn't care whether people believed or not because what God did for me couldn't be denied by anyone.

A few days had gone by and it was time to see Dr. Morgan. Silently I sat in that warm and bright room on the table waiting for Dr. Morgan to enter. He came in with his head buried so far in my chart that he didn't notice that there were no crutches standing in the corner nor a brace on my leg. Well Diane it's time, are you ready? Ready for what Dr. Morgan! For the surgery, what else would I be talking about? I don't believe I need to have the surgery. What are you talking about? Dr. Morgan looked at my legs and then around the room. Hey! Where's your brace? I thought I made it clear that you weren't to take that brace off; and where are your crutches Diane? I don't need them and I definitely don't need the surgery because I'm healed. What on earth are you talking about? I smiled and continued on with the conversation. God has truly healed me. I went to a prayer clinic with my church and while I was there God answered my prayers and healed me. Dr. Morgan put his hand over his mouth and sat there staring at me in silence. His eyebrow rose as his eyes examined my legs closely. He closed his eyes briefly and when he opened them he demanded some things of me. Diane, stand up. I leaped off the table and onto the floor. Now give me some squats. I squatted and sprung back up like a frog leaping through the air. Okay Diane get back on the table and lay on your back. I complied and Dr. Morgan began bending and turning my legs every which way but loose. This is impossible! A few weeks ago you couldn't bend the left knee. You had lost muscle and strength in both legs and I was preparing you for surgery. This can't be! You were crippled and in pain! Dr. Morgan sat down in his chair, placed his hand over his mouth, and sat in silence once more. Diane, what am I supposed to tell the compensation board? They are going to think I'm crazy or something. What will I say…that I was going to operate on someone who really didn't need surgery? How can I explain this without sounding like a quack? It's simple Dr. Morgan. Just tell them exactly what I told you. God had mercy on me and healed me. He touched me with His glory and I'm grateful. I'm not ashamed to tell anyone. Dr. Morgan sat back with a confused look on his face. Diane I did everything in my power to heal you, but I couldn't. I don't understand. I can do these surgeries blindfolded and with one hand tied behind my back, but for some reason you were crippled by the surgeries. Dr. Morgan, God had to show us both something and that something is that He is God and He will be surpassed by no one. He is real and He is faithful. So you mean to tell me that you prayed and asked God to heal you and He did. Dr. Morgan, He did it for His glory. He did it because I belong to Him and I believed He would do it for me. He did it because He is God and decided to give me His favor. It wasn't as easy as it sounds because I was full of myself and pride had consumed me. God had to knock me off my high horse and when I fell on my face I was forced to examine the ugly things about me. I came to a very low point in my life and the only place I could look was up, right into the face of God. Wow, you know I've heard about God, but never really placed that much emphasis on Him. Dr. Morgan began to ask questions concerning God, and the Holy Spirit used my lips to give him the answers to his questions. Diane can I publish this story in the medical journal. Yes sir, you most certainly can. When Dr. Morgan got up to leave his face seemed broken. Diane you are a walking miracle. Thank you Dr. Morgan, but remember it was God who did it for me and He'll answer you if you turn your life and problems over to Him. He thanked me, shook my hand and bid me farewell. I guess you don't need me now huh? No, I'm in good hands. Dr. Morgan smiled and then left the room. I walked out of his office with the realization that God not only taught me some things during this trial, but He also used this situation to witness to others to draw them nigh unto Him. I now know it was all for His glory and I consider it an honor and a privilege to serve Him in this capacity.

<u>Journal Insert</u>

Oh God who am I that thou shalt be mindful of me? I truly thank you for your faithfulness and your love toward me. You healed me although I doubted you. You blessed me when I acted ugly. You touched me although my heart was filled with pride. James 4:6 says, "But He giveth more grace. Wherefore He saith, God resisteth the proud, but giveth grace unto the humble." Thank you for humbling me and not turning away from me. Although we change and become disobedient toward you, you have always remained the same. My God, forgive me and give me to know the power of your resurrection. I know my steps are ordered in your Word. I humbly submit my entire being unto you Lord. Thank you for your peace in the midst of my storms. Thank you for the miracle, my new legs. You are God and you are bigger than life. You are large enough to hold this mean old world in the palms of your hands, yet small enough to live inside of me. I wanted a divine healing. I wanted only to be touched by you Lord. Hallelujah you did it for me. With my wretched self; you did it for me. Thank you Jesus! Please teach me thy precepts and transform me into the vessel you would have me to be. I love you Lord and I give you my life for the rest of my life. I am reminded of 2 Corinthians 5:7, "For we walk by faith and not by sight." You've taught me a valuable lesson on faith and because of that lesson I've grown as a Christian. I've learned to be still and to wait on you no matter what the situation may look like. Lord I thank you for the miracle that you've given me, but I will not get so caught up in the miracle that I forget it was you who performed it. Thank you Lord for your love and for giving me all that I needed to obey and believe you for all that you said you would do. I give you all the honor and praise because it rightfully belongs to you. Amen.

Diane

25
<u>UNCONDITIONAL LOVE</u>

The snow was coming down very hard and within minutes it had painted everything white. Eddie and I had a lovely intimate morning together. We had breakfast and long conversations about our future together. Things were really starting to come together for us as a family. With daddy's birthday just a few months after his funeral and a few weeks before Christmas I was happy we all got through it together. I had a lot to contend with all at once, especially Eddie's infidelity. The Lord gave me a special gift through all of this turmoil, my healing, His presence, and His peace. The only reason I made it through was because God was with me. Eddie and I got dressed and decided to take the kids shopping and then go for dinner when they came home from school. I sat patiently in the window waiting for my children. The weather was getting bad and I was concerned about them. Diane what time will the kids be in? In about 15 or 20 minutes, why? I'm going next door for a minute to sit with Mrs. Bea and Mr. James, you know they were secretly married and I want to say congratulations. Why are they keeping it a secret? I don't have a clue Diane, maybe it's because she's in her 50's and he's in his 70's. Well hurry up Eddie, the kids will be here momentarily. When Eddie left I sat in silence and began picking at my brain concerning the thoughts that used to haunt me. As the time came close for Xavier and Kayla to come home I put my boots on and while tying them a still, but small voice spoke to me, "Go next door." I sat up. In my heart I knew it was the Holy Spirit. Lord I don't want to go next door. I really don't feel like engaging in any conversation with Mrs. Bea today. I sat there gazing out the window when the Holy Spirit said again, "Get up and go next door." Okay Lord. I'll go. I apologize for not adhering the first time and I apologize for being rude to Mrs. Bea and Mr. James by not going over to say congratulations. I got up, grabbed my coat and as usual I strapped on my off duty weapon and walked through the snow to their house next door. The garage door was open. I walked right in and up to the door. Usually, I would knock and then just go on in, but because I really didn't want to be bothered in the first place I opened the screen door and went to knock without entry. I raised my fist to the window on the door and as I glanced down into the basement something caught my eye. My eyes followed the rug, which lead to the green leather couch, which lead to them. Somehow my mind didn't process what was actually going on because I thought Eddie was helping her with something until I stood there and watched. In the midst of the cold winter air beads of sweat rolled down my face as the tears within me raced to the forefront of my eyelids. I stepped back from the door and went to walk away. I didn't get two steps before I became completely enraged. I turned and went back to the door. I cried at the very sight of them together. I reached for the door with my left hand and with my right hand I reached for my gun. The only thought that entered my mind at that very moment was to blow them both away. As my fingers wrapped around the pistol grips of my .45 automatic they quickly came loose and my hand lifted off the gun and was placed at my side. It was as if someone was standing next to me orchestrating my moves and keeping me from grabbing it. The Lord wasn't going to allow me to do it. I snatched the door open and watched them scatter like two rats from the top of the stairs. While out of breath Mrs. Bea spoke as if nothing happened. Oh, hi Diane. I took each stair slowly, contemplating erasing her existence from this earth permanently. Where's Eddie! Oh, he's in the washroom fixing something for me. As my face emerged from the dark shadow of the stairwell it was evident to her that I knew what was going on. Mrs. Bea watched me as the tears streamed down my face and then she began to back up. If I looked the way I was feeling and I were her I would've knocked me down and got out of there as fast as possible. When I reached the bottom of the stairs Eddie slid out of the washroom like a slimy snake still trying to fix his pants. Eddie I told you not to play with my emotions! I told you that if you couldn't be right, then to leave me alone, didn't I! Diane...I... Eddie, don't say anything else to me. I want a D-I-V-O-R-C-E! I turned to Mrs. Bea and she was crying. Mrs. Bea you should to be ashamed of yourself and when Mr. James gets home I'm going to let him know what kind of woman he married. Eddie attempted to grab my arm. Diane you don't know what you're talking about. I pushed him away from me and out of anger I slapped him so hard his face turned white. Don't tell me I don't know what I'm talking about, I saw you! With my own two eyes I saw you! I stormed out of the house and into the garage. I could feel the hurt bubbling inside of me and a woman screaming to get out. Just as I was going to scream I bumped into Xavier. I needed some time to myself, so I sent him to the corner to wait for his sister. He sensed something was wrong and questioned, however, I insisted that he adhere to my request. When I walked through the doors of my house the woman inside of me pried open my mouth and let out a monstrous scream. My hands grabbed hold of my head as my mind refused to remove the picture of them together from my memory bank. I couldn't erase it nor could I blink it away. Just that quickly it had become a permanent fixture upon my eyes and my soul. My knees buckled and carried me to the carpet beneath my feet. Lord why did you have me to go over there? What was the point? What was I to learn from that? Why would you have me to see that? Lord! Lord! Why do you remain silent now? I need you. Why did this have to happen to me? Why now? I thought I'd gotten past all of this? For the last few years it's been one thing after the next. What purpose is my life serving by remaining on the receiving end of torment? I need your help Lord. Please help me. I wept continuously as I picked myself up off the floor. I went straight to our bedroom, stripped his closets and drawers of his clothing and began to throw it out as I mumbled nothings to myself. Eddie I told you not to play with my emotions. I told you that if you couldn't be faithful, then to just leave because I'm tired of you dumping all of your garbage on me. I forgave you the first time, so there ain't gonna be a second time.

Mommy what are you doing? The sound of Kayla's voice silenced me and stopped me in my tracks. Then I heard Eddie telling her and Xavier to go to their rooms. His feet gradually climbed the stairs as he made his way to our bedroom. He stood there in the doorway watching with his face as long as death row. Diane I'm sorry, please don't do this and please don't make me leave. My heart was numb and my words were cold and loud. Diane the kids are gonna hear you so please stop. Why Eddie? So you can look like the hero leaving me to look like the villain for throwing you out. I went to walk past Eddie to get out of the room and he wrapped his arms around me pleading with me to hear him out. Eddie, get your filthy hands off of me. You have her scent all over you and I don't want you touching me! Okay I won't touch you, but please give me a chance to explain. There is no sense in explaining anything because my mind is made up. Diane, that didn't mean anything to me. I was talking and then the next thing I knew it happened. You know that I don't find anything attractive about Mrs. Bea. When it was happening I had a feeling that I was going to get caught. It was like I was standing on the outside of myself watching what was going on and the whole thing made me sick. I love you Diane and I don't want to lose you. Please don't leave me. I'm begging Diane; please don't leave me. I don't want to hear it Eddie, get out of my life and my house. If you are going to put me out then let's at least go to dinner as a family one last time for the kids. No! Can you at least come down stairs with me so I can explain this to the kids? Eddie called the kids in as we assembled in the living room. I didn't want to see the hurt in their faces when Eddie told them he was leaving, so I held my head as low to the ground as possible. He began with, I have to leave and I'm not coming back because mommy and daddy aren't gonna be together anymore, but I'll still see you. When Kayla caught the gist of what he was saying she wept like I never heard her weep before. Xavier stood in shock as anger imprisoned the tears in his eyes. Kayla began to moan and at that point I just couldn't take it anymore. I looked over at Eddie as if to say, look at the mess you've created; was it worth it? He got up to console Kayla and Xavier as I sat there bewildered, trying to figure out why my life has been shattered into pieces. Their broken faces gave me a glimpse into their broken dreams and at the very sight of it I decided to go to dinner as a family one last time. Eddie tried to repair the damage done with conversation and lots of attention, but the kids were sitting on the edge of their seats wondering what was going to happen to their family. They watched me as I ate. They even counted the tears that fell into my plate as I desperately fought to hold them in. I didn't want him sitting next to me. His cologne used to tantalize my senses, but now it was making me sick. I couldn't take it anymore. I was tired of pretending, so for the third time I excused myself to go to the restroom. My intention was to call someone to come and get me, but he followed me each time as if I needed a bodyguard. I was two feet away from the restroom when I felt his breath on the back of my neck. Eddie, would you please stop following me. I don't want to let you out of my sight because I know if I do then I will lose you forever. You have already lost me. Don't you get it Eddie; we're finished! Eddie began crying and begging me not to leave him in the middle of the lobby. People gave looks of concern when Eddie blocked my way. Eddie you are making a scene. So What, I don't care! I want my wife! Please say you'll give me another chance. Eddie move out of my way before these people call the police. If you can tell me you don't love me anymore, then I'll move. Eddie I don't love you anymore, you took everything I ever felt for you and threw it away. Well I'm still not leaving. I'm not giving up that easy, so you're gonna have to put me out. We went back to our table, finished our diner, and went home.

For weeks we slept in separate bedrooms and held separate conversations with the kids. The tension between us was as thick as a brick wall and noticeable to everyone. I couldn't sleep and my appetite took an indefinite leave of absence. One night after getting my paperwork and finances in order in preparation for my singleness I grew tired. I went to my four-cornered room and lay across my bed with thoughts of vengeance. I began planning how I was going to tell Mr. James about his new bride and her rendezvous with my ex-love. The hatred within my heart began to filter throughout my thoughts. Then, in the still of the night after a period of silence the Spirit of the Lord spoke. He said, "Remember when, forgive, and stay." What am I to remember Lord? Why do I have to stay when your Word clearly says that divorce is permitted when adultery or sexual immorality is involved? Then He began to speak. I said to stay because that is my will for your life. Do you remember how you felt when Katrina's husband wanted to hurt your husband so bad he didn't care about how you would be affected by his actions when he tried to tell you about their affair? Yes Lord. Well imagine how Mr. James would feel. What is your motive? Is it to uplift or tear down? And just as I've forgiven you of your sins you must forgive them of theirs. Shame filled my entire being when God showed me how much hatred and revenge hurts the innocent. Lord, wash me and make me clean again. I don't want to hate. Lord, please forgive me for touching the evil that lies within this flesh. Forgive me for the wrong motives I've entertained. I want to forgive them, but I can't do it by myself. I can't erase what happened. I can't erase the pain. I really don't understand why you would tell me to stay with a man that can't love or be faithful to anyone, nevertheless, because I love you Lord I'll do it. I've always said that if you called me to go, then I'll go. Lord I'll do as you've requested, but help me to erase the images in my head and replace it with your love and the beauty of your holiness. Help me to see them as you see them. I need your help Lord. I really need your help because I can't do it without you. Tears of repentance carried me off to sleep as the Lord cradled me in His bosom. On the next day I phoned Mrs. Bea and gave her my forgiveness. We cried together and she thanked me for not telling Mr. James. It felt as if a load was lifted off my shoulders the minute I said I forgive you. However, as time passed I began hiding from her and doing whatever I could just to keep from bumping into her as if I did something wrong. I refused to go outside or leave the house if she was outside and I purposely hid my face from her. Then the Holy Spirit asked, "Why are you hiding?" I didn't know. He said, "What have you to be ashamed of?" I replied, nothing. "So why are you running from the enemy, she should be hiding her face from you?" That was all I needed to break the yoke of shame that was keeping me bound. Forgive me Lord for not tapping into the power you've given me. They that wait upon the Lord shall renew their strength. They shall mount up on wings as eagles. They shall run and not be weary, walk and not faint. Lord, thank you for the victory. Days, however, turned into weeks as I allowed the Lord to work on me. I spent the majority of my time in church where I kept myself busy with different activities. Wednesday night prayer was something I really enjoyed. It was my middle of the week refresher.

Mommy I don't want to be late for teen Bible class. Xavier I'm sorry, but you're going to be at least 10 minutes late because this traffic is murder. I looked back at Kayla and she was lying across the seat. She'd been quiet ever since she came home from school. Kayla, are you okay? Mommy I don't feel so good. What's wrong? My head and my stomach hurts, but it's not that bad. It just feels like everything is moving. Maybe I should take you home. No, it's not that bad, really! Okay, but if it worsens let me know. When we walked in, the church was full and prayer service had already begun, but I wasted no time in dropping to my knees. I always feel elated whenever the Lord communes with me. I don't feel worthy of the privilege He gives me by allowing me to be in His presence. He's given me peace in the midst of all my trials and sufferings, and His love overshadows my pain. When I got up off my knees I sat on the pew to prepare myself to receive the Word of God from the man of God. Five minutes into the message Kayla came up to me crying, clutching her stomach and gasping for air. Kayla what's wrong? There was no answer, just gasps. She drooled at the mouth and her eyes were as wide as a constipated owl in the tree. Quickly, I grabbed Kayla's hand. I wanted to get her to the bathroom in case she was going to vomit. When I passed through the doors at the rear of the church Kayla fell to the floor and went into convulsions. Her arms were flying back and forth while her legs were doing their own thing. Moans and groans emanated from within as her teeth clamped down onto each other and locked in that position. Several people rushed to her side praying and interceding on her behalf. I cried when the ambulance came and took my little girl away. Xavier rode in the front seat of the ambulance as I followed in my car and watched the red flashing lights spin around in circles. Satan the Lord rebuke you in the name of Jesus Christ my Lord and my Savior. I command sickness to loose my daughter right now, for it is written…No weapon formed against us shall prosper, in the name of Jesus Christ I pray. Lord, I thank you for making everything alright. Amen. The hospital was crowded with parents and sick children. Doctors were giving orders and nurses were running all over everywhere. Immediately, I went to the telephone and called Eddie and every family member I could think of, and soon they flooded the emergency room with concern for Kayla. A man in a white coat came out of the back and approached us. Mr. and Mrs. Camden you can go and see your daughter now. Can you tell us what's wrong? No, but it looks like she had a seizure. I've called the neurologist to come and take a look at her, but it's going to be a while seeing that he's 60 minutes away with a patient right now. Eddie and I proceeded to Kayla's room as the others followed. Kayla lay helpless upon the white hospital bed dressed in a white and blue hospital gown. Her mouth twisted to the side and her speech slurred as she attempted to talk. As she uttered little nothings that didn't make since we knew without a doubt that something was dreadfully wrong. It was as if she had a stroke. I anointed her head with blessed oil, held her as best I could and prayed. Afterwards the nurse asked me to sign some papers for Kayla's treatment. Eddie stood in the corner with a bewildered look on his face as Michelle attempted to talk to him. Sam kissed Kayla on the forehead and left. Lottie questioned the doctor using medical terminology that only they understood concerning Kayla's condition; and mama just held her hand and talked to her as if nothing had happened. However, after hours had passed by everyone eventually left. Mama took Xavier home with her while Eddie and I stayed with Kayla. I thought it would be awkward to share conversation with Eddie, but we were talking as if we'd forgotten about the wall between us. After some time Kayla drifted off to sleep. A period of silence enveloped us until the neurologist came in to examine her. He confirmed that she had a seizure, but wanted to keep her in the hospital to run more tests. When the doctor left the room Eddie and I sat in silence once more. Our eyes met with sadness, regret, and humility. Eddie turned away and fixed his eyes on Kayla, as she lay fast asleep. Diane what's wrong with my baby? Why is this happening to her? As he wept I turned away. Diane, I never meant to hurt you. I really love you and I miss you dearly. Though I wanted to respond pride rendered me speechless, so once again I turned away. Over time Kayla's condition seemed to worsen. She had been tested for just about everything under the sun, but the doctor's couldn't find anything. They couldn't even give us a definitive diagnosis for epilepsy although she was still having seizure-like episodes. She woke up confused, not knowing who, what, when, where, or why. She missed a great deal of school, which caused her grades to go down. She felt alienated and alone. The children began teasing her and calling her names when she had a seizure in school. Her frustration grew because she had to take medication all day, everyday. It was as if her brain just shut down and left her to do for herself. Kayla was acting like a totally different person and it was hard on everyone. Somehow during this trying time we managed to come together as a family. I was so preoccupied with Kayla's illness that it was difficult to concentrate on Eddie's sickness, "Infidelity."

Mommy can I ask you a question? Yes Kayla. How long do I have to take this medicine? Just for a little while. When is a little while gonna be over? I don't know Kayla, but don't you know the Lord also heals through doctors and medicine? Yes mommy. Well then, trust him and stop worrying. Okay mommy. Now take your medicine and then you and Xavier hit the hay. Okay mommy, good night. After the kids retired for the evening I went to my four-cornered room. Eddie sat up on his bed and watched me as I passed by his doorway. I went into my room and shut the door and softly laid my head on my pillow. I watched the stars above me through the open skylight and marveled at their beauty. Lord, everything you created is so beautiful I want to cry every time I'm reminded of your greatness. I love you so much; I can't see myself apart from you. Then the Spirit of the Lord spoke. "If you love me, then keep my commandments." I was quickly reminded of what the Lord told me to do. Lord I don't hate them anymore. I've forgiven them both and I have stayed here just as you have asked. "Diane, rise up and go back to your bed." My mouth hung open as a tear slid down my face in response to the Lord's command. I didn't move and I didn't say a word, however, my thoughts were screaming no way. My flesh wanted to ignore what the Lord said, but I couldn't, no matter how unfair I thought it was. God had spoken so there was nothing left for me to say. However, the command was a difficult one. It humbled me and because I love God I obeyed the Holy Spirit. I walked up to our bedroom door and reached for the doorknob. Lord, the only thing that matters to me is pleasing you. You know what's best for me; I don't know anything and I acknowledge that I am absolutely nothing. My prayer is, Thy Will Be Done. When I entered the room Eddie rose up. I climbed into bed with him and cuddled under him. He wrapped his strong arms around me and wept crocodile tears. We cried ourselves to sleep as the Lord God cradled us in His bosom.

26
<u>MY COVENANT FRIEND</u>

The coffee house was tucked away in a small corner by the lake. The walls were covered with all sorts of pictures and memorabilia. People of all nationalities decorated the tables with their heads in newspapers while others were involved in idle conversation. The cashier stood behind a glass counter with a huge smile. She offered a Danish to go with my coffee, but I took a bagel instead. I sat at my favorite table next to the window waiting for my very best friend, Evangelist Matthews. We were accustomed to having coffee together at a moments notice. Sister Matthews really doesn't know how special she is to me, but Lord you do, so I ask that you bless her and keep her, and please save her husband and children. Her only desire is to please you and I admire her for that. I continued to thank God for her inwardly because we had become very close and I knew our friendship was truly a gift from Him; one that I knew I didn't deserve. One thing is for certain, God is perfect and the gifts He gives can't be anything less. As I sipped on my coffee I searched the faces that passed by the window. Finally, she emerged from within the crowd on the street. Her golden brown skin glowed as the light of God burst forth from within and her eyes reflected truth and sincerity. She noticed me and smiled as she passed by the window. We greeted each other with an embrace and sat down. Sister Diane it's always a pleasure to see you. I want you to know I enjoy these moments where we can sit and talk. I feel the same way because you're the only one I can talk to about anything. Girl I know what you mean because you're all I have too and I thank God for your friendship everyday. As the waitress approached, Sister Matthews grabbed her hand and began placing her order. Her eloquent speech alluded to her being an educated woman and her accent revealed that she was indeed from the South. While the waitress poured her coffee into a large mug Sister Matthews rummaged through her purse for her creamers and sweeteners.

So what's been up with you my dear? I didn't answer her. The question caused me to remember the turmoil smothering my life and my

235

smile slowly turned upside down. In an attempt to keep her from seeing the water that covered the surface of my eyes I lowered my head. Sister Diane what's wrong? Where do I begin? You can begin with just opening your heart; you know you can talk to me. Okay, I walked in on Eddie and Mrs. Bea. What are you trying to say? I'm saying I walked in on them having sex. I explained the situation in its entirety to her and when I lifted my head Sister Matthews' face was covered in tears. I knew then that she truly loved and cared for me the way that Christ does because she immediately identified with my hurt like no other friend I've ever known and shed true tears as if this problem were her own. Sister Diane I am so sorry you had to go through that; my heart literally broke in two after hearing it. What are you going to do? I want to leave, but the Lord said to stay and I don't know why because it seems that my marriage has been stripped away from me already. What am I to learn from this? I keep going through this same thing over and over again, only to hear the Lord say, "Stay, forgive, and know that I am God!" I know you're upset, but you must know that if God truly said that, then He has a purpose for it. You have to remember you've asked God for some things regarding your ministry and I've heard you say, Lord wherever you take me, I'll go. Well, before God can use you He has to try you in the fire like pure gold to get all of the impurities out of you. Do you understand? Yes I do, but my heart really hurts right now. There are times when I look at Eddie and all I see is the two of them together. That scene seems to be permanently framed in my mind, which then fills my heart with hate and I can't erase it. I don't want to hate because I know I can't please God in a condition such as this, but it happens when I least expect it and anger begins to consume me. As I wiped the tears away others quickly replaced them. Diane I want you to know that while I don't like what Brother Eddie has done I still love him and I think you do too. Well, I would be lying if I said I didn't. Of course I still love him, but what difference does it make! If he loved me he wouldn't have done this to us. Besides, we will never be the same again; this is the second time that I know of and I'm tired. Diane God has your life in His hands. He's ordered your steps; all of them, so I want you to stop saying you're tired because in a sense you're saying that you're tired of the way that God has prepared for you to go. Okay, I understand and I thank you for being bold and honest enough to tell me that. Sister Matthews flagged the waitress down for another cup of coffee as we shared our inner most thoughts with each other. Sweetie, I believe your husband loves you dearly. This is nothing but the Devil because none of it makes any sense. If the Lord told you to forgive, then that's what you have to do. I'm not saying it's going to be easy, but be the loving wife God has called you to be. I know for a fact that God will see you through it. He will even help you get rid of that anger. Well, to be honest Sister Matthews, He's already spoken to me about it. Yeah! What did He say? I was in prayer when the Spirit of the Lord said, "Anger is like a flame of fire that starts in the pit of your stomach. If you don't put it out; before you know it it's engulfed in flames, and every time you open your mouth to speak, instead of words flowing out...fire shoots out; and every time you attempt to think on good things the fire burns it, leaving nothing but smoldering ashes of the peace you used to have." Wow! That's what I said after He gave it to me. He told me to write it down and I did. I hung it on the wall in my prayer room so I would never forget it. Sister Matthews smiled and continued to tell me about the goodness of the Lord, how God will never leave us nor forsake us, and how we as Christians may have to go through some traumatic things for God's greater good. I found myself listening attentively as a child does to a parent. We talked for hours and pretty soon we were both laughing. We left the coffee house only to sit in my car for more conversation.

Diane you remind me of someone. Who would that be? Do you remember the testimony of Job? I smiled and she closed her eyes and began to speak. There was a day when the sons of God came to present themselves before the Lord and Satan came also among them. And the Lord said unto Satan, whence comest thou? Then Satan answered the Lord and said, from going to and fro in the earth, and from walking up and down in it. And the Lord said unto Satan, hast thou considered my servant Job? Hast thou considered my servant Diane? Ummmmm. Whenever Sister Matthews began to minister she'd stop and say, ummmmm in the middle of her sentence as the Holy Spirit began moving through her. It was as if she was eating something delicious and in the midst of chewing on it she'd say, ummmm, portraying how good it was

237

to her. To me this signified God's goodness and grace upon her and I knew that it was God's words she was chewing on and spewing out to me. She held my hands and we bowed our heads in prayer. Her sincere petitions filled the car and knocked boldly on heaven's door. She spoke as an angel who knew the Lord intimately. Tears fell from her face and splattered upon my hands as she poured her heart out to God. The wall I'd worked so hard to put up tumbled down. My Amen's turned into moans, of which, could only be interpreted by God Himself. His presence overwhelmed me as my friend held my hands and accompanied me to the feet of Jesus.

Journal Insert

(A letter to a special friend)

Dear Sister Matthews,

In the book of Ruth, Ruth loved and cared for her mother-in-law Naomi and she never left her side. They had a bond like no other. Naomi was her friend, a sister, and even a mother. She made a wonderful example for Ruth to follow. She taught her obedience, patience, and love by modeling a holy lifestyle in front of her. Ruth watched and gleaned from Naomi's life experiences, which gave her firsthand knowledge on what it takes to be a woman of strength. Naomi was a true woman of God; exceptional in grace and beauty, anointed and gifted to do the will of God and draw others nigh to Him.

Sister Matthews, I have learned so much from you. You are my Naomi and I will not leave your side either, whether it's to assist you or just learn from you. I will always be here for you whether you're here or ten thousand miles away. If you need anything and I have it, it's yours. If I don't have it, then I will find a way to get it for you. I've never known a friend as wonderful, kind, and loving as you. You've given me a piece of your heart that I will treasure forever and always. I truly thank God for you. You speak as an angel softening the hard hearts of many. Your smile is full of joy and your laughter sings in heavenly places. I truly believe that you are one of God's prized possessions and I see Him in the reflection of your eyes. The Lord has anointed you and empowered you for His kingdom purposes so don't ever doubt the gift or the way in which He leads you. Use everything He's given you to His glory and hold onto His unfailing hand. He has chosen an intelligent woman as you to do His work. However, the difference between you and the intellectuals of the world is simple, they allow their heads to get in the way of their hearts and God knows that your heart is perfect toward Him. He has humbled you and we both know that the attitude of humility is a prerequisite for walking in the anointing. So walk on my sister, stand on God's Word and walk on. Life's a journey that no one makes alone. The more people you touch along the way, the more meaningful and rewarding your time will be.

Thank you for touching my life in a very special way. Thank you for allowing the Holy Spirit access to your heart while teaching me how to be a true devout woman of God. I thank you for teaching me how to be a good wife to my husband and I thank you for listening when no one else would. You will always have a special place within my heart. I love you and I will never forget you.
Diane

Every good gift and every perfect gift is from above, and cometh down from the Father of lights, with who is no variableness, neither shadow of turning.

James 1:17

27
<u>SAM I AM</u>

Sam's drinking worsened over the years and his health became a major concern for all of us. He drank for breakfast, lunch, and dinner; and just in case he wanted to snack while out and about he carried a cooler full of beer in the trunk of his car. Sam began drifting away from everyone that loved him and attached himself to people who only loved his misery. Year after year I watched Sam waste away. His life was being sucked into that bottle and he couldn't see it. I prayed night and day for weeks that he be delivered from the demonic stronghold that was crippling him and then I turned him over to God. It's a wonderful thing to be able to trust God with everything and to know that he hears you and is going to work it out for your good. Not that He will give you everything you ask for, but He will do what He knows is best for you. Whatever His will is, that's what I want. I made a conscious decision that I was not going to allow Sam and his problem to drive me crazy because I had enough problems of my own to contend with. I got up early as usual and went into prayer to fellowship with the Lord. After some time I emerged from my prayer closet and got dressed. I was on my way out when the telephone rang. Hello Diane, what are you doing? I was getting ready to leave the house, why mama? Sam called and said he was being admitted to the hospital. What happened? He said he had been there since last night for his stomach because for two days straight he'd been vomiting non-stop and when there was nothing left in his system his body was still convulsing. What did the doctor say? They said he had gallstones and they need to do emergency surgery. What! Mama you know that Sam's problem stem from his drinking. I know, but he's had problems with his stomach for a while. In the back of my head I was thinking, I wonder why. Mama, are you going up to the hospital? Yes, we might as well go together. After you talk to Lottie and Michelle let them know that I'll swing around and pick them up in a half hour. I climbed upon my knees and began talking to God. Lord, I guess you already know that Sam is in the hospital and I know you're with him even as I speak. As your child I need to know what it is you would have me to do? I know whatever you need accomplished you're going to do it with or without me, but as your representative let them know that it is you who walks with me. When I pray, please allow them to hear you and not me. When I speak let them hear your words of wisdom and when I touch let Sam and all who stand idly by know without a doubt that it is by your power they are and can be healed, according to your will, of course. Lord I pray that this wonderful opportunity be used for your glory, honor, and praise. As always, your will be done.

Visiting hours were almost over when we arrived at Mount Mercy Hospital. The corridors were just about empty except for the maintenance man who had begun waxing the floors. The elevator groaned as it slowly took us to the eighth floor. I figured it had to be pretty old considering it took us five minutes to get to our destination. The nurse smiled as we walked around the desk to Sam's room. All four of us peered into the room as if we expected to find Sam hooked up to a ventilator, but instead he was lying across the bed with his legs crossed as if he was on a beach. He reminded me of a child rebelling on the first day of school where the child refused to take off his coat. It would be too much like acknowledging that he would be there for a while. Sam wore the hospital gown, but refused to remove his slacks and shoes. How are you feeling? I feel like someone put a grenade in my stomach. While mama questioned Sam I sat back and watched him with a keen eye. He trembled like a human earthquake. Michelle's concern for her older brother was exemplified through the worried look on her face and her quiet demeanor. Lottie was listening attentively to Sam's answers, but stood behind mama as if she was her guardian angel. Acknowledging Sam's trembling, Michelle asked the question that was floating around in the air ever since we arrived. Sam why are you shaking like that? Mama quickly interjected. He's always been a nervous wreck. Everyone agreed except for me. I knew there was much more to it than just nervousness. I stood up and walked over to Sam as mama got up and went to the bathroom. I looked him dead in the eye and made sure I had his attention before I spoke. Sam you know this is a warning from God. Yeah I know. How many warnings do you think you're going to get? This is probably it Diane. It's not a joke Sam. God wants you to stop worshipping that bottle and turn it over to Him. Sam had a humble look on his face. He was actually receiving what I'd said. When I turned around Lottie and Michelle were agreeing with me. I motioned for them to gather around Sam's bed so we could pray together. I looked around for mama, but she hadn't returned. Sam where is your pain? It's around my side and into my back. He guided my hand to where his pain was and we bowed our heads as I sent prayers up to God. By the power of God and the faith He's given me to believe in what the world says is impossible I rebuked the spirit of infirmity and claimed a healing for Sam. I closed the prayer with thanksgiving to God for doing this wonderful thing. When we lifted our heads mama was coming back in and a nurse with a wheelchair followed. Come on Sam it's time for you to have another ultra sound. Are they going to do the surgery in the morning? We have to see what the doctor says because you have some pretty large stones. I know; I saw them on the screen earlier. The nurse chuckled as she rolled Sam down the hallway. We watched until they disappeared into a room. Mama stood there in the hallway as if time had stopped. Mama we might as well go home now and come back tomorrow. We gathered our purses and headed toward the elevator. Ladies, can you wait just one moment please? A dark haired nurse dressed in pink and white flagged us down. Candidly mama answered. Yes, what is it. Can you guys take Sam's personal belongings? He has on a very expensive necklace and we would prefer it if you didn't leave it here. How long is he going to be in testing? He shouldn't be that long, just wait by the nurses' station and I'll get back to you in a minute. I stood back and briefly listened to mama, Lottie, and Michelle talk about how badly Sam was shaking. They attributed everything to him being nervous. Sam has basically shut his eyes on his problem, but have they refused to see the truth also? I felt I had to say something because if they continued to distort the truth I was going to pass out. Listening to them make excuses about Sam's condition made me feel as though someone had placed a noose around my neck. Mama, Sam may be nervous, but that is not why he's shaking. He's going through some kind of withdrawal and you all know it. One of the nurses looked up over her glasses at me then lowered her eyes like a shy dog confirming what I'd expected all along. Mama's eyebrows joined together creating three creases across her forehead. Her tongue was sharp and her tone was heavy. Diane I agree with you regarding Sam's drinking. It's a bit much, but the boy ain't going through withdrawal, not now and not ever! He drinks, but he's not a drunk. My eyebrow rose as I began to refute her rationale inwardly. Lottie folded her arms and lowered her head before speaking to mama as if she was afraid to look her in the eye. Mama now that I've had a chance to think about it Sam does seem like he's going through withdrawal. Out of anger and frustration mama raised her voice without knowing how loud it actually was. How could he be going through withdrawal; wouldn't the doctors have said something? Not necessarily. They can't discuss his condition with you unless he gave them permission to. I just don't believe he drinks that much. Michelle sternly interjected. Mama yes he does! He keeps it hidden from you, but we've seen it for ourselves; Sam is a functional alcoholic. Mama's face drooped so low I wanted to reach out and catch it before it hit the floor. As his mother I believe it's my responsibility to tell his doctor what's going on. Lottie gave her opinion and let mama know that after the doctor's received Sam's toxicology reports his drinking problem was no longer a secret. Questions soared from mama's lips as we began to discuss the reasoning for all of this. As Sam and the nurse emerged within the hallway we shushed each other silent. What's wrong Sam; you have a puzzled look on your face. They said the stones are gone. My eyebrow raised in response to Sam's last statement. Gone? That's ridiculous, how could they be gone! I questioned his healing, forgetting the request I made of God as if my faith had vanished. The dark haired nurse came back to retrieve Sam's valuables. Sam can you please give your family all of your valuables because we don't want to be held responsible for it. The only thing I have is my keys and my cross and I'm not removing my cross from my neck. As he clutched the silver cross dangling from his neck we gave him a hug and told him to get some rest. What Sam doesn't realize is...it's not the cross that saves. Jesus is the only one who can save him. That cross becomes nothing but an idol if you worship it and not God and we fail to worship God each time we disobey Him. What sense does it make to wear the cross and refuse to carry your own cross and follow Jesus? To knowingly sin is to rebel against God. You can't worship the cross, because worship belongs to the one who shed His blood on the cross for our sins. Jesus is the way, the truth, and the light. No man can go to the Father, but by Him.

Mama and Michelle found Sam's car and took it to his house. I thought about the situation in its entirety as I made my way back to my car. As I placed my key in the ignition I quietly said, Lord I give it all to you. It was as if the Holy Spirit sat down next to me instead of Lottie because I heard Him so clearly. He said, "Have you?" My first response was yes Lord. He replied, "Then why did you question Sam's healing after you asked me to do it?" With a broken face and a heavy heart I asked the Lord to forgive me and then thanked Him for honoring my request. My conversation with the Holy Spirit was interrupted by Lottie's whining voice. Girl what are you staring out into space for? Start the car and let's go! As bad as I wanted to put Lottie in her place I couldn't say anything demeaning for the grace of God was upon me. My eyes were weary and my brain was shutting down, so I dropped Lottie off and rushed home. I was welcomed by snores and pig grunts as I entered my bedroom. Eddie was sleeping like a baby and could care less that I was home. I'm surprised he didn't drown in all the drool his face was swimming in. However, I was glad I didn't have to climb into a cold bed. The sheets were nice and warm. I exhaled as my head sank into the pillow and within minutes I was snoring like Eddie. I had just entered la la land when the telephone rang. It was so loud it almost gave Eddie and me both a heart attack. I glanced at the clock and its neon green light brightly said 3:00 A.M. The only calls that come in during this time of the morning are emergencies or death notifications. When I heard mama's voice I knew something wasn't right because concern stifled her words. Mama what's wrong? It's Sam. What about him? The nurse just called and said Sam was trying to escape and then threatened to shoot her. What do they want you to do? They want me to come to the hospital to calm him down because he's barricaded himself in his room and won't allow anyone near him. Do you want me to go with you? No, I'll call you mid morning; I want to make it up there before the police get there. They called the police! Can you blame them? Besides, they finally told me he was going through withdrawal. Mama I told you that already. I know, but I just didn't want to believe it.

I hung up feeling guilty about not going with mama to the hospital because I didn't want her to go through this ordeal alone. In a way I felt that I should bear the load because I was the oldest and it was my responsibility to take care of them. Eddie rolled over with a huge yawn and then offered his 10 cents in blurbs and half sentences. Sam is going to have to deal with his own problem and until he's ready to do that there is nothing that you or your mama can do. Eddie yawned again and then dozed off into the coma he was once in. Early the next morning mama called to give me a report on Sam. She sounded as if she had a rough night. She whispered as if what she had to say was top secret. Mama where's Sam? They're taking him by ambulance to another facility for more testing because they said they found the gallstones again. Mama your voice sounds weird, what's wrong? She sighed and then went on to explain. I was up all night long dealing with Sam. What was he doing to keep you up? He was talking off the top of his head, staring at the ceiling, and talking to people that weren't there. He practically drove me crazy. Just when I dosed off he'd wake me with a crazy question or start walking around the hospital. I'd say, lay down Sam and rest your nerves and then he would ask, why did Lottie leave all of that Halloween candy all over my table? Mama, Lottie didn't have any Halloween candy and it's not Halloween. Exactly my point Diane! We went through that all night long. Did you get any sleep at all? No, and I can't do this anymore. I'm going home to rest before he comes back. Well, you go on home mama and I'll check on Sam in a few hours after my meeting. Before I made it to my meeting my cellular phone was ringing; it was mama. Sam had pushed the nurses out of his pathway, struggled with the security officers, and ran out of the hospital wearing nothing but a hospital gown, slacks, and socks. I grew angry as my mind showed me pictures of Sam in a bar nearby trying to satisfy that urge within him. Hours later Sam showed up at mama's door without an explanation. He was adamant about not going back to the hospital although his doctor phoned and declared it a life and death situation if he didn't return. Nothing we said convinced him to go back. I made the assumption that since I was his older sister he'd listen to me, but that turned out to be a disaster. He cursed me as if I was a stranger about to attack him and demanded I give him his keys so he could go home. I told him that I didn't have his keys and if I did I wouldn't give them to him anyway. Mama hid them from him because if he got out of our sight we would never get him back to the hospital in time. I watched him in silence as he lay shaking across the bed in the guest room. His lips and face were two shades of purple. I knew then he had been drinking. I turned my face to the window and glanced down on the street. I came across a small hole in the screen and remembered Sam as a child. This was his room as a young boy and this is the window he used to hang out of as he shot several bystanders with his B-B gun. I chuckled to myself and wondered what happened to the silly little boy that was so full of life. It's ironic how things turn out because Sam couldn't stand the smell of alcohol when we were younger and now he acts as if he can't function without it. He was being stubborn and unreasonable so I left the room and phoned his best friend, John. I really didn't care about him getting upset with me. I just wanted him to get the help he needed. When John arrived, he went straight upstairs to talk with Sam. I don't know what he said to him, but whatever it was it worked. Sam went to another hospital, they admitted him immediately, and scheduled him for surgery. However, the surgeon did inform us that they had to deal with Sam's withdrawal first. I sat on the edge of Sam's bed inquiring about how he felt when a priest walked in to visit the man on the other side of the curtain. Sam almost jumped out of his skin and his eyes bulged 10 times their normal size. Did you see that? What are you talking about Sam? Sam pointed in the man's direction. Him, he's not really here you know. Sam leaned over to whisper in my ear to keep the priest from hearing what he had to say. Diane, when you came in the building it was light outside, but up here it's dark because this floor doesn't exist. Before I could respond to him mama was practically spitting fire. Sam, don't start that mess again! I grabbed Sam's hand hoping it would calm him down. Sam it appears to be dark out because it's raining and there's a building close to your window, which is blocking any real light from getting in. Oh yeah, I'll prove it to you; what time is it? It is 4 o'clock in the afternoon. It was 4 o'clock when you all came in, but its 9 o'clock up here. Sam what in the world is the matter with you? A sinister grin formed on Sam's face and then he burst into laughter. Before we could blink Sam jumped out of his bed and attempted to leave. However, John caught up with him and brought him back. Sam was going through withdrawal, but in the spirit I knew it was a crazed evil spirit of addiction and rebellion that was driving him. Once again, Sam had begun to scare the nurses and upset the other patients, so they moved him to a private room. Mama wanted to speak with his doctor concerning the hallucinations, so Lottie, Michelle, and I waited patiently with her as John left for home. Sam tugged at the tubes going into his arm and pushed every button on the monitoring machines. Mama smacked his hands as if he was two years old and commanded him to leave those things alone. He went from one extreme to the next. His blood pressure was soaring through the roof and his mind seemed to have taken a brief vacation. Sam held conversations with people who weren't visible to us and seemed to be amazed by their jokes. We, on the other hand, certainly weren't laughing. He jumped up, stood in the middle of the floor and began shifting his weight from side to side.

Sam, what may I ask are you doing? Can't you see this building is about to fall? It's leaning; see I can push it from side to side. Sam this building isn't going to fall. Yes it is. Sam you're hallucinating again. You can't make this building tilt by shifting your body weight. His behavior became erratic and unexplainable. The only diagnosis we came up with was that Sam had lost his mind. He called the police on several occasions because he said the building was crumbling and there were children on the train tracks who were hurt. Sam stuffed his window with the mattress from his bed to protect us from the impact of the fall. It was a sad situation. We ended up laughing to keep from crying. Sam laughed with us, but when he began imitating Herman the Monster's laugh we cried. Sam's mind had taken off and it didn't appear to be coming back. I stood in front of the window captivated by the dazzling lights of the city. The world appeared to be peaceful from up there. Sam pulled up a chair next to me and ordered all of us to sit down on his plane as he began announcing that he was the captain and he was taking us in for a landing. My eyes slid away from the heavenly scenery outside and down to Sam. I tried avoiding the fact that Sam was moving his arms back and forth as if he was driving an airplane by drawing attention to what was on the television, but Sam kept driving and giving out instructions as if he were a real pilot. We're coming in for a landing;

everyone put on your seatbelts. Mama! Mama! Sam I'm tired, what is it? Look how pretty the runway looks with all the lights. Mama looked out the window, rolled her eyes and then sat back down. She looked like she wanted to cry. Michelle walked over to Sam and peered out the window. Oh my goodness! It does look like a runway; maybe he isn't crazy after all. Lottie cringed at Michelle's comment and sighed really loud before speaking. Now we've got two nuts to deal with; Michelle why don't you climb in Sam's bed because it's obvious that whatever Sam's got it is definitely contagious. Lottie always did have a way of breaking the tension. Mama snapped out of her shell and we all laughed together. As the night passed on, the nurse thought it best to give Sam a shot to help him sleep. She assured us it was strong enough to knock him out. After the nurse administered the drug Sam sensed himself losing control of his body and began walking to lessen the effects of the potent drug. He stumbled and his knees buckled, nevertheless, it didn't overtake him. As a functional alcoholic that shot was nothing but kool-aid to Sam. He ran through the hallway and tried escaping down the emergency exits, but mama caught him. What are you trying to do Sam? Do you want to end up dead somewhere? Sam stared at mama just like daddy did when he knew he was wrong. A similar smirk rose upon his face and then a laugh. He looked just like daddy. Security was called to keep Sam from roaming the halls and being disruptive, but Sam went back to his room only to move all of the furniture around and into the hallway. He had gone back 10 years in his mind when he worked for the airlines...Why are y'all sitting around doing nothing? Load these planes so we can get out of here. He took chairs and stacked them on top of each other in the hallway. Mama thought Sam's behavior was extremely abnormal, so she requested a psychiatric evaluation from the psychiatrist for his well being. We were exhausted and had come to realize we couldn't continue to fight with Sam to keep him in the hospital and since the hospital couldn't hold him against his will we had no other choice but to have him committed to the psychiatric ward.

When the psychiatrist came down he wouldn't allow us in the room while examining Sam, but we stood at the door to hear the conversation in its entirety. Hello Sam, I'm doctor Marzo and I would like to talk to you for a minute, so why don't you have a seat. Sam, do you know where you are right now? Yes sir, I'm at the airport in New Jersey. I'm getting ready to fly back home. Where is home for you Sam? My home is in Detroit, Michigan. Why are you staring at the window Sam, please direct your attention on me. There's a man out there doc. Sam where do you see a man? He's in the cloud. Don't you see him; he just walked through a door. The doctor along with everyone else thought Sam's last statement was abnormal. Nonetheless, I thought it was possible that he might have seen a man walking through a door in the clouds. I felt that if a person was having a near death experience, then it was highly possible to see what Sam was seeing. Sam how are you feeling? I feel great, but we better hurry up and leave because the building is going to collapse. Dr. Marzo approached us with concern stamped on his forehead. I'm going to have Sam admitted to the psychiatric floor for evaluation, but I need him to be in a calm state before he gets up there, so I'm going to ask the nurse to give him another injection. Mama shook her head in disagreement. I understand the need to have Sam in a calm state, but I think the bulk of Sam's problem is the narcotics you guys keep pumping into his system. Mama went on to explain to the doctor that according to our family history, we tend to have bad reactions to narcotics which bring about hallucinations along with other medical problems. Dr. Marzo, I believe this is the cause for Sam's sudden mind loss and irrational behavior. I understand your concern as his mother; however, it's necessary for us to take these steps. Mama hesitated before asking the next question. Rage painted her face red and lines of frustration ran zig zags all over her face. Are you going to treat his medical condition along with the withdrawal? Yes, we most certainly will. Dr. Marzo called for the nurse and ordered an injection for Sam and also summoned more security officers in case Sam took a turn for the worse. Sam continued to pace the hallway, talking to himself while mama sat in a chair nodding. Within minutes the nurse was marching down the hall with several security guards at her side. Her eyes displayed fear with an unexpected twinkle of mistrust. She didn't walk with confidence, nor did she try to hide her lack of. The commotion woke up mama and she came out into the hallway to investigate. I knew they were going to be forced to restrain Sam so I asked mama to go back into the room. She folded her arms in front of her chest and walked away. The frail nurse whined when speaking with Sam. Excuse me Sam, but you're going to have to take this injection. No I'm not! Sam can you please do this for me; you'll feel much better when it's over. That would be a negative; I told you I'm not taking no shot! Sam shoved everyone out of his way as the nurse followed behind him with her squeaky voice. They tried to rationalize with Sam as if he was in his right mind and able to respond sanely. Finally, they decided to grab him and hold him down, but mama had come back by this time. Sam went berserk and they couldn't hold him. He threw an officer to the left and then one to the right. The nurse ran away and mama dove into the pile of officers to save Sam. Lottie and Michelle let out loud screeches and my face fell into my hands. Mama, what are you doing, move out of the way. We grabbed mama, but she had a tight grip on Sam's arm and was screaming the words let him go. Don't do that to him! The security officer's released Sam out of fear of hurting mama. I walked away shaking my head because the whole thing seemed like a nightmare. I sat Sam down and convinced him that we were taking him home, only he had to go with us to sign his release forms. Sam grabbed his jacket and poked his chest out as if he had been named victor over a huge battle. He took each step with pride. His face was bold and hard like a triumphant soldier. When the light in the hallway hit his face I saw my daddy again. My heart groaned as he strolled away. He looked and acted so much like daddy I wanted to cry. I looked into mama's eyes and felt her pain. I knew if I saw daddy in Sam, then she had to see him too. It was at that moment that I made a real connection with her grief. I wanted to fix everything and let her know it would be fine, only I lacked the ability and the power to do so. The light and energy that had encompassed about her face when I was a child had begun to diminish. The orange and red tones in her skin faded as a cloud of tension covered her face. Her eyebrows now clutched each other and gave no evidence that they would let go. Sam placed his arms around mama and kept his eyes on the security guards as they followed us down the hall. In his mind he was protecting her from them. We arrived at the psychiatric ward and stood outside two blue doors, waiting to be buzzed in. When the doors opened Sam entered with the security officers, but they kept us out and locked the doors behind them. After patiently waiting for at least 20 minutes, the doors opened and the officers appeared before us. Sweat dripped from their foreheads and their uniforms were disarrayed as if they'd been in a bar fight. They bragged and laughed about how strong Sam was and how they each contributed in defeating him. They passed by us as if we weren't there. Mama jumped up and demanded that someone talk to her. Excuse me, but what happened to Sam? They stopped in their tracks and when they turned around I cut them with my eyes as if to say, you better not have hurt my brother. Cowardly, they lowered their heads and walked away except for one. He explained that Sam had to be forcibly subdued in order to give him a shot to help him relax, after which he was placed in a padded quiet room where he was just walking around. The security officer escorted us out and had another officer escort us to our vehicles.

Sam didn't have much to say when we went back to visit him. He appeared to be much better, but seemed a bit angry. He ignored me and directed his attention toward the television in the gathering room. How are you feeling Sam? Sam looked at me with no expression before opening his mouth. Why did y'all put me in this crazy ward? Sam we had no choice. You didn't have to put me in here! Mama sat with Sam and explained everything to him. Later Sam thought it was funny and began cracking jokes regarding the whole ordeal. He couldn't believe half the things we told him that he did. We talked to Sam about getting help for his alcohol problem, but he was convinced he could stop without anyone's help, especially after this. The doctors wanted to prepare him for surgery after his body had overcome the withdrawal symptoms, however, they could no longer find the gallstones. They simply disappeared! I felt real good because I got a chance to minister to my family and Sam got a chance to experience for himself the healing hand of God. I don't have the words to describe Him, but God is awesome and His love is from everlasting to everlasting.

28
THE NEXT JOURNEY

Eddie and I sat on the porch enjoying one another's company as Xavier and Kayla played out in the yard. Things were finally beginning to shape up in my life and what I was now experiencing was an overwhelming sense of joy and peace. Only Jesus could've healed my heart, mind, and spirit like this. Only He could've pieced my broken life back together. As I laughed to myself Eddie reached out and held my hand while his face stayed in his book. I watched Kayla run around the yard with so much energy it reminded me of the time she couldn't because of the epilepsy and the fear of falling or bumping her head. God I thank you for healing my baby. It's been over a year and the doctors can't figure out what happened. It's as if the epilepsy just decided to disappear, however, I know it was you who took it away. My face glowed with the onset of happiness and my mind drifted away with many thoughts. Time has a way of healing old wounds, but laughter plays an intricate part in helping you to overcome adversity. My marriage had suffered a great deal and I remember feeling like I was drowning without any hope of rescue. Eddie and I were trying, but something was missing; we were missing. The two kids who were madly in love with each other and life were gone forever. We needed a boost over the ditch we'd fallen into; if not for us, then for Xavier and Kayla. Through this series of heartache and rejection I've learned a great deal about myself. I'm weak and incapable of being perfect, but through Jesus Christ I am made perfect. He is my strength and my salvation. Looking back over my life, I now realize I developed a false sense of responsibility to my husband and whoever touched my heart. I made myself believe I could fix everything and I became the dependable rock for everyone to lean on. I became everyone's protector. I believe that's why I chose my particular profession. Being a police officer made several statements. It said, I am the law and you can't touch me...you can't hurt me without suffering sever consequences...and I'm here to serve and to protect. Eventually I set out to bring all evil and wrong doers to justice. In all actuality the badge empowered me to stand up for myself and others, something I was afraid to do as a child. When I look closely at my life I realize I did all of those things to keep from dealing with my own problems and also to make up for past hurts. Eddie and I made several mistakes in our relationship. He wasn't really ready for a commitment and I needed to heal and love Diane before making a commitment. I also wasn't ready for the responsibility of rejection. We drained each other emotionally and psychologically by basing our happiness on the stability of the other person. We became a safe haven for each other, a pit stop between work and the kids, which made our relationship very unhealthy. I found out quickly how much work a marriage actually takes and neither one of us was prepared to pay the expensive price of sacrifice. When I look back at the night before my wedding when Monique phoned me to inform me of her and Eddie's relationship, I was actually standing at the crossroads of my life. Looking down both roads, I found one that appeared dark and lonely while the other was safe and familiar. I chose the familiar path and married Eddie. The warning signs were there along with several red flashing lights saying, "STOP!" Yet, I continued. Was God giving me a choice? Did I choose the right path? Only God knows. There is nothing I can do to surprise God. He knows what I'm going to do before I even think of the thing and He works everything out for my good. I am quite aware that sometimes we suffer because of our own choices and failures. However, I do believe that no matter which road I chose on that day, because God made choice of me before the beginning of time, He'll bring me to the place He has for me because He has ordered my steps. He'll use my bad choices to work some things out of me, to cleanse me and make me whole. I now know what unconditional love means. It means to love in spite of. It means to regard others before you think of yourself. Forgetting what you need and what you want to love someone who may not love you back.

It was my children's laughter that revived my own and it was the love of God that showed me how to love my husband in spite of his destructive behavior. As I ponder over my life and the paths that I've taken I've come to understand one very important thing; God is and has always been in control of my life, which is not my own, nor is it without purpose. My steps, which include my joy, my tears, my pain, and my sufferings, were all chosen for me before I was formed in my mother's womb. I know that I was predestined, chosen to be a joint heir with Christ and to serve God at all costs. When I think about all the things I've been through, I count it a privilege and a joy to have suffered for Christ. I am aware of God's presence in my life to such a degree that I'm very careful with the words I choose to speak, the thoughts I ponder over, and the way in which I respond to others. It is very important for me to exemplify holiness in all that I do and say because my God who is holy is always watching, listening, and is always by my side, and if I'm going to be pleasing to Him then I must be holy like Him. Nothing else matters outside of doing the will of God and throughout the years He's developed in me a spirit of humility of which I am eternally grateful. The Lord has done great and marvelous things for me; I couldn't possibly pay Him back for His goodness. He's healed me spiritually and physically. He saved me, sanctified me, and filled me with His precious Holy Spirit. There is no one and nothing that is able to separate me from my God. I love Him with my entire being and I am committed to Him forever. I gazed into the heavens and smiled with amazement; the beauty of God's creation captivates me every time. He made all things perfect and beautiful. My life, as ugly as it seemed to me in the past is now the most beautiful thing I can look back on because God not only created it; He ordained it to be so. Trivial as it may seem to the world and to all those who know me, I've grown closer and stronger in the Lord because of my trials. During my child rearing years I was very much aware that God existed, but I didn't fear Him, obey Him, nor did I reverence Him. I couldn't because my lack of knowledge concerning Him kept me from loving Him. This view of God proliferated on into my adulthood. I was content with just being religious, however, when God called me to holiness I knew there was a distinct difference between the two because religiosity allowed me to sin and do whatever I wanted to. I found that being religious was the way of man and I could practice evil while pretending to belong to God, but holiness was the way of God and in it I had to abstain from the very appearance of evil.

My thoughts began to fade away as Kayla bounced the basketball up the driveway. She reminded me of myself when I was her age. Her brown satin face sparkled under the sun as she desperately tried to get her father's attention by shooting three pointers. I thanked God again for healing her and making her whole and I know she thanked Him for delivering her from all of that medication. Xavier was washing the car in front of the house. He was attempting to eat candy at the same time when the candy spilled all over the ground, but that didn't stop him; he turned around swiftly and picked up the candy, placing it in his mouth one at a time. I thought, how disgusting, he's such a boy! Eddie yelled out to him, but Xavier threw him that handsome smile and walked away. As he gets older he reminds me of his father, headstrong and as charming as can be. Eddie grabbed my hand and gently kissed it. Inwardly I thanked God for His guidance through all of our troubles. My heart was beginning to slowly turn back toward my husband and by the grace of God it felt as if we were becoming a family again. I haven't forgotten the hurt, the pain, the disappointments, or the ugly pictures in my mind, but the Lord has overshadowed all of that with His love and because of that I am free and I have peace. Through this whole process I learned that in order for God's will to be done in my life I had to let go of my will. Finally, I got up to join Kayla in a friendly game of basketball. Come here Kayla, I want to show you how to play the game. My daddy used to tell me to treat the basketball like it's your best friend. Don't pound it like you hate it. Let the tips of your fingers gently bounce it, controlling its movements with a gentle touch, left hand, then the right hand, and back and forth. Soon the ball fell under her control and she was defying the very essence of gravity. As small as she was she was soaring over my head. S-W-I-S-H. In your face mama! I almost cried. It reminded me of when my daddy played basketball with me. Oh, I see you catch on fast. Now I'm going to teach you my famous hook shot. Mama, are you talking about the hook shot grandpa taught you. Of course I am! I already know how to do it mama. Well I'm going to show you anyway so step aside little girl. Eddie gazed at me like a man does when he really loves a woman and it warmed my heart. I went to the middle of the driveway, which we called mid-court. Kayla sized me up and said mama you are not getting that hook shot by me this time. I threw the ball at Kayla so hard it almost knocked her down. Check! She threw the ball back at me and bent over with her arms stretched out like Magic Johnson on the prowl. I turned my back to her and bullied her with my size as I bounced the ball up and down. Kayla put her left hand on my waist and with her right hand she attempted to strip the ball from me. I pushed off on her, lifted my right hand and threw a hook shot over her head. Kayla ran beneath the basket hoping I would miss when the net wrapped around the ball and spit it out. I stood at mid-court listening to my daddy laugh in my heart. His laughter echoed in my head and his smile shined in my eyes as I twitched my mouth to the side just as I did when I was a child. Mama you cheated. No I didn't, you just can't play. Kayla went around the driveway like a mad woman and threw up at least a thousand hook shots until she got it.

The sun had gone down and left amber streaks all across the face of the sky. It was so beautiful my eyes would not release its splendor. Eddie and I decided to take the kids for a drive to get some ice cream. We drove down to the waterfront just as my parents did when I was a child. We found a nice spot and parked. The kids ate their ice cream, then darted out of the car and ran around in the grass like two young squirrels. Look Eddie, look at what we created; aren't they beautiful? They are more than beautiful; they are a blessing to us both. I smiled and cuddled under Eddie's arm. We sat there talking a great deal about life and marriage and came to one conclusion, love does conquer all. Every time I look into Eddie's eyes I fall in love with him all over again and remember why I love him so. However, we could never go back to the way things were because the both of us had changed. Those two people died along with the shattered dreams that were built up on false pretenses. Our lives glistened with empty promises, lack of communication, lack of commitment, and lack of love. Sin destroyed our marriage; however, I was starting to feel that God was giving us a new one. Xavier and Kayla switched from the grass onto the pavement where they were racing in the cool night air. Kayla jumped up and down and did a victory dance because she won, but I knew Xavier played his big brother role and allowed her to win to make her feel good. Although I was proud of him, in the back of my mind I was saying, humph, there is no way in the world I would've allowed Sam to win, especially not on purpose. Laughter wrapped around my tonsils as I reminisced about Sam. He, Lottie, Michelle and I have done some crazy things as children. They got on my last nerve back then, but my love for them can't be measured by anything. My thoughts led me to the face of my mama and daddy. Every thing they did was done for us because they loved us. I didn't always understand that, however, I know that I wouldn't be the person I am today had it not been for their care, provision, guidance, and love. I will always respect and love them deeply for the way in which I was raised, even if our home was dysfunctional. I adopted some of my parenting skills and principals from them and now I have two beautiful children to show for it. It was getting late and it was time to go home. As usual the kids fell asleep in the back seat of the car and when we got home they went straight to bed. Eddie and I retreated to our room and consummated our new marriage and new life together. Infidelity in a marriage not only leaves permanent scars on the heart of all involved it can also cause a woman to feel inadequate where intimacy is concerned. However, through the renewing of my mind and my heart God taught me that none of this had anything to do with me, but it had everything to do with His purpose for my life. In these trials I learned to be still and to wait on God to move. Any time I called myself assisting God I set myself up for destruction. Before drifting off to sleep Eddie wrapped me up in his arms and whispered the words I love you in my ear. I looked into his eyes and found the truth staring back at me; I felt he was sincere. I knew without a doubt we were going to be fine. I allowed my head to sink into my pillow and fell asleep marveling at the miracles of God. At 3:30 in the A.M I heard the words, "Come to Me" and my tired eyes popped open. I relished at the awesomeness of God because I was out like a lamp, yet His voice penetrated through my comatose state of mind and awakened me. I entered my prayer room and sat down in silence. As I meditated I asked God to touch my mind and free it of all thoughts so I could hear His voice clearly. Worship usurped my entire being and then His peace fell upon me. In the quiet of the early morning the Spirit of the Lord spoke to me. "Do you love me?" Yes Lord, I do. Then He asked, "If you had to make a choice between your marriage and Me what would you chose?" Pain ran through my body and tears fell from my face, each with its own burden. With trembling lips I looked up as if God was standing over me. I knew in my spirit that He was not asking me a question; He was giving me a command; a command that I thought would possibly cost me my marriage. I fought desperately within myself to keep from attempting to figure out what the Lord meant because in time He would reveal it. Sometimes we get ourselves all tangled up inside because we think we know what the Lord means and we don't. We don't have the mind of Christ, yet we always think we know where He's coming from and then He comes from another way entirely different than what we assumed. I would've asked why now Lord or why would you do this right now...Eddie and I have just begun a new marriage, or have we? Instead of questioning Him I was humbled in His presence. I looked up and opened my mouth to speak. At first nothing came forth, but then a whisper and then a word. Lord above all else I choose you. It's not in me to choose any other. I didn't answer right away because the question posed stung me, and by the weight of its content I knew it would cost me much more than I could ever possibly expect. I don't want to lose my husband, but I will not disobey you either and I'm not sure it will even come to that. All I know is...You can see everything and you know everything. Lord I belong to you and whatever you require of my life; it's yours. I will obey. Whatever is in store for me, I will obey. Wherever you're sending me, Lord I will go. I fell to the floor, clung to the feet of Jesus and wept until I could weep no more. After countless hours I slowly pulled myself up and left my prayer room. I walked up to my bed where Eddie lay sound asleep and wondered where God was about to take me. My heart reached out for Eddie as tears slid down my face. Eddie I will always love you. I don't know what God is doing or what He has in store for us, but I do know it's going to be okay. I'd rather be in His will than live a life opposite that. I won't worry and I will not fret because my God will never leave me nor forsake me. I climbed into bed and as I cuddled under Eddie the dream I had a few years back began to flash before my eyes and the Spirit of the Lord began giving me the revelation knowledge to the dream.

I saw myself standing in the yard with Eddie while we were working. I had climbed upon a wooden fence when his attention was directed to a box of shiny, bright pink cans. Eddie took these cans and walked away. The fence represented protection and restraint while the wood represented Christ. Therefore, no matter what trauma awaited me up ahead, the Lord Himself would give me His protection and anoint me to restrain myself from doing what I felt was best for me. These cans were the women he lusted over and had affairs with. When Eddie walked through the lame lions and the barren land I hesitated in following because I was afraid of the lions and I didn't want to do what it took to go after Eddie. I was looking at the circumstance that I was in instead of the promise given to me by God. I allowed the enemy to place fear in my heart regarding the lions and because of their fierceness and boldness I was afraid to approach them or go through them to get beyond my dilemma, but because they were lame they were ineffectual and couldn't hurt me. The decent across the desert represented a long journey through difficult times, famine and judgment, and at the end of that decent I looked up and saw the Lord. The red rose He was handing down to me through a cloud represented Christ, His suffering and sacrifice. He gave me the authority to represent Him, to suffer for Him, and to give myself as a sacrifice to Him. The cloud is symbolic of the Lord divinely covering me and guiding me in the paths that I must go. When the rose turned into a sword it symbolized the Word of God, of which I girded around my waist. The white robe I was wearing represented purity and holiness. It was my covering, my priestly garment for which the Lord clothed me in. When I turned around Eddie was kneeling in tears and I've come to understand that no matter how rebellious you may be and no matter what you've done; when the Lord shows up every knee will bow and every tongue will confess that He is Lord. When I turned to Eddie to show him what the Lord had given me I was in turn confessing my discipleship to Jesus Christ; equipped with everything I needed for the next journey. Lord I thank you for comforting and sustaining me through these difficult trials in my life. I know you are always by my side and I know without a doubt that you won't leave me, so I gladly answer this call with "Yes Lord." Lead me where thou wilt. Anoint me and strengthen me to pass the tests that have been fashioned for me. Anoint me to obey you that I may please you in all that I do, say, and think. As I closed my eyes a tear ran down my face in the dark of the night. With my heart, I tightly held onto the hand of the Lord knowing this journey would be a difficult one. This journey would not only call for total submission and obedience on my part, but it would also be one of great Spiritual Warfare.

Journal Insert

And we know that all things work together for good to them that love God, to them who are the called according to His purpose. For whom He did foreknow, He also did predestinate to be conformed to the image of His Son, that He might be the first-born among many brethren. Moreover whom He did predestinate, them He also called: and whom He called, them He also justified: and whom He justified, them He also glorified.   Romans 8:28-30

I can say with conviction that what I've been through doesn't dictate who I am, because I identify myself with Christ and not my past hurts. I struggled with the way you were leading me Lord because I couldn't see where I was going and I didn't think I could make it, but you gave me the faith I needed to believe and a heart after your own; thank you. I've learned to trust and depend on you for everything because you know what's best for me. I know what seems impossible for me is not impossible for you because you center in on my availability and obedience, not my ability. I have become a stronger Christian through my trials and adversities. Thank you for molding me and making me into the vessel of honor you've chosen me to be. Lord, my suffering has not been in vain because I know if I suffer with you, then I will reign with you. It is for you that I live and for you I'll die. Amen

Diane

Printed in the United States
28479LVS00007B/43-75